ILS - LEARNING SERVICES
MARITIME GREENWICH

So

This book must be returned or renewed by the last date stamped below, and may be recalled earlier if needed by other readers. Fines will be charged as soon as it becomes overdue.

TELEPHONE RENEWALS 020 8331 7788

the
UNIVERSITY
of
GREENWICH

Social Proprieties

Social Relations in Early-Modern England (1500-1680)

David A. Postles

New Academia Publishing, LLC
Washington, DC

New AcademiaPublishing, LLC
P.O. Box 27420, Washington, DC 20038-7420
www.newacademia.com - info@newacademia.com

Contents

Acknowledgments

Although I had previously read the work of Erving Goffman, it was only during conversations with my colleague, (Professor) Eric Dunning, about the figurational sociology of Norbert Elias, the social interaction ideas of Goffman, the sociology of Mead and the symbolic interactionism of Blumer, that I began to realize how the relationship between micro-sociology of social interaction could inform the macro-sociology of 'social structure', or, to reflect early-modern concerns, social ordering in all its facets and meanings. To Eric, therefore, I owe an immense debt of gratitude, although he would not, I'm sure, subscribe to the approach that I take. His rôle has been that of a master to an errant pupil. What our exchange of ideas—mostly in one direction—reflects is the vitally important role that discussion over lunch in the Senior Common Room can contribute to the life of a university, the dissemination of ideas, true interdisciplinary transactions and the realization of research. It's interesting that another retired academic has also stimulated my thoughts and indicated areas that I have neglected: (Professor) Charles Phythian-Adams. Colleagues do not *have* to have retired, however, to inspire, and my indebtedness is as great to (Professor) Greg Walker. The inter-relationship between dramaturgy and social activity is extraordinarily interesting and Greg both instigated my interest and provided unfailing advice in a convivial way, again over lunch in the Senior Common Room. It would be remiss of me then not to acknowledge those who enable that environment: Odette; Gaz; Sue; Liz; Peter; and (sometime) Catherine. Whilst I have recently been spending much time researching at the University of Nottingham Library, Tina Adams has been convivial. The writing of this work has been facilitated by the congenial presence of Audrey Larrivé in the Centre for English Local History, her kindness, efficiency and friendship. Discussion of these matters with Paul Griffiths has always been profitable, although they diminish because of distance, and Richard Smith has been as supportive and inspiring as always. Then there are the innumerable inadvertent contributors to this study who will not realize the part that they have played. Observing how people address and interact with each other within my institution has provoked questions of how to approach the past. Sharing ideas with second-year undergraduates bravely taking HS2202 in the School of Historical Studies has been entirely rewarding for me, if not for them. The interdisciplinary milieu of the M.A. in Humanities has also had an impact on my approach and I thank all the staff involved in and all the participants on this fascinating course.

On a very practical level, I would like to acknowledge the superb work of Kate Holland and Kathryn Summerwill in making available through electronic delivery the churchwardens' presentment bills in the archdeaconry of Nottingham, which has facilitated my use of that particular source.[1] Archivists at many archives offices have exhibited their accustomed grace and courtesy, for which I am truly grateful.

My initial foray into this area of research was kindly accepted for publication by the editors of *The Journal of Historical Sociology*. That article forms the basis of chapter 1, although now in a heavily expanded version, incorporating much new material and new lines of thought.

I have had the great good fortune to have a partner of extraordinary patience and intellect. When we met in 1969, neither of us could have anticipated that some of our interests—similar then—would converge so closely. Both academically and emotionally, Suella has made an immeasurable impression on this small book. I dedicate it, however, to George Ramsay and Michael Palmer, two people who were formative influences on a young man fascinated by early-modern economic and social history, who has now returned to that fold after a hiatus of over thirty years.

Dave Postles, University of Leicester, March 2005.

Abbreviations

Place of publication is in parenthesis

BerksRS	Berkshire Record Society (Reading)
BHS	Banbury Historical Society (Banbury)
BrisRS	Bristol Record Society (Bristol)
BucksRS	Buckinghamshire Record Society (Buckingham)
CHS	*Collections for a History of Staffordshire* (William Salt Archaeological Society) (Stafford)
CRS	Cambridgeshire Record Society (Cambridge)
CWPRS	Cumberland and Westmorland P. R. Society (Kendal)
DNPRS	Durham & Northumberland P. R. Society (Durham)
DRS	Derbyshire Record Society (Chesterfield)
DS	Dugdale Society (Stratford-upon-Avon)
EETS	Early English Text Society (Oxford)
ERO	Essex Record Office
HRS	Hertfordshire Record Society (Hertford)
KR	Kent Records (Maidstone)
LPRS	Lancashire P.R. Society (Preston)
LRS	Lincoln Record Society (Lincoln)
NNRO	Norfolk and Norwich Record Office
NRO	Northamptonshire Record Office
NRRS	North Riding Record Society (Northallerton)
NRS	Norfolk Record Society (Norwich)
ORS	Oxfordshire Record Society (Oxford)
P.R.	Parish Register(s)

RSLC	Record Society of Lancashire and Cheshire (Liverpool)
SfRS	Suffolk Record Society (Woodbridge)
ShPRS	Shropshire P.R. Society (Shrewsbury)
SoRS	Southampton Record Society (Southampton)
SPRS	Staffordshire P.R. Society (Stafford)
SRS	Somerset Record Society (Taunton)
SS	Surtees Society (Durham)
SuPRS	Surrey P. R. Society
SxRS	Sussex Record Society (Lewes)
ThS	Thoresby Society (Leeds)
UN	University of Nottingham Manuscripts and Special Collections
WHS	Worcestershire Historical Society (Worcester)
WRS	Wiltshire Record Society (Trowbridge)
WSRO	Wiltshire and Swindon Record Office
YASRS	Yorkshire Archaeological Society Record Series (Wakefield)
YPRS	Yorkshire P.R. Society (Wakefield)

Introduction

[she denied] that ever she made any rhyme but she said a certeyne ryme and for goodwill she told the same to goodwife Willyams and her daughter and to the goodwife Cadman and her daughter because she thought it was made to there discreditt, and she hard it as she came to the markett to Oxford abowte Christmas last of one Robert Nevell who did singe it by the waye, and the ryme is this viz. yf I had as faire a face as John Williams his daughter Elsabeth hass then wold I were a taudrie lace as goodman Boltes daughter Marie dosse, and if I had as mutche money in my pursse as Cadmans daughter Margarett hasse then wold I have a bastard lesse than Butlers mayde Helen hasse...[2]

Remember that Fyneux C.J. in Michaelmas term [1515], 7 Henry VIII, said that where I am once estopped in my name of baptism I shall be estopped for ever against the whole world.[3]

For the purpose of this report, interaction (that is, face-to-face interaction) may be roughly defined as the reciprocal influence of individuals upon one another's immediate physical presence.[4]

The fundamental way in which people interact socially is how they address each other (or, when not in face-to-face situations, refer to each other). In their interaction—circumscribed and influenced by emotional responses and (the avoidance of) embarrassment—social actors employ a variety of forms of address: names, nicknames, social titles, which impute familiarity and closeness; distance and respect; courtesy; or dismissiveness.[5] Many of those responses are dispersed through the deposition in the archdeaconry court of Oxford above. Reported social address can thus furnish an insight into the praxis of social relationships with an elemental poignancy.

Quotidian social interaction through the "speech community's" language use in addressing individuals, when considered in its totality, moreover, can take us further than the relationships between individuals. The accumulation of this social interaction can reveal something about the ordering of local society.

Two perceptions of early-modern social ordering—through "national" and local lenses (though not necessarily antithetical) have been suggested, the one established on a social language of "sorts" and the other of "chief inhabitants," "core" or "focal" families.[6] When reduced to great poverty by a fire which consumed his barns and goods, John Throe of Hitchen, a weaver, addressed the justices of Hertfordshire in 1626 for a brief for collecting assistance. In his support, he adduced a petition testifying to his character, certifying that he had been a man who had lived by his labor and had maintained his wife and children. The appeal was importantly subscribed by the "better sorte of the same towne."[7] In this context of the language of "sorts," for example, the charge was addressed to the constables in Norfolk for enforcing the Book of Orders in 1596 to sustain "the poorer sort."[8] "The names of such recusantes as be either married wives or of the meaner sorte whose estates wee finde to be meane & uncertayne" were certified to the justices of that county in 1586.[9] "The better sort of people beinge muche greived & offended that the ruder sorte would not be stayed nor by the magystrates restrayned..." was a complaint to the assembly of Norwich in 1604.[10] "And that the poorer sorte of people and others may not be oppressed by an unequal proporcion..." exercised the minds of the aldermen of Northampton in 1605.[11]

By the late sixteenth century, then, informal descriptions of English social differences existed alongside the formal classification of degrees and estates. Prominent amongst these colloquial distinctions was the language of "sorts."[12] This development reflected the instability and transformation of social relationships occurring in early-modern England, so that fluidity of terminology ensued.[13] During the late sixteenth century, the language of sorts was itself transformed into a more elaborate and rhetorical form of social distinction through the association of adjectives of discrimination.[14] Inspiring this process was the use of this language by hegemonic social groups to demarcate themselves from the less privileged or the less compliant: it became deployed in a hierarchical and polarizing manner, particularly in the late sixteenth and early seventeenth century.[15]

A different paradigm conceives of a more localized social description characterized by the use of terms which identify the principal inhabitants within villages, expressed in locally-produced documents such as manorial court rolls and parish records. Such chief inhabitants were described purely in terms of their local position—as officeholders—rather than with reference to wider society.[16]

What we may be observing in these descriptions is two different, but co-existing perceptions of social ordering in early-modern England. They need not be exclusive; they might even be commensurate. To these formulations and perceptions, we might add a third, again in no way precluding the other two, but complementing them. The language of address and naming informs any consideration of the ordering of society, but perhaps also avoids two principal issues.[17] First, although all language use consists of rhetoric, the self-acclamation of "chief inhabitants" persuasively projected a self-representation of a particular group.[18] Secondly, those social categories hitherto formulated were problematically and resolutely male-centered. Now, although local society's use of names and forms of address was no less imbued with rhetorical overtones, it allows some penetration into the world of quotidian exchange and how female actors were incorporated into local social ordering—all at an elemental, fundamental social level.

In selecting the categories of analysis below, the primary objective has been to build up from social relationships rather than read back from social structure. Contemporary descriptions of social organization—or social structure—are freighted with rhetoric and thus may constitute ideological constructions of social organization. The intention here then is to look at social relationships as they were negotiated and worked through in practice, and only then to relate those social events to "social structure." It is the politics of address which take precedence here and those politics are best illustrated by forms of colloquial address negotiated between social actors, the attribution and reception or acceptance of nicknames and aliases, and the expectations of and respect for forms of address as titles.

During the later middle ages, a certain amount of fluidity developed in the ordering of society, one of the consequences being the implementation of the Statute of Additions in 1413, which required all defendants in criminal cases to be attributed an occupation or status. By the early sixteenth century, so much ambiguity had arisen that in 1520, More K.B.J. could opine that the statute should be understood that: if the son of a knight was engaged in husbandry, he should be designated "husbandman," not "gentleman," whilst, conversely, the son of a husbandman who attained an office associated with gentle status (an officer or clerk in a common law court) should be denominated "gentleman," not "yeoman," for everyone should always be described according to actual occupation.[19]

Throughout the discussion of address, illustrative examples are extracted from contemporary dramatic performances. In one sense, this recourse is felicitous, for Goffman likened social interaction—both verbal and through gesture—to theatrical performance. Indeed, that analogy was intrinsic to his observation.[20] That sort of justification, however, would be, on its own, rather spurious. The real justification for importing material from contemporary theater is that by doing so, we are observing the observers.[21] To that end, material is derived only from the City Comedies and Jonson—what on the surface appear to be two radically different political and social perspectives.[22] Concentration on the City comedies, of course, begs the question of metropolitan influence over a wider space. No doubt there are arguments for perceiving some cultural influence of the City in other areas of the country. The point remains, however, that the City was extraordinary. Here then the use of the City comedies is allusive. What we know of provincial theater does not yet allow us to make more categorical statements about the theater and society elsewhere.[23]

How the playwrights can inform our comprehension of social

interaction and relationships can be illuminated from a single play: Thomas Middleton's *A Trick to Catch the Old One*. The central male figure, Witgood, exclaimed: "I have rins'd the whoreson's gums in mull-sack many a time and often ..."[24] As will be confirmed below, that sort of social reference fractured social relations, even in its deployment against the clergy. When Witgood addressed the two usurers as "O Master Dampit" and "Master Gulf," even "Kind Master Gulf," Middleton was, amongst other meanings, reflecting how the category of gentility and the title master had become obfuscated and transformed by the late sixteenth century, by the intrusion of new commercial wealth—a social critique of contemporary social trends exhibited in aspirations for this title.[25] That social ambiguity and fluidity was elucidated further by Middleton:

> The son, once a gentleman, may revel in it, though his father were a dauber.[26]

When Witgood adopted a more familiar register, addressing Dampit as "my old Harry," he engaged in another social discourse: the use of hypocorism to express (false) closeness and the *double entendre* of "old," intending familiarity, but also expressing Dampit's age.[27] So too, Witgood's avaricious uncle, Lucre, referred to his adversary, "old Hoard," and it is clarified later, not least at his marriage to the anonymous Courtesan, that Hoard was indeed of advanced years—and Hoard is undoubtedly "the old one" in the play's title.[28] Finally, the terms of abuse bandied about in the play were principally "knave," "rascal" and "villain," common words of rebuke in direct social interaction which challenged male honor and character.[29]

The relevance of the playwrights to social practice is, of course, ambiguous. Dekker was probably the closest to the quotidian life of the populace of London, although little is known of his origins. His career was checkered, including a spell imprisoned for debt, and he never enjoyed the patronage which Jonson acquired. His work perhaps best represents "citizen values and low life realism."[30] Superficially, Jonson appears as the opposite. His traditionalism longed for the aristocracy to stand to its obligations as he imagined it had in a previous era. He aspired to and achieved courtly patronage, particularly through masques. Jonson returned to classical forms of literature.[31] On the other hand, his earlier life had been punctuated with dissolute episodes when he most certainly acquired a knowledge and understanding of London life. He had, indeed, followed a criminal existence, close to the gallows.[32] In the case of Middleton, his background was intimately connected with the City, since his father, William, had been a citizen and bricklayer, who had achieved gentle status in his later years. Nonetheless, because of his earlier career, William's status was ambiguous. For Thomas, however, fortune smiled less kindly because of the second marriage of William's widow, so that Thomas descended the City hierarchy. Even when he achieved some recognition as a playwright, his social position remained ambiguous and he, indeed, emphasized the craft quality.[33]

We can agree then with McLuskie that the City Comedies of Dekker, Heywood, Middleton and Rowley "enacted and articulated the beliefs and aspirations of the society which produced and consumed them" and attracted an audience from diverse sectors of London's population.[34] The difficulty is, of course, differentiating representation and realism. None of the playwrights eschewed ideology: Dekker was empathetic to the City and its values; Middleton was critical, ironically or otherwise; and Jonson, with his conservative mentality, desire for high-level patronage, and demand for the aristocracy to stand to its obligations, had an entirely different agendum. All, nonetheless, inevitably introduced into their works an element of "dramatic realism."[35]

What these literary sources thus provide us is direct speech—if imagined—in social interaction. The parts played convey the meanings of address. That direct—or reported—speech is only otherwise available when court cases—in Quarter Sessions and ecclesiastical courts—or the minutes of meetings of borough councils reiterated the alleged words. Such are the sources examined below for direct or reported address in social interaction.

Otherwise, we are dependent on references to people rather than direct address between them. Principally, some parish registers and some parochial accounts—of churchwardens and constables, for example—furnish references to people which inform us how they might have been addressed. For example, shirts and smocks were provided by the corporation of Reading in 1624 to "Blynd Sample" and "Old Harrison."[36] In 1625, a complaint about an apprentice to the Corporation involved the testimony that Goodwife Symes and "the Runinge begger called Cowper" had purchased shoes.[37] An example of the informality of address is presented in the reference to "bawld Lewes wife" in the Hall papers of the borough of Stratford-upon-Avon in 1594.[38] Now, although these are references in written records rather than direct face-to-face address, there is sufficient evidence, not least in the plays, that those were also forms of direct address to these individuals.

We have been appraised, of course, of the narrative strategies that are embedded in depositions in legal *fora*.[39] Attention to contexts and claims are as advisable here as when dealing with literary texts. Those strictures apply no less in forms of address *represented* in depositions. It was contended in Chancery in 1566 that when Edward Baily walked with John Taylor in Stotfield (Staffordshire), Taylor enquired: "goodman Baily how happeneth the high way to Tamworth to be changed?" - to which Baily responded: "Mr Bretten requested me saying, Neighbour Baily, the way was altered by means of Agarr for his case..." [40] These alleged terms of address were reported to persuade the Orator's case—parties in disputes in Chancery were denominated Orators. Whether the forms of address were actually spoken, remains uncertain. What we can, however, deduce is that such terms were contemplated and would have been deployed in favorable circumstances.

The rhetoric of language use in courts is also exemplified in proceedings about land in Barton-under-Needwood (Staffs.) in 1561. The nub of the different claims depended on whether John Holland otherwise called Great John Holland and John Holland otherwise called Crabb John Holland were the same person or two different people. We can, nonetheless, assume that one or more people were recognized by these nickname affixes—Great and Crabb—in local society.[41]

To substantiate that claim, the material from the churchwardens' accounts in particular is likely to express the form of address of local society. Even parish registers, although composed by the incumbent, might well reflect a wider social usage, since the incumbent was part of local society and so might well have inculcated local usage, and the churchwardens inspected the registers. For good measure, however, we can recite debts owed to George Daniell, yeoman, deceased, as enumerated in the probate inventory of his estate in 1592, consisting of arrears from "ould good wyffe Dodge of the hill toppe" and "litell John Henshaw."[42]

Below, then our concern is how address reflects how far social actors were integrated into local society and how address was expressed in social interaction. In the latter investigation, two issues are paramount: how address was informed by an attempt to manipulate social interchange; and how address informed the social status of the actors.[43] In chapter 1, the emphasis is on titles of address, formal and informal. The former—formal address—principally engages with the contested and fluid status of Master and Mistress as titles of address reflecting some status of gentility—contested because of social flux at this time which brought these titles into the aspiration of more social groups, particularly in the urban context. Formality in address is consistent with social distance.[44] Thus, although he received a "cordial reception" in 1618 on his journeying through England and Scotland, the "water poet," John Taylor, consistently referred to his hosts by their formal title of Master where such obtained.[45] Within this section, however, are also investigated the semi-formal titles of Goodwife and Goodman, but it is divulged how these forms were attributed discretely and selectively, often dependent on context. Finally, more informal "titles" are considered, especially "old" so-and-so, but also the use of adjectives (sometimes from disability) in referring to some social actors (as "Blynd Sample" above).

We should also acknowledge that these expressions existed before 1500 – that being a purely arbitrary *terminus a quo* to make this project manageable. For example, the churchwardens' accounts of Saint Mary at Hill, London, introduce us to these forms of address in the late fifteenth century. At the top echelon constituted by formal titles, the status of Mistress Agnes Breton was expressed in her financing the painting and gilding of the lady tabernacle in 1488, amounting to £27.[46] Correspondingly, the alderman of the ward was constantly titled Mr. Alderman or Mr. Remyngton.[47] If we move down the scale to semi-formal address, in 1487-8 Goodwife Blyn paid the standard 6s. 8d. for her husband's burial.[48] The interment of her son was expensive for Goodwife Mascall in 1500.[49] For her service in making up four albs, Goodwife Hunt was remunerated with 1s. in 1504-5.[50] In 1550-1, Goodmen Derhame, Howtyng and Collyns contributed for the burial of their children, whilst Goodman Proyse had been compensated for rope in 1492-3.[51] Considering next informal titles, Mother Selbye was involved over the matter of one penny in 1485, 1s.had been exacted from Mother Boyis in 1492-3 and 10s.was received from Mother Browne in 1494-5.[52] Assuming another sobriquet, "olde Mouce" in 1487-8 took the tenancy of a house which required the carpenter's attention.[53] These forms of address—both formal and informal—were not then novel in the sixteenth century. Their inclusion in written records depended, to some extent, on the wider use of the vernacular in documents, although court records, even when composed in Latin, had included and continued to include direct speech in Middle English. Accordingly, then, the first part of chapter 1 is concerned with informal or colloquial address (such as "old so-and-so") whilst more formal titles are the subject of the second section of chapter 1.

From the certainty of those titles, both formal and informal, chapter 2 is concerned, in contrast, with people imperfectly acknowledged in their local society. So, in comparison with the full forms of address above in the accounts for the parish of Saint Mary at Hill, there is the payment in 1493-4 of £6 13s. 7d. to Constantine the carpenter for constructing all the new pews and enclosing the font.[54] Various degrees of ignorance of people's identification become visible: from no knowledge at all of a person's names ("anonymity"), through information about either forename or surname, but not both. Here too are discussed issues of ambiguity about names: the varying approaches to imposing a name on the bastard; changes of name and its motives; and the significance of the *alias*. The issues encountered here were of great consequence, marking out or labeling people at the margins, indicating their reception into and inclusion in local society or their exclusion from it; or alternatively providing social cohesion of small groups.

The issues of social nearness and distance are also well illustrated in some personal memoranda. We might single out here—purely for the purposes of exemplification—the account and memoranda book of Edward Don.[55] In his transactions with people, Don adopted a variety of forms of reference: occupation and habitation of the person; surname only; surname and habitation; forename and surname; pet form of forename and surname; and surname and occupation. He employed these forms consistently for each individual, reflecting their closeness or distance in the relationship. His personal shaving was always performed by Carow the barber.[56] Shoes were constantly repaired by Hykman.[57] Disbursements were made to Robyns.[58] Comestibles, especially fish, were purchased from Bate, once Bate of Risborough.[59] On the other hand, those closest were identified in his household book by their forename—often by a hypocorism or pet form—and their surname, profusely his servant Dyk Furberer for his many journeys and errands.[60] The Middleton household accounts included the expense of dispatching "lyttle Dyckez" to collect a gelding in 1556.[61]

From titles of address—formal and informal—and the ignorance of identification, the discussion next considers, in chapter 3, expressions in social interaction which had an emotional content: either love and friendship, or denigration. As explained below, recovering genuine and sincere articulations of amity and devotion is complicated by context and source. Some situations (and sources) are suffused with formalism (requiring expected expressions) or dissimulation (attempting to manipulate through a false rhetoric). As explained below, then, attempting to differentiate instrumentality from affection is not always achievable: the motives for articulating friendship were complex. Early-modern society, moreover, had ideologies of neighborliness and community which, even if themselves only rhetorical, had an impact on language use. Those obligations are exhibited by a Yorkshire testator who in 1544 desired not only a mass and dirige for his own soul and those of his "good frendes" but also "to make a dynner to my frendes and goode neghbors the same day..."[62] The contexts and implications of those discourses and complexities receive fuller treatment below, in chapter 3, and so are not elaborated here.

In the later parts of chapter 3, the discussion moves into the realm of unbridled responses in which a failure to manage the emotions brought forth incandescent abuse of authority.[63] For the most part, these subversive speeches occurred in Quarter Sessions, in ecclesiastical courts and in borough council meetings. Their com-

mon thread was the denial of deference. What was at issue was how these speech acts undermined social honor, credit and status. It might be considered that words were but words, but in fact every attempt was made either to punish the miscreant who made the obnoxious utterances or to ensure the submission of that offender to the authority in question. In the fifteenth century, both the good wife who taught her daughter and the wise man who instructed his son reflected on the power of words in an honor society.

For þⁱ tonge may be thy fo[64]

Fayre wordes wreth do slake;
Fayre wordes wreth schall neuer make;
Ne fayre wordes brake neuer bone,
Ne neuer schall' in no wone.[65]

Assuredly, the implication was that conversely insalubrious comment would cause perturbation.

In the final part of the book, we move to well-trodden ground, surveyed particularly by Scott Smith-Bannister. Despite the extensive nature of his discussion of forenames between the introduction of parish registration in 1538 and his arbitrary *terminus ad quem* of 1700, some interesting interstices remain about which much more can be established. In this present context of social interaction, the most significant issue is the question of the use of pet forms of forename—hypocorisms—particularly important for forms of address (chapter 4). In what circumstances were full formal forenames and pet forms respectively employed? What do they signify about the relationship between social actors and social intercourse? Although Smith-Bannister recognized these aspects and cursorily alluded to them, they can be explored more expansively.[66]

After all these proposals, what follows is not an attempt to replace analyses of social ordering ("social structure") by a microsociological emphasis on social interaction. It is, rather, an effort to complement and refine. Moreover, the "domain" of social interaction is not fixed and immutable; it too is influenced by discursive transformations in society.[67] In our own context, we might consider the forms of address and language use associated with the "gallants" of the late sixteenth and early seventeenth century.[68] Although abrupt and not often expansive, forms of address as social interaction inform us about how people were negotiating their place within local society.

1
Forms of Address

Dogberry Goodman Verges, sir, speaks a little off the matter—an old man, sir, and his wits are not so blunt as, God
help, I would desire they were; but, in faith, honest as the
skin between his brows.[69]

Colloquial and informal address

Baptismal registration merely divulges the official form of naming of a child. It has been maintained that naming constitutes one
means of socialization of the child – into the kinship and society.[70]
Whilst, to a certain extent, that supposition has some validity, the
socialization of people into local society often involved a further
and later stage in naming and forms of address which involved col-
loquialism, the alias and hypocorism. Recovery of that social aspect
of address remains successful in only a fragmentary way, that is, for
only a small number of inhabitants in a local society.

In a rather florid form and higher register, the incumbent of
Penkridge acknowledged this colloquial address in 1640:

Senex Henricus, extravagans Mendicus.[71]

No doubt, the wandering beggar buried was customarily addressed as Old Henry. Similarly, then, was recorded the burial of
"Old Blake, a poor man" in the same parish in 1622.[72] Age (but not
necessarily authority and respect) thus contributed to colloquial
forms of address.[73] In both these cases in Penkridge, what was al-

most certainly at issue was the indignity of old age rather than its dignity.[74] Thomas Hylles was presented before the Ely consistory court for alleging that "olde John Dand" was "one nawghty bawdy knave."[75] Since his local acquaintance was in this manner, "Ould Hobden" was entered thus in the burial register of Blackburn in 1605.[76] A generation later, the burial was inscribed there of "Old Booth wife."[77] Aged women were susceptible to this form of address, as when in 1598 and 1599 "Ould Mother Whithead" and "Ould Mother Smith" were registered as buried at Guiseley.[78] The incumbent of Chipping accordingly recorded the burial of "Ould Siseley Bradley" in 1667.[79] For the maintenance of her daughter's bastard son, "ould Ellen Smith" of Nottingham, already in the bedehouse, received a quarterly allowance of 6s. for two years from 1632.[80]

That astute Dutchman and metropolitan playwright, Thomas Dekker, observed this usage in *The Witch of Edmonton*, co-authored some time after 1621 with William Rowley and John Ford, for Act 1 Scene 2 is the conversation about pre-nuptial agreement between Old Thorney and Old Carter, the parents of the betrothed.[81] This use of vocabulary was not merely a dramatic device but a reflection of social practice. In his will of 1571, Richard Northey, an alderman of Colchester, recollected that he had purchased tenements and land in Mile End from old Rennell.[82] It was part of accepted social discourse to use this form of reference, sometimes reverentially, sometimes with familiarity, often neutrally.

Most poignantly (because constantly), the incumbents of Garstang engaged in this language of age which no doubt reflected the colloquial form of address in the parochial speech community. Commencing with the burial of "Ould Barrow wife" in 1595, they inscribed a litany of senescence in their registers: "Ould Cottom wyffe," "Ould Rychardson wyffe," "Ould Threllfall wyffe," "Ould Jenet Sturide," "Ould Artcher wyffe," "Ould Jenet Lea," "Ould Edward Bladgburne," encompassing forty other such designations of "Ould" parishioners before concluding with, in 1647, "Ould Bee wyfe."[83] In another northern parish, the incumbents of Leeds remarked on burials in the same fashion:"Old Wright"; "Old Grannam widow"; "Old Ryshe wyffe"; "Old Christabell"; "Old John Browne" (both poor and blind); "Ould Elzabeth"; "Old Raphe

Foster"; "Old Thomas Bircktwisle"; "Old Newall wyffe"; "Old Sybell Walker"; "Old Cuthbert Hidrythe"; "Old Ellen of the Moore Towne"; "Old Whithead wife"; and "Old hummay."[84]

The adjective was employed almost as repetitively in the register of burials of Saint Oswald, Durham, from 1576 into the seventeenth century: "Old Thomas Bell"; "Old William Barrame"; "Old Henrie Burthere"; "One Old Agnes"; "Old Agnes Sawer wyddowe"; "Old John Markhame"; "Old Margaret Till widdowe"; "Old Margret Warde"; "Old Thomas Howsone"; and ultimately "Old Hugh," but with a multitude of other "Old" parishioners.[85] The appellation was also applied in the record of fourteen burials in Eyam (Derbyshire) between 1633 and 1640, beginning with Old Mrs Hatley and Old Anthony Wilson.[86]

In another context, in the dispute between Nathaniel Bacon and James Calthorpe in the early 1580s, it was alleged: "Also that old Baniard did burne the hurdells of old James Calthrop reared within Styfkey."[87] Bacon received notification from Downey in 1587 that "olde Smyth is not yett come from London... The olde man will sell his office if he can."[88] In yet a different setting, the common council of Salisbury in the late 1570s agreed that "olde mother grafton" should have a life tenancy of her house.[89] A decade earlier, the Assembly of Boston had resolved to fine for forestalling "Old Kamock of Lincoln."[90]

Of course, what we encounter here is the potential polyvocality of "old": were the contexts in which it was applied and used homologous? Some might have considered it a term of mild disparagement – with the implication "no longer relevant." Others might have insisted on it in a sense of respect, distance and dignity. Its meaning was contingent and depended on the perceptions of both user and described. Undoubtedly, it did import in some contexts affection and value. Hassall in 1615 referred to the burial of Elizabeth, wife of "owld Gehesy whilst he lived."[91] It eventuates that "Gehesye" had been Thomas Gissy, buried at the age of 87 in 1613.[92] Not only had Hassall calculated the exact age of "Gehesye," but he memorialized him elsewhere: "coming afterwards by a traditionall report (especially by old Gehesey the clerk who had some 50 years belonged to the church and seen the translation of 5 or 6 vicars)...."[93] Unreservedly, Hassall expressed an admiration and "old" remained an affective term.

This association between age and experience in the informal title "old" is illustrated further by events at Morebath (Devon) in 1536. At that time, the parish was in a quandary because of the lack of a clerk, which caused endless discussion. On one occasion, to facilitate mass, "old J. Waterus" was fetched to assist the vicar.[94]

Whether or not it was considered a term of disparagement and incapacity, the form of address occasioned some veneration in some contexts — as the repository of local memory.

> Owlde Agelsfeild towlde William Vydian 3 martii 1609 he knew one there buried in the chauncell. That half the slaughter howse standeth upon the churchyard ...[95]

In a dispute about Saint Faith's churchyard, the burgesses of Maidstone gave some credence to the antiquity of remembering of Old Agelsfeild.

The ascription of "old" can be refined further. It should not be presumed that "old" always intimated single and alone, although often it did. The justices of Somerset in 1607 corresponded about binding over "old Pricket his wife and his daughter" to appear before sessions.[96] Despite the status of "old Gehesye" and "old Pricket," nevertheless, the insinuation of "old" usually entailed not only aged, but also single and incapacitated. The compiler of the registers of Saint Augustine the Less in Bristol thus referred to "the old widow Brown an Almeswoman."[97] In Reading all of Old Bennet, Old Agnes and Old Sparkes were almsman or almswoman.[98] In 1547-8, the parishioners of Bishop's Stortford requested the churchwardens specifically to allow alms of 1s. 8d. to old John Patryk.[99]

Clarification of the status of 'old' is contained in the parish registers of Cuckfield (Sussex), which, between 1601 and 1615 recorded the burials of seventy-seven persons accorded the prefix "old," beginning with "old Robert Thornedene."[100] Here, "old" seemingly imputed very old: old John Michell at least eighty years old; old Thomas Winpenny reputed to be ninety-six; old Christine wife of Thomas Harlan, about eighty; and old Edward Vaux, over eighty.[101] The incumbent of Brighton was so impressed as to record of "ould John Browne housholder this man was as hee sayed an 105 years ould" in 1624.[102] The service of surgeon was contracted in Bury St Edmunds to old Wretham, who received £1 as part of his stipend in 1605 and 1607. Robert Wretham occupied this position there between 1595 and 1607. Indicative of his age in 1605-7 is the probate of his will in 1610.[103] The feoffees of Bury, who remunerated "olde Wretham," also purchased a sheet for the burial of Old Hanson in 1622.[104]

Charitable bequests in wills remembered those who were aged in local society, sometimes described as Mothers or Fathers as below, but otherwise simply as old so-and-so. The nature of the legacies reflects age. To old William Brewer was left a frieze gown by Peter Dawbye of Barking in 1558.[105] A best black coat was to be received by old Jooll a year later.[106] In 1538, "olde mother Oke" benefited from a will, receiving a shirt and two petticoats and "old Jone Voureacre" was remembered as a legatee in another Somerset will of 1558.[107] The imperfectly named old Margaret was, however, to be the recipient of money, 2s. 6d.[108] In his will of 1571, Thomas Finche bequeathed 1s. 8d. each to old Dowesett, old Sparrowe, and old Furlaye, to alleviate their poverty, it would seem.[109] A Staffordshire will of 1578 allowed a pair of shoes and 1s. to the old woman called Mother Barbour.[110]

Even so, sometimes the epithet old was a substitute for an imperfect knowledge of the person, for the churchwardens of Thorney presented Old Taylor, whose forename they could learn, as an absolute recusant in 1621.[111] This aspect can be discerned through the parish register of Winwick (Lancashire) in 1635: initially, the incumbent registered the burial of "old John of the Hey," but corrected this to Old John Edge.[112]

Extending past 1640 for a specific purpose, we can see how the epithet insinuated even into tax lists which were compiled through local inquest. In the late-seventeenth-century Hearth Tax exemption lists for Norwich are encountered old Chrithood, old Mose, old Flude, old Harper, old Smeth, old Touly, old Hackney, old Pye, old Cutter, old Thirtrekle, old Simpson, old Bishop, old Dowsing, old Chroch, old Riches, old Hogskin, old Sparke, old Blackamore, old Hudson, old Samond, old Shead, old Abbetts, old Wigginton, old Read, old Beamont, old Kidd, old Nicolls, old Moy, old Carr, old Miles and old Watson.[113] Most were accounted for a single hearth, although some for two, but all certified exempt—presumably for poverty resulting from age. In the more formal taxation listings for the hearth tax in the late seventeenth century, the adjective old occurred but infrequently, however, although it *did* occur and its occurrences reveal the characteristic of the epithet by that time. In fact, in its few incidences it referred exclusively to poor old people: Old Brede in Stowmarket who had a single hearth but was certified exempt; Old Ormes who had two hearths in Ipswich but was also discharged; the pauper Old Sayre in Wenlock; 'Ould Carr', discharged for two hearths in Seale; and Old Hunt also exempted for two hearths in Bromley.[114]

A further complication of old is confronted occasionally, for it sometimes differentiated two homonymous males—usually males. Jane Schache thus made bequests under her will to her brother, young John, and to the children of old John.[115] Similarly, Joan Denton, widow of Shenfield, in 1570 referred in her will to her sons, old John and young John—so that old simply reflected seniority rather than age in this particular context.[116] John Bucke had, by his wife Margaret, three sons, the eldest William, and the next two his namesakes, old John and young John, both Johns appointed his executors in 1561 by the description of young and old John.[117] That situation obtained in another Essex household, for the testator in 1566 left 10s. to each of his wife's sons, old John Cheston and young John Cheston.[118] Although William Pollard, an Essex husbandman, had six children, his eldest sons included old William and young William, mentioned in his will of 1569.[119] So too, Robert Shinglewood of Boxted in Essex in 1570 bequeathed a ewe to each of young John Shinglewood and old John Shinglewood.[120] How much resonance the adjective might have conveyed is illustrated in an entry in the Woodstock chamberlains' accounts in 1647. Then, old Hickes received 4s. of the money bequeathed by old Master Hiorne for the poor in the almshouse. Indubitably, then, Hickes was an old man in the almshouse, the epithet indicating his age. Old Master Hiorne has more complications, for Edmund Hiorne had died in 1629, succeeded by his son another Edmund who died in 1669. In this case, old Master Hiorne imputed both the expiry of Edmund the father and his seniority to the living Edmund.[121]

Less frequently employed was the adjective little, but some Essex wills divulge its use. One testator left a "wennel" to little Bess Sawman in 1564, whilst in that year a great hutch comprised the legacy to little John Francke.[122] Without any concrete evidence, it might be supposed that little referred not to stature but to age—an alternative to young. This assumption is probably confirmed by a legacy in a Banbury will to little Richard, the testator's sister's son, in 1607.[123] It also accords with the legacy of the remainder in a house to "litill John Longe my brother" in 1529, although it is less obviously so with the legacy to the testator's hine, "litill John Catill" in 1554..[124]

Other marginal people in local populations were only partly recognized by their formally-given names. In the year of the Armada, "Georg the Swynherd" was interred at Bishop Middleham.[125] At Manchester in 1598 was buried "Jane the aple woman 70 yeres and neverr maried."[126] Some forty years earlier the registers of the same parish recorded the burial of John "the sonne of Hyndle the pyper of Skipton."[127] A similar sort of periphrasal description was applied to "Thomas ould sheapard of Dunkenhalghe" when his burial was entered in the register of Blackburn in 1624.[128] The incumbent of Haslemere in Surrey resorted to the same convention in 1606: "the Old Cowpers wife was buried" and "Jones the old Cinder picker" was interred.[129] Burials at Tamworth comprehended "Margaret the swinherds daughter of Wiggenton" in 1572 and "Gabriel a musition" in 1591.[130] With even less decorum, a burial was recorded in 1591 in Durham as simply "the swynherdes chylde, not chrystened."[131] Quite extraordinarily, a few of those assessed in the taxation of 1524 for Buckinghamshire suffered the same indignity: Bennet the sawyer, Atwell the capper, Thomas "of that ferme," and Rowland "servyngman."[132] Since all were assessed at the lowest level (£1) their incidence confirms the association of the poorer sort with imperfect recognition. Rather than remembered by their formal surname, therefore, these marginal people were recollected by a periphrase describing their occupation, almost a reversion to the unstable and flexible occupational bynames of the high Middle Ages.

Less emotively remote, but still maintaining social distance, was the employment of an affix of occupation. Sir Hugh Smyth was advised by letter that "Hedges the Carier" was bringing him a new scarlet suit in 1620.[133] In 1578, Heydon wrote to Nathaniel Bacon: "Wheras this bearer, Blogge, a brickmaker, informeth me that he hathe a servant...."[134] Although this form of address occurred most frequently in accounts, it is probable that it was encountered too within the normal usage of the speech community. At Norwich, then, two aldermen were delegated on behalf of the council to inspect the work done by "Arnold the Carpenter" in 1632.[135] In that same year, the bailiffs of the hospital there were ordered to remunerate "Fisher the Carpenter" for paling.[136] When notice was intended about his stall in 1633, the minutes recorded him as "Whatlock the Bocher."[137]

How it was employed to denote tradesmen is illustrated well by the financial accounts of Ipswich, which frequently recorded payments to "Palmer the plumer" in the 1560s.[138] Those accounts compensated also "Cutberd the scavell man," "Martin the musician," "Harpam the pynner," "Smythe the laborer," "Becket the carpenter," "Clarke the mason," "King the thatcher" and "Smithe the brewer."[139] Such cursory and perfunctory identification of tradesmen was common. Not only did they occur as forms of reference in accounts, but also in colloquial oral communication, for the presentment of Thomas Ansloe for baking without license or freedom of Liverpool qualified him as "called otherwyse Thomas the Baker," presumably, given his offense, so addressed by local inhabitants.[140]

Semi-formal address

Although the "forename" was conferred as the official and formal name, to what extent was it superseded by forms of address during the life-course?[141] If we consider widows, for example, a proportion, it seems, would not be addressed by their forename, but by their status. When the unfortunate Thomas Watson was slowly expiring in 1596, allegedly after suffering a beating from his master,

> ... some Wedensdaye morning the sayd Thomas Watson prayed his wyfe to goe to the widdow Franke *alias* Carye and to get of her some thinge for her [sic] for an inward bruse which was upon the right side.[142]

Although not all widows were described in this manner, numerous were, so that, for example, in the register of burials of Chipping in Lancashire between 1620 and 1661, twenty-four of the elderly female deceased were registered as Widow with surname, as "Widowe Parker" in 1629.[143] Comparable entries in the register of burials of Saint Mary, Shrewsbury, accounted for at least seventeen female deceased between 1597 and 1616.[144] In the parish of Saint Oswald in Durham, between 1551 and 1603, twenty-five interred women were described by the epithet Widow and their surname.[145]

Although the register of burials for Saint Mary, Reading, commences in 1538, it was not until 1595, with Widow Grantame, that the formula of Widow plus surname first appeared in written form. Thereafter, a succession of thirty-six Widows with surname followed.[146] The same number of female deceased who were buried at Gainsborough was also designated as Widow in combination with surname, after 1568.[147] In Grantham, in 1604, where 102 females were interred, thirty-three were wives, fifty-one daughters, accounting for eighty-four; another seventeen were described as Widow plus surname.[148] Before 1640, twenty of the females interred in Richmond, Surrey, were described by the formula of Widow and surname.[149] Seventy women buried at Chesterfield in the first thirty-five years of the seventeenth century, moreover, were described by Widow plus surname.[150] At Bishop's Still's visitation in 1594, those apparently presented—a long list of inhabitants—included seventeen women who, like Widow Dolpen, were identified by the title Widow and their surname.[151]

Designation by Widow and surname was not, however, a permanent and irrevocable form of address, but depended on remaining single. When Nathaniel Bacon, as J. P., was taking depositions about the murder of Edward Stone, he included the examination of Elizabeth Spicer, the wife of John Spicer of Kings Lynn (1601). Her deposition commenced: "the said examinate saith that about seven yeres since she being then called the widdow Hyll...." [152]

After the destructive fire in Banbury, the citizens of Coventry dispatched assistance which was distributed to named recipients in 1628. Amongst the female beneficiaries, twenty-two were described as Widow plus their surname and four by their forename, surname and the status of widow. Only three other women (forename and surname) obtained this compensation.[153] Widows were predominantly known, then, by the formula of Widow and their surname and they lived for the most part close to the margins of existence.

In the late seventeenth century, the convention of describing these women as Widow and their surname was consolidated and their association with poverty can be further demonstrated – through the hearth tax listings (See Table 1.1, page 141. Widows in the Hearth Tax for seven southern and Midland counties, 1664-1674[154]; and Table 1.2, page 142. Widows in the Shropshire Hearth Tax, 1672[155]).

In all the tabulated material above, the number of widows, chargeable and non-chargeable, represents the number of female heads of household identified by the title Widow and their surname.[156] Equally, in all those tabulations, those women are principally associated with one or two hearths with a predominant number exempted from the tax, reflecting their poverty.[157] One exception, however, was the listings for Oxfordshire, for here only about half of the three hundred or so widows were denominated as Widow with surname. An equal number were represented by a different form: "Elizabeth Wallis widdow" of Headington defined by her three hearths, is an exemplar.[158] Moreover, widows in Oxfordshire did not experience the same degree of poverty; fewer of them received the concession of exemption, it seems, and the proportion restricted to a single hearth was much lower here, although there was variation across the *pays* of the county.

In Dorset, about 53 percent of all the 850 or so widows were listed as Widow with surname, whilst a further 3.5 percent were included as Mistress with surname and widow. Although in this county also, the distribution was concentrated on one or two hearths, a significant proportion was also responsible for three hearths. Moreover, a very small element was exempted or discharged from the tax. In Dorset, the reason for exemption was very specific: poverty ("pauper"). All the widows exempted were described by the formula Widow with surname and they were associated predominantly with a single hearth (See Table 1.3, page 142. Widows in the Oxfordshire Hearth Tax, 1665[159]; and Table 1.4, page 143. Widows in the Dorset Hearth Tax, 1662-4[160]).

In several urban places, an amended distribution is apparent, with a smaller proportion of widows discharged or exempted for poverty than in rural villages. What the figures demonstrate then is the *opportunity* for a higher extent of independent widowhood in urban locations, since a higher proportion of women had more than two hearths and the proportion of exempt widows, although still high, was lower than in rural locations. The mean number of hearths held by urban widows remained, nonetheless, below the mean for all households, at about a mean of 1.8 hearths per widow, compared with global means of 2.32 hearths per household in Worcester, 3.08 in Cambridge, 2.59 in Exeter, 2.4 in Leicester, 2.06 in Newcastle, 2.38 in Norwich, and 3.2 in York.[161]

In most of these urban centers, widows in the hearth tax lists were recorded as Widow and their surname, but the anomaly was Shrewsbury (See Table 1.5, page 143. Widows in the Hearth Tax for some urban places[162]).

In that urban location, widows were inscribed in three different forms: "Mistress Wood widowe"; Widow Jones; and "Margaret Griffithes widowe."[163] To some extent, these distinctions reflected residential segregation, for the form Mistress … widow was largely located in the central precincts of Castle, Stone and Welsh Wards and associated with higher numbers of hearths.[164] By contrast, the form of Widow and surname was reserved, by and large, for poorer widows inhabiting the suburbs, predominantly with one or two hearths.[165] Overall, then, the hearth tax for Shrewsbury enumerated 127 widows chargeable to the tax by the title Widow with their surname and thirty-one by the formula Mistress…widow. Rather surprisingly, widows who were certified exempt for poverty (just under thirty) were predominantly registered by their forename, surname and the status of widow, as Margaret Griffithes, widow. Quite the reverse obtained in Leicester as it was an exception to this relative urban prosperity of widows. Of 131 widows in Leicester, eighty-three were discharged, often explicitly because of their poverty; 103 had but a single hearth. Of those 131, ninety-one (70 percent) received the description Widow and surname[166] (See Table 1.6, page 143. Women in the hearth tax exemption listings in Norwich, King's Lynn and Great Yarmouth 1673-4).

Even more emphatic was the social situation in the second city, Norwich, where in the exemption lists for the hearth tax more than

1,100 women were described as Widow and surname, all exempt and 82 percent having a single hearth. Quite in contrast, the tax collectors in Worcester used this designation (Widow with surname) for merely a small proportion of the women assessed to the hearth tax in 1678 – only twenty-seven women.[167] We might assume here that the collectors were disguising the normal address for these women under a more formal register of description.

For people at a certain life-course stage, address by the forename was too familiar; what was necessary was some title of respect and early-modern people supplied several. These courtesy titles conferred both dignity and social distance to the elderly.[168] What we must take into account, however, is how, although the intention might have been respectful, such colloquial titles might have been appropriated and subverted.

Amongst the category of widows, a few were accorded the colloquial title Mother. Hassall in 1606 registered the burial of "Mother Fuller alias Taylor" of the almshouses.[169] A deposition at Nottingham in 1588 declaimed that Richard Wryghte of Cambridge had lodged "at one wyddoez house named Mother Jane dwelling in the Butcherye."[170] Accordingly, a select group of widows was designated in this way in the burial register of Gainsborough between 1570 and 1587: "Old Mother Warde"; "Mother Magham"; "Olde Mother Lyndsay"; "Mother Hameltone Wyddowe"; and "Old Mother Normantone."[171] Between 1579 and 1607, sixteen of the females interred in East Grinstead were titled Mother (and two Father).[172] By contrast, only four were so designated in the burial register of Bishop's Cannings, compressed in 1592-6.[173] Half a dozen occurred in the burial register of Shotley, five between 1571 and 1589.[174] A full dozen mothers were interred in the parish of Hunsden in Hertfordshire between the burial of Mother Jones in 1548 and Mother Walet in 1629, although most occurred after Old Mother Brande in 1597.[175] The combination of old and Mother – as also with old Mother Nicholson in 1585, old Mother Gibson in 1602, old Mother Wood in 1609, old Mother Swyere in 1611 and old Mother Biggs in 1615 – merely confirmed the characteristic of the age of mothers. Almost superfluously for us, but significantly for local society, the clerk recorded at the burial of old Mother Bearman in 1611 "an auncient widdow of this parishe" and of Mother Wood "an auncient old woman" in

1615, as if not to qualify Mother, but to emphasize their longevity and status. As elsewhere, fewer men were accorded the title of father—half as many during the same period, commencing with the burial of Father Homes, servant to Sir John Carye, buried in 1549.[176]

Instances in the registers of burials in Reading expand upon the status of "Mothers." In addition to Mother Mary (1574), Mother Justice (1587), Old Mother Twitt (1610), and Old Mother Weston (1611), none of whom received any further definition, Mother Margery Stokes was a "pore almeswoman," Mother Tomes shared that experience and status (1615) and Mother Prince was the widow of Henry (1617).[177] On her burial at Haslemere in 1649, Mother Woodes, widow, had attained a venerable age: *circa anno centessimo* (in about her hundredth year).[178] Aged and often impotent as they were, Mothers received assistance from the churchwardens, illustrated by payments at Cratfield to Mother Grene during her illness and wood for Mother Smyth.[179]

The accounts of the borough of Stratford-upon-Avon reveal further the real association of the colloquial titles Mother/Father and age, but also experience. In 1563, Mother Margaret deposited 3s. 4d. for her chamber in the almshouse.[180] In the following year, Mother Helen too made a contribution towards her chamber.[181] In 1573, Mother Locke was admitted to the almshouse (and, in the following year, Father Bunney).[182] Entry to the almshouse was permitted to Mother Ashwell in 1584 and by 1593 she had assumed the role of sweeping before the chapel.[183] Father Degge paid the customary amount of 6s. 8d. for admission to the almshouse in 1597.[184] In the City parish of St Mary at Hill, the annual wage of "olde father mondaye" amounted to £4 in 1554-5 and he received an additional 4d. for providing drink for the singing men of the choir, but described then as "olde mundy."[185] In Bishop's Stortford, old father Lute in 1520-1 acquitted to the churchwardens what appears to be a concessionary rent of 1d. In subsequent years (1522-9), he was referred to simply as old Lewte.[186] These payments might indicate the preference of some older people to maintain their independence through work, although we should also be sensitive to the compulsion and expectation of their time and also to the issue whether that kind of work preserved their dignity in old age.

This connotation of Mother/Father with age is further demonstrated by the census of the poor conducted in Ipswich in 1597, in which Father Herley was described as able, a laborer, but aged 70, Mother Ingram as aged 80, but capable of spinning and carding, Mother Forde, aged 80, as an oakum picker, as also Mother Bunche, a widow, aged 70.[187] Age, in some cases, implied impotence and lack of dignity. Father Tofte, deceased, had before 1589 occupied a room in the almshouse of Tooley's foundation in Ipswich.[188] The poor and sick indigent had received support: Mothers Harryson, Taylor, Glood, Martin, Copsey, Ingram (six times in great sickness), Orgon, Collen, and Antonye.[189] Allowances or pensions explained the regular appearance of Mothers in the Layston parish memoranda book in 1616, when amounts were allowed to Mothers Buckhame, Dobs, Batsford, Wynne, Cooke, Stringer, Pets, Pelham, Fleminge, Lynsell, Turner, Hocke, Browne, Chappell, and Hills, as well as Fathers Fleminge and Holgate.[190]

As acts of charity and beneficence, Mothers and Fathers were recipients of small testamentary bequests from other villagers. Often such legacies consisted of clothing, such as those coats directed to Fathers Holte and Deathe in Essex wills of 1560 or the doublet and pair of hose left by Philip Genno, a husbandman, to Father Humfray in 1570.[191] Cash amounts of 3s. 4d. were included in the legacies of William Locke, husbandman of Great Bentley, to six poor women, including Mothers Denmark and Page—associating this informal title with poverty in these instances.[192] Poverty too is implicit in the bequests of small amounts of grain provided by an Essex husbandman to Fathers Golde and Gyles and Mother Leawin in 1564.[193]

In another Essex will, the beneficiaries included old Father Chekin and Mother Jones, both receiving 1s.[194] An old groat comprised the legacy to Mother Elkyne in 1559 in one will and in another Mother Dawber was remembered through a bequest of 1s.[195] In 1560, Fathers Spayn and Bryon were the beneficiaries of money legacies from an Essex husbandman.[196] Similar pecuniary legacies were afforded under wills to Mothers Jomme, Harkone and Campe in 1564: 1s.; 1s.; and 1s. 4d.[197] In 1571, 1s. each was the entitlement of Mother Townsend and Father Trymynge under an Essex will.[198] The singleman, Barnard Payne of Little Bromley, allowed under his will

1s. each to Mother Cartwrighte and Mother Stone.[199] Old Mother Clarke was recipient of 1s. under a will of 1567.[200]

The examples can be multiplied, although perhaps only a few more will suffice to make this connection between Mothers, Fathers, the aged and poverty. When Elizabeth Wealls of Corringham ordained legacies of 1s. to the poor of that village, she nominated Mother Shepard (who actually received 2s. and a frock), Father Corine, and six widows.[201] Mothers Lillye, Hewet and Clarke had allocations of 6d. each under Gilbert Pere's last wishes.[202] By the same impulse, a brickmaker of West Bergholt, Thomas Gale, in 1571 remembered seven poor folk, specifying amongst others Mothers Sparlinge, Butler, Freman and Hall, to receive 4d. each.[203] Inspired in the same way, the yeoman, John Bridge senior, designated a few pence each to Fathers Wever, Water, and Sparowe, Mothers More, Selbye, Carter and Hoord, old Clement, and numerous widows.[204] Perhaps in accordance with the imperatives of a more evangelical religion in Essex, these testators were anxious to remember the less fortunate and aged in their local society, especially those reverentially addressed, if fallen on harder times, as Mother or Father.

All these small amounts suggest the remembrance of the poor, aged members of local society. Indeed, a testamentary bequest to the poor of Mucking in 1571 specifically mentioned Mother Brewar and Mother Sawken who were to receive half a bushel of rye each.[205] An Essex will which made provision of 4d. each to the poorest people in Ramsey in 1568 named *inter alia* Father Wallesse and Father Lounts (as well, in reference to anonymity, the lame maid).[206]

Under the will of Agnes Mannynge, widow of Ranford, in 1561, the gifts to these older women were no doubt intended to recollect female social networks, for the widow ordained that her gown be passed to Mother Foster, a kerchief to Mother Laylande, and a cassock and smock to Mother Gosby. It was precisely the symbolism of the personal items of clothing to her female peers that was important and reflected meaning in their relationship.[207] The same symbolic value inhered in the bequests by another widow, Thomasine Astyn, in 1561 to Mothers Coke, Cutbarde and Curtys, the first two obtaining a single petticoat and the last two old ones. Ordaining her will in 1564, Alice Lavor of West Bergholt made provision for three women titled mother: a smock, kerchief, apron and 1s. for Mother

Freman, a petticoat, smock, apron, kerchief and 1s. for Mother Am-field, and to Mother Butler an apron, kerchief and 1s. In contrast, she made a cash benefaction to Father Hall (1s.).[208] So too, the wid-ow Margaret Over of Barking cemented at her death her association with her female peers through her will in 1574, leaving kerchiefs to Goodwives Byrde, Marshe, Gowson, Tyrrey, Somerskale, Hub-berd, Lynlye and Clifton, but also to Mothers Garse, Marshall and Gyllet.[209] The intimacy of the personal items of clothing marked the intimate nature of the female networks.[210]

Some bequests obviously related back to services provided by Mothers, as the smock left to Mother Randes for her pains.[211] Doubtless because of their expertise from long experience, some Mothers continued to serve the local society, laying out the dead, as did Mother Sparham at Cratfield in 1598 and 1603.[212] Despite the circumspection of others about a body infected by plague in 1531, it was "Mother Gryffythe whiche dyd kepe and wynde the sayd corpus...."[213] Mother Creswicke was provided with wood to make up the fire at the last reckoning of the churchwardens' accounts there in 1622.[214] Surplices and rochets were fabricated by Mother Wynday at Lydd in 1533.[215] At Saint Peter's in Hertford, Mother Hickman furnished bread for communion and constantly washed the surplices, communion cloths and linen in 1580-4. There too Mother Gray cared for Carter's children, presumably orphans.[216] It was Mother Quayle who occupied the position of governess of the Spittle House (keeper of Saint Peter's, the "sicke house") in Bury Saint Edmunds, receiving her wages from the Feoffees there, from at least 1608-12, perhaps having retired at the last date because of her sore leg.[217] Mother (sometimes Widow) Snowdon was respon-sible for the custody of the Bridewell (House of Correction) in Bury between 1597 and 1607—a decade of service—and she continued to appear in the Feoffees' accounts down to 1622, indicative of her age.[218] Other Mothers in Bury provided more occasional assistance: Mother Erle had custody of a poor child; Mother (Widow) Shipp provided for two others; Mother Snowden cared for Pratt's wife in her mental distress and also healed Many's son.[219]

In multiple instances, those dignified as Mother acted as mid-wives. In the early 1560s, Mother Alden acted as midwife at the labor of Katherine Dingle and elicited a confession that the father of the child was "Browne of St Martin's at palace gate."[220] John Childe, son of Thomas Childe, entering the world in 1578, was baptized at home by the midwife, Mother Tood, as also the infant Francis Cowper was baptized by the midwife, Mother Tarne, in 1576—both in York.[221] In Norwich in the mid 1560s, a deposition about the alleged father of a child was made by Mother Alden, the midwife at the child's birth.[222] Through such activities, these "Mothers" actually acted out a rôle as maternal elders in local society.

Mother, nonetheless, was not exclusively associated with one particular social level. When corresponding in about 1632 about her projected marriage, Elizabeth Phelips informed Thomas Smyth that "hee [her intended] will not be fooled by no precice matron or bussie balde patted knave, you know I am sure that I mean Mother Caple and frier Claxton..."[223]

Implicit in the attribution of this "title" was age, often imputing venerable status. Dekker could, for dramatic effect, invert the meaning of this address in referring to "Mother Witch."[224] The principal characteristic of age was expressed in the description of Mother Agnes Gryne, aged eighty, in 1570.[225] It was probably no more than tautology when the incumbent registered in 1605 the burial of "Emmott commonly called old mother Carter."[226] Age must also be inferred for the half a dozen women, headed by Mother Clarke, who inhabited the almshouse in Cambridge in the early seventeenth century.[227] Both the titles Mother and Father often imputed the incapacity of age. In Boxford, therefore, Father Baker received 4d. from the churchwardens when he was sick and Mothers Sare and Medowe a quarterly allowance of the same amount towards her rent.[228] Relief was delivered by the Feoffees of Bury to Mothers Muriell and Spere in 1595, although the former, already sick, died shortly afterwards.[229] Mother Shilling benefited there in the same way in 1608.[230] Succor was furnished to Mother Thompson of Bury after she had been hurt by a falling wall in 1609.[231] Mother Glover was interred in the same borough in 1609.[232]

As might be expected, Mother was not an exclusive title of address. Women of this age and status might be addressed by more than one title. In *Gammer Gurton's Needle*, then, the character Dame Chat was also referred to by other characters as Mother Chat and Goodwife Chat, although by far most frequently as Dame.[233]

The corresponding appellation for men—Father—was deployed in an even more selective manner.[234] In 1576 at Gainsborough, "the old father William Luptone" was interred.[235] Although infrequent, men described as Father existed in Reading: Father Burchame and Father Diggrie, both buried in Armada year, and almost thirty years later Father Toten.[236] At Worksop, the passing of Father Sawell in 1584 was noticed.[237] In the burial register for Richmond, Father Colman (1592) was outnumbered by Mothers Burgis, Spechin, Gwillam, and Washington, in the late sixteenth century.[238] Occasionally, someone designated "Father" still had family responsibilities, for Father Stubbard at Cratfield was entitled to a payment for his daughter in 1581.[239] Infrequently, one of these senior inhabitants (by age) remained active and purposeful, for Father Cobbe of Lydd was remunerated for mending the bellows of the great organs in 1530.[240]

Formal address

Equally, the courtesy address of Mistress was denied to all but a tiny minority, merely four deceased women buried at Saint Mary in Shrewsbury between 1602 and 1618.[241] The significance of the title is epitomized by the burial of their husbands inside the church of Saint Mary at Hill in the City in 1531-2 by Mistresses Ideall, Goodwyn and Johnson.[242] When Mistress Margaret Grace died, the incumbent of Saint Oswald, Durham, described her as "a verye honest nighbore and about the aige of one hundreth yeares or their aboute," indicating the sort of criteria for this respectful form of address.[243] In most cases, however, the courtesy title was a consequence of their husband's status: "Mystris Elizabeth Chater wife of Mr Christopher Chater"; Mistress Claxton wife to Master Robert Claxton; Mistress Eleanor Newton wife of Henry Newton of Rilly, gent.; and Mistress Ann Richardson wife of Master John Richardson, the elder, esq.[244]

Master, however, had other contexts. It was demanded of servants, in the widest connotations of that term, that they refer to their employers as master. As a consequence of this meaning, some wives were addressed as dame.

My maister suppeth herbie at a gentylman's place
And I must thither feache my dame, Maistres Boundgrace.[245]

A singlewoman of Little Waltham, Jane Schache, accordingly
appointed her master, Mr Francke, the overseer of her will, and bequeathed to her dame Francke a worsted kirtle.[246] About the same
time (1559), another Essex testator selected as his overseer his master, Robert Steven of Leigh, but also made a legacy of one old royal
and one old angel to his dame Stevyns (sic).[247] In the same manner, William Heigham intended to leave 10s. to his master Lawrence, whom he made executor, and the same amount to his dame
Larance in 1564.[248] When, in 1560, John Webbe of Sible Hedingham
constituted his master, John Thryft, his executor, he also ordained a
legacy of his best hat for his dame Thryft.[249] Some eleven years later,
Elizabeth Smallewoode left her worsted kirtle to her dame Allen.[250]
As a servant of John Thursten, John Browne of Frinton felt compelled under his will of 1570 to proffer 5s. to his dame Thurstone.[251]
It is significant in all these cases that the bequest was made to the
dame, the master's wife, rather than to the master, who might, however, in a few cases act as executor or supervisor. The gift of grati-
fication was indirect and to a woman. Displeasure of the master's
wife, however, might lead to complication. Robert Myller, referring
several times to the dissatisfaction expressed by his dame, asked
his master, William George, in 1563 that he might then be released
from his service.[252] In this context of trade, industry and commerce,
then, the equivalent title associated with Master might well be the
less prepossessing dame.[253]

Dekker again perfectly represented this social propriety, reflected in Hodge's speech to his master's wife after her social elevation:

Roger [Hodge] Aye, forsooth, dame – mistress, I should say,
but the old term so sticks to the roof of my mouth; I can
hardly lick it off.[254]

Of course, position was most assured through the title Master,
reserved for a local elite in the inscription of burials in the parish
registers. A very select few were accorded this honorific status in
the register of the urban parish of Saint Mary, Shrewsbury, not al-

ways explained, but sometimes justified by the incumbent: Master John Perch "Senior Allderman of this towne" and Master Andrew Lewis "one of the Alldermen of Salop."[255] In Reading those designated Master also tended to be office-holders and principal inhabitants, such as the former Mayors Master Richard Aldworth and Master Richard Watlington, interred respectively in 1594 and 1601.[256] Indeed, the title Master largely differentiated chief from secondary burgesses in that borough in 1616.[257] In 1612, the body of Master William Okham, bailiff, received burial, followed in 1616 by Master Richard Turner, J.P., and in 1617 by another J.P., Master Bernard Harrison.[258] The title was accorded to comparable males in the register of Saint Oswald, Durham, referring to the burials of, for example, Master John Lambton, draper and former mayor, and Master Henry Shaft[o]e, J.P., esq., in 1629 and 1631.[259]

By the late sixteenth century, the status of Master might have been extended more widely than earlier in the century. When the members of the councils of Oxford were "invited" to subscribe to Dame Margaret Northern's Coffer—a charitable bequest—in 1547, the title of Master was reserved exclusively to the Mayor and seven of his brethren at the head of the list, whilst the remaining sixty-six—bailiffs, chamberlains and common councilors—were allowed no such honorific address.[260] As the Easter book for the parish of Saint Mary in Nottingham was compiled in 1582, the aldermen in each ward consistently received the title Master.[261] The distinction between aldermen and other councilors of the Hall meeting of Stratford-upon-Avon was maintained also by the attribution of the title Master to aldermen and no title to the other burgesses of the Hall, a differentiation established by 1564.[262] The composition of the convocation of the City of Wells also made a demarcation—although inconsistently—between aldermen (Master) and others (no title), particularly in the early seventeenth century.[263] When, moreover, a taxation was assessed by the acre towards "his Majesty's provision" in 1618, the fifty-eight contributors were distinguished by status. The restricted number of assessed denotes their local elite status. Twenty-one were accorded the title Master (and three Mistress). Of this distinctive twenty-one, eleven belonged to the current aldermanry in convocation.[264] Perhaps more surprisingly ambitious was the self-appellation of all the leet jurors of Manchester from 1592 as *generosus* (of gentle status).[265]

The dramatic utility of the term was deployed by Udall in *Roister Doister*, in which the deceitful Merrygreek constantly addressed Ralph Roister Doister as your mastership or, in elision, "your mash-yp."[266] This Matthew, of course, was quite possibly, in the light of his later confession, mockingly addressing the self-indulgent Ralph, so the dramatic purpose may reflect on the ambiguity of the title at this time, a form of address to which all and sundry aspired.

Since status in rural society continued to depend on landed estate, it is not surprising that Nathaniel Bacon, in delivering his charge to the jury at sessions in 1595, proclaimed:

> It is not unlike but manie of you do knowe of a contencion which resteth in this corner of our contrey between two gentlemen, the one Mr Forrest, who marryed the widdow Mistres Wyndham and was sometyme wife unto Mr Wheatley, and the other Mr Wheatly....

for the issue concerned the inheritance of land.[267] Incidentally here were demonstrated the meanings of several honorific titles, of which Mistress was one.

The titular address of Mistress for women cannot be totally separated from an association with males. Although conferred in deference to the status of the husband or late husband, the honorific title permitted a public recognition of women. When he narrated her interment in the upper end of the chancel near her husband, Hassall not only described Mistress Isabel Goodman as the widow of Master John Goodman, but acknowledged her abilities: she was writing a letter when she had a stroke. Moreover, he recollected, she had outlived her husband by twenty-four years, with the implication of her own merit.[268] When he referred to Mistress Bridget Stevenson in 1602—she was also buried in the chancel—he reflected only that she was "an auntient widdowe."[269]

In the urban context, the association of Master and Mistress with formal status was expressed through burial inside the parish church, as demonstrated at Saint Michael le Belfry in York. Between 1599 and 1630, twenty-one men buried in the highest part of the choir were inscribed in the register of burials as Mr. Of the remainder designated Master, four were interred in the nave aisle, eight in the north part of the choir, one in the transept, nine in the south part of the choir, two in the north aisle and one in the south aisle, whereas six were buried inside the minster. The pattern of burial of women described as Mistress was similar: six in the south choir; one in the south aisle; six in the highest part of the choir; two in the transept; two in the north choir; the same in the north aisle; one in the nave; and one in the minster.[270]

Again, Dekker perceived the meaning of Master and its connotation of gentle status in *The Witch of Edmonton*.

> *Old Thorney* You offer, Master Carter, like a gentleman,
> I cannot find fault with it, 'tis so fair.
> *Old Carter* No gentleman I, Master Thorney; spare the Mastership, call me by my name, John Carter. Master is a title my father, nor his before him, were acquainted with. Honest Hertfordshire yeomen, such an one am I.[271]

Whilst both Thorney and Carter, from their different social stations, correlated Master and gentility, Carter vehemently declined to accept the title. In fact, Carter's retort suggests something suspect about the status of gentleman (and the "new" social differentiation in general) and the playwrights here might well have directed their moralizing to the contested nature of that status by the late sixteenth and early seventeenth century, since so many aspired to the titles of gentleman and Master, as has been described above for the urban elite, and as is vividly illustrated by the adoption of the title masters of the convocation of Wells by the leading councilors in that city from 1604 and the ascription gentlemen of the twenty-four of the council of Worcester in 1621.[272]

The playwrights' script, moreover, accords with Sir Thomas Smythe's *De Republica Anglorum*, published almost forty years previously (1583), although compiled by Smythe in the early 1560s. When referring in chapter 23 to the yeomanry of England, Smythe maintained that:

> These be not called masters, for that (as I saide) pertaineth to gentlemen only: But to their surnames, men add goodman
> ...they are called goodman *Luter*, goodman *White*, good-

man *Finch*, goodman *Browne*, amongest their neighbours, I
meane not in matters of importance or in lawe.[273]

Such was this association with status that Chapman, Jonson
and Marston could reproduce it, somewhat bitterly, in *Eastward Ho!*
Although of gentle origin, Quicksilver was a younger son and thus
apprenticed in the City. His disdain for his Master and peers was
evident, erupting in conversation:

> Marry, foh, goodman flatcap! 'Sfoot, though I am a prentice
> I can give arms, and my father's a justice o' peace by de-
> scent.[274]

The title of goodman thus corresponded with middling status,
in this context with trade, industry and commerce, symbolized by
the flat cap.

Now, although Smythe began his exegesis of English society
when he was a classical scholar at Cambridge in 1562-5, despite
opinion that his was a rhetorically traditional treatise, he was indeed close to social practice in these comments. Indeed, Edward
Vaudrey, a Sussex vicar, in his will of 1557 equated goodmen and
goodwives with householders: "to every other housholder in my
parishe...betwixt the goodman and the goodwife..."[275] The title
goodman was, furthermore, an indication of good neighborliness.

Perhaps, then, the most affective titles in early-modern society
continued to be goodman and goodwife, usually reserved for social
peers—often, in the case of males, parish officers—who performed
some service. For that very reason, the address is encountered most
frequently in churchwardens' or constables' accounts.[276] "Item for
Goodman Filbie and William Newsom cargies when they rid to Sir
Francis Boldinge giving the account for colecting for the pore...,"
as entered in the churchwardens' accounts for Cratfield in 1576.[277]
A churchwarden commented of himself and his co-warden in 1541-
2: "memorandum whan the Goodman Dowsyng and I dyd ryde
to the Erle of Sussex..."[278] In 1596-9, payments were rendered to
Goodman Rouse, the constable levying the musters for Ireland.[279]
Accordingly also, expenses were redeemed for Goodman Taylor in
the churchwardens' accounts of Market Harborough in 1607-8.[280]

Those who lodged poor travelers at the request of the constables —a legitimate demand—were accorded the same title, accounting for the payments to Goodman Pake for hospitality for three and Goodwife Wymant for seven in 1612 and 1620.[281] Goodman Alsop received his costs for carriage of a cripple to Great Bowden in 1612.[282] In its listing for 1616, the churchwardens' account for Saint Mary the Great in Cambridge recited twenty males identified by Goodman with surname, such as the first encountered, Goodman Palmer.[283] When Thomas Talbot in 1592 wrote to William Sabbe and Bolt, the *incipit* of his letter addressed them as "Goodman Sab & Bolt."[284]

Service in local society also distinguished those entitled Goodman in some churchwardens' accounts in Oxfordshire. Payments for carrying stone were consequently made at Pyrton in 1548 to Goodmen Yeates, Carpynter, Laene and Devens and again fifteen years later for the same service to Goodmen Eates and Reddinge.[285] In the same parish in 1586 Goodmen Wigginton and Barnie were recompensed for making repairs to the churchyard gate and inside the church.[286]

In the early sixteenth century, Goodman Grenewey received expenses for washing the church vestments of Lydd. It transpires that he was one of the churchwardens at the time (1526) and the title was retained for him for many years after this official service.[287] Goodman Cawston, who received his costs for carrying and melting lead in 1532, had become a churchwarden in the subsequent year.[288] Another service—supplying a baldrick (leather strap) for the great bell—was performed by Goodman Catlyn.[289] Similarly, the churchwardens' accounts for Saint Mary at Hill in London reinforce the association between the conferral of the title goodman and good works or particular circumstances for the parish in the early sixteenth century. Goodman Edmondes paid for the burial of two children in 1505-6 and Goodman Halthorppe for his child—conditions which called for empathy.[290] In 1511-12, Goodman Mershe was remunerated for half a day's labor.[291] In the late 1520s, Goodman Wild was compensated for maintaining the choir for a year.[292] We might compare this courtesy with the abrupt account of contract workers in these accounts: "Sutton, founder," "Benet, mason," "Smart, carpenter," "Gymbold the Joyner," "William the Browderer," "Rogers

the plomer," "Whyte the donge man" and so on.[293] The occasion
for Goodwife and Goodman as titles of address in the churchwar-
dens' accounts of another London church, Saint Andrew Hubbard
Cheapside, was predominantly sorrowful circumstances—burials:
Goodman Clarke; Goodman Gester's wife; Goodmen Bygat's and
Green's wives; and Goodmen Caron and Ewerd.[294]

This affective use of the title goodman occurred too in testamentary arrangements. When a neighbor was recruited to some
service in a will—especially as overseer of the will—then the title
goodman was appropriate to the context. Included in the legacies
of Joan Cooke, of Warley (Essex), widow, in 1560 were bequests of a
grindstone and a cheese press to Goodmen Bryte and Fyssher who
were also nominated as joint executors.[295] Goodman Boode was appointed joint overseer of an earlier will (1559).[296] For his prospective
role of overseer, Goodman Levett received the testator's best boots
in 1560.[297] Others who acceded to these roles of overseer or executor
included Goodmen Hunter, Pytce, Wryghte, Lytman, Nevell, Joolle,
Stamar, Norrys, Hendan, Younge, and Foller (1556-66).[298] Goodman
Rattell was entreated in a will not only to act as overseer, but also to
monitor the upbringing of the testator's son, as was Goodman Elly
in 1566.[299] The government of another testator's daughter was entrusted in 1562 to Goodman Whytynge.[300] It was in association with
neighborly acts that the title goodman figured in testaments. When
women mentioned in wills had the title Goodwife, the circumstances also suggested that the motivation was service rendered: Goodwife Peachie thus received 5s. from a testator for tending him in his
(presumably final) sickness.[301]

Where, consequently, other services were mentioned in wills,
the titles goodman and goodwife were also occasionally elicited.
John Pierson, tanner of Barking, thus remembered his nurse, Goodwife Laurence, with a legacy of 3s. 4d.[302] In their capacity of witnessing a will, two neighbors were described as Goodmen Bruar
and Gyffard in 1560.[303] Goodman Hearde was requested through a
will in 1564 to act as governor of a son should the testator's wife die
before the son achieved the age of majority.[304] It was only in these
contexts of neighborly assistance that men and women mentioned
in wills were accorded the title of Goodman or Goodwife.

Somewhat later, the accounts of the Newbury workhouse in

1628-33 constantly referred to disbursements to Goody Clinton, Goody Paine, Goody Foch, Goody Curre, Goody Spencer, Goody Paice, Goody West, Goody Cally, Goody Charlocke, Goody Butler, Goody Collet, Goody Rombilow, Goody Jeffry, Goody Nitingale, Goody Renes, Goody Jones, Goody Stimpe, Goody Perring, Goody Hadway, Goody Hayes, Goody Prin, Goody Holmes, Goody Frinch, Goody Holland, Goody Jiet, Goody Bemham, Goody Croke, Goody Deale, Goody Baring, Goody Shaw, Goody Nalder, Goody Forster, Goody Smith, Goody Simones, Goody Whiting, Goody Arlet, Goody Dickerson, Goody Grimes, Goody Parnell, Goody Brookes, Goody Baige, and Goody Sanders. All were goodwives engaged in the processing of textiles—spinning and carding—for the workhouse.[305]

Perhaps an exemplification of this relationship between address by the title of goodwife with good work was the nuncupative will of Rose Leach, a singlewoman, of Bury Saint Edmunds, in 1637. By her oral disposition she intended Goodwife Cadge to receive all her personal estate as some little recompense for the care and attention which Susan (Goodwife Cadge) had afforded her during a long and tedious illness, as well as defraying her rent to Susan's husband. It was further reported that Rose had maintained that had she more, it would all have been allocated to Susan to compensate her more fully for her help (great pains and costs).[306]

Nonetheless, Goodwife Adams was reduced to stealing cabbages and carrots in Weymouth in 1621.[307] Allegations against Goodwives in the borough of Reading involved theft and receiving stolen goods, threatening behavior and even infanticide.[308]

It seems likely that the titles of Goodman and Goodwife were relinquished during the middle of the seventeenth century and gradually disappeared.[309] They appear but disparately in the hearth tax and poll tax returns of the 1660s and 1670s, although the predilection of the clerks about titles might have been a significant influence in their recording. For this reason—the probability of the decline in this semi-formal title—it is important to consider the apparent fortunes of these titles—good, goody, goodman, and goodwife—in the late seventeenth century, through the hearth taxes which, furthermore, allow some perspective of the social position of these inhabitants through the number of hearths assessed against them. Exceptionally, they recurred in some profusion in some of the central wards of the City of Norwich (See Table 1.7, page 144. Occurrences of the titles good/goody/goodwife/goodman in the Norwich hearth tax, 1671-4[310]).

The persistent use of the titles good, goody, goodwife and goodman in the Norwich hearth tax returns is remarkable. These titles recurred in the assessment for Great Yarmouth, although with less intensity: fewer than forty listed in the entire assessed population.[311] Although the returns for Cambridgeshire almost consistently neglected titles of address, three goodwives were listed in Newmarket.[312]

It is interesting too that the title survived in Suffolk, although in declining numbers and highly selective use, in the Hearth Tax return of 1674. Amongst some 28,400 heads of household, 101 were represented by the title and surname, mostly Goody, but the occasional Goodman.[313] Two other observations—other than the selective appearance—can be advanced: first, that in contrast to Norwich, the distribution of these goodies was mainly in rural rather than urban places (see Fig. 1, page 145, Goodies in some Hearth Tax assessments); second, that the goodies as often as not held the mean number of hearths of the whole population of Suffolk – that mean of all hearths estimated at 2.11.[314] (See Table 1.8, page 146. Rank order of goodies by hearths in Suffolk in 1674).

In fact, the mean of hearths held by goodies slightly exceeds the mean of hearths throughout the total population of the county: 2.149 (standard deviation 1.203) compared with 2.11. Goodies therefore belonged to the "middling sort" of rural Suffolk. That distribution in rural locations is illustrated in Fig. 1, but can also be demonstrated by the clusters in some locations, mostly within the Hundred of Blackbourne: eight goodies in Hopton; thirteen in Redgrave; and six in Stanton[315] (See Table 1.9, page 146. Rank order of goodies by hearths in Kent and Hampshire in 1664-5[316]).

In addition to the returns for these East Anglian counties, the lists for Kent also contained the titles, but more sporadically and perhaps with more complexity of status. In Kent, the preponderance of goodies subsisted with but one or two hearths, but more importantly for the ambiguities of their position, the higher proportion was also not chargeable to the tax. That pattern was replicated in Hampshire, where also goodmen and goodwives were mainly discharged from contributing to the poll tax and generally had no more than a single hearth, indicating some decline of their fortunes.

By contrast, the returns in the 1660s and 1670s in many other counties contain no use at all of the titles Goodman, Goodwife or Goody: Derbyshire; Rutland; Dorset; and Shropshire, for example.[317] That complete absence in many counties in this sort of record is not conclusive proof that the form of address had lapsed entirely into desuetude, but it is an indicator. In the listings for Nottinghamshire, goodwives (but not goodmen) appeared in only Newark on Trent (a single one) and in nearby Staunton (three).[318] In only two villages in Bedfordshire—Silsoe and Woburn—did the clerks refer to a goodwife or goodman.[319] In Oxfordshire, Gude Penn at Middle Aston might represent the title, but was a solitary instance.[320] The sporadic resort to the term in East Anglia thus appears to be a survival which continued to be used more affectively there. The relative absence of Good, Goody, Goodwife, and Goodman in many counties must also be set into the context of the confirmation in the hearth tax returns of other titles, including the formal Master and Mistress, but in a very pronounced manner too Widow with surname.[321]

The persistence of goodwife into the late seventeenth century is perhaps—but only perhaps—confirmed by one of the multitude of pamphlets attributed to Sir Roger L'Estrange (1616-1704) in the late seventeenth century. About 1680 appeared the homiletic address *Goodman Country: to his worship the City of London*, a satirical critique of the shrieval elections in the City and a declaration about religious orthodoxy. The valediction of the anonymous pamphlet was signed off "Honest Country." The author's intention here might have been to contrast the traditional allegiance of the country with the novel latitudinarianism of the City, associating the title goodman with integrity. If so, it was likely to have been conservative counsel. Less substantive evidence is contained in *The good-wives lamentation: or, the womens complaint on the account of their being buried in woollen*, printed in London in 1678: "'Twas the other day at a *Gossiping* that I over-heard a whole Conclave of Good-wives..."[322] In immediate response, that profuse pamphleteer, L'Estrange, concocted *The good-*

wives vindication: or, an answer to a late saucy pamphlet intituled The womens complaint on the account of their being buried in woollen. By a person of quality (London, 1678). What L'Estrange revealed was that the initial pamphlet too was composed by a man. The term goodwife, moreover, was used descriptively rather than as a title or form of address.

Some idea of the relative proportions of all these forms of address can be obtained from the Norwich rate book of 1633-4, at least for an urban entity.[323] Enumerating about 1,250 eligible to contribute, the rate listed 129 titled Master who usually headed the lists for each parish. A comparable number—twenty-three—were addressed as Mistress and heads of household, therefore singletons, either widows or never married. In contrast, merely three were designated Mother. Most prolific of those with a title were Widows, some 294 in all, the majority further described or implicated as poor. Over a dozen others were addressed as Old so-and-so, some with the imputation of poverty: "Olde Cooper...so as he begg not" and "Olde Munford...yf his wife beg not."[324]

Furthermore, a series of lays or rates in the parish of Saint Mary, Cambridge, in the early seventeenth century, allows another opportunity to estimate the frequency of these forms of address[325] (See Table 1.10, page 147. Titles of address in rates for Cambridge, St Mary, 1620-4[326]).

Internal consistency appears through the years, so that an individual designated Master, for example, will consistently be so described; as constantly, a title continued to be withheld from those refused a title of address in any year. Transfer across titles was infrequent, although Master Higney, known as such in 1620 to 1623, developed into Father Higney in 1624 and 1626.

In particular, the rating lists divulge how the meaning of gentility was changing, contested and expanding in the urban context. Amongst the wealthier town-dwellers, this title had become desirable, to which many aspired. Indeed, this urban (and urbane) attitude might be profitably compared with Dekker's portrayal of the stolid refusal of his yeoman to accept this title. Increasingly, therefore, Mr. or Master had become a contested and ambiguous title.

What the listing further reveals is that, although Goodman was attributed quite widely, still it was not applied to all males below the level of gentle folk. The imputation is that it did depend on characteristics of neighborliness. Its selective use can be illustrated further. In the churchwardens' accounts for Strood (Kent), Goodman demarcated those who had made a contribution to the affairs of the parish. For example, Goodman Standly had previously served as churchwarden and he stored lime and made a gift of boards towards repairs in 1556 and the 1560s. Included in the legacies in his will was provision for distributions to the poor which took effect from 1579.[327] The term of office of churchwarden James finished in 1571, but he continued to serve the parish in a voluntary capacity, entitling him to the title of Goodman through the accounts.[328] When a contentious issue arose, the accounts recorded the journey of the churchwardens there: "when Goodman Punnett and I went to Grenewich to my Lorde Bisshop."[329] In 1604-5, the distributions under the will of Master Goodwin were received by forty-two recipients, three of whom were addressed as Goodman, twelve as Goody, seven as Widow, two as Mother, one by old and a surname, and another by old with forename and surname; in contrast, two were denominated by their surname only and the rest (fourteen) by forename and surname.[330]

The sparing allocation of these forms of address is also reflected in the registers of Boston in the late sixteenth century. In 1587, 363 interments were registered, but included only Father Mody and Mother Eshton; of the two hundred burials in 1588, only Goodwife Benne was listed; Mother Gee occurred alone amongst the seventy burials in 1589; Mother Bradshawe in 182 in 1590; amongst 137 in 1591, Goodwives Owstinge and Kempe and Mothers Farrer and Petty; and Father Wilson of 127 in 1592.[331] Between 1584 and 1602 the burial register for Richmond (Surrey) contained only sporadic references to seven Mothers, one Father, six Goodwives, and one Goodman.[332]

We can quantify the extent of the use of Goodwife in the burial register of Brixworth (Northants.) between 1546 and 1640.[333] Only two interred women were dignified with this title: Goodwife Collins (June 1622) and Goodwife Markame (April 1623). Five other deceased women were accorded the title Mistress. After 1597 (but not before), the title Widow plus surname was employed too: applied to twenty-five deceased women, but throughout 104 women were described simply in the form the wife of John Smith, without any revelation of their own forename. Equally, 110 other women were recounted as the daughter of a specified father. Another 149 women were accorded an independent status by their forename and surname. Disclosed by this register of burials then is that in this context the title Goodwife was only exceptionally attributed—and that feature is consistent with other burial registers.

Although also occasional, payments for ringing of the bells at funerals at Stratford-upon-Avon confirm the relationship between these informal titles "old," Mother and Father. Mother Denes' burial was thus announced in 1576; old Winmerys, old Barratt, and Mother Healie in 1580-1; Mother Hannes and Father Asholle in 1584; and Father Taylor and Mother Pattricke in 1593-4.[334]

Now, how these informal titles might be related to the life-course can be detected in the case of Margaret Smith of Stratford-upon-Avon. In 1577, for the same service, she was alluded to as Mother Margaret.[335] In 1578, she was imperfectly identified as "a pore woman" who was allocated a small amount for sweeping outside the chapel.[336] In 1579, she was partially acknowledged: "to Margaret for sweeping without the chapel."[337] In 1583, her full identification was attributed: Margaret Smythe who swept about the chapel.[338] By 1584, when she received the higher amount of 1s. 4d. for clearing the street in front of the chapel, she was described simply as "old Margret."[339] In 1595, however, when she entered the almshouse, her description had become "Lame Margaret."[340]

Although it pertained to a particular social stratum below gentle status—perhaps what later became the "middling sort"—the title of Goodman (and -wife) was employed discretely and selectively; it had an almost honorific import, and demarcated a select status within a social level, based on service and neighborliness. These characteristics are exemplified by the petition of Goodwife Bartram "the carpenter's wife," for an additional allowance for looking after a child in Southampton in 1607.[341] The title was reserved for such as Goodwife Clayton who supervised the hospital and sustained poor children in Reading in the 1620s.[342] For that reason, the title was likely to be more visible in some records—accounts of payments—than others (parish registers).

In comparison, the attribution of the titles Mother and Father contained more ambiguity. Certainly, these titles imputed age. On the other hand, the ambivalence inhered in what were the characteristics of age: experience; dignity; frailty; lack of dignity? Some old women accorded the title Mother continued to perform valuable service in local society. Other Mothers were relegated to a more fragile existence, succumbing to illnesses of old age, and its related poverty and indignity.

Those forms of address were informal (old, mother, father, widow) or semi-formal (goodman, goodwife) ascription, but address as Master or Mistress possessed the formality of position and status. These two titles, however, were also affected by social aspirations in early-modern England, particularly urban commercialism which led to many aspiring to the status of gentility.[343] Increasingly, holders of high urban office expected the dignity of the title Master, whatever their origin. All these titles and forms of address embodied recognition of integration within local society. Other people were less fortunate and form the subject of the next chapter.

2
Imperfectly Known

Titles such as goodman and goodwife discussed in chapter 1 were associated with what became in the middle of the seventeenth century the "middling sort."[344] Some of the informal titles examined above were attached to more marginal inhabitants in local society. By and large, however, the most marginal elements of local society were imperfectly known, for a variety of potential reasons. One explanation of their incognito status resided in their recent arrival —they had not had time to form social networks and their links in local society were weak. On the other hand, it seems also that in many cases those integrated in local society had neglected to discover the identities of the more marginal elements. That supposition might apply, for example, in cases of records of burial of unnamed or incompletely identified people who had expired whilst lodging locally—no one had troubled to find out who they were, not even the host. Now, in the case of bastardy, it was also partly a case of lack of knowledge, in that the father, unless he confessed, was an alleged, and thus not certain, one. In the case of this sort of marginal, people in local society reacted in a number of different ways in recognizing the illegitimate child, some informed by the notion of stigma. In yet other instances, however, particularly name changing and *alias*es, the incomplete knowledge was a subterfuge perpetrated by the marginal. So it is with these categories connected to marginal people—anonymity, the identification of bastards, name changes and the *alias*—that this chapter is concerned.

Anonymity[345]

> A poore Mayd whose name we could not learn borne as some say at Wellington in the county of Hereford.[346]
>
> Pauper stranger, name and place of abode unknown, died at the home of James Bate, where he had been hospitably received.[347]
>
> A poore man his name we know not but borne nere Bromyard in the countie of Hereford.'[348]
>
> A pore man being a Welshman & a beger his name not knowen.[349]
>
> Cateren, Nameles, of Wiggenton.[350]
>
> A poore woman was buried whose name we know not. She was brought into the towne from Ellaston.[351]
>
> The next [day] the povre begery woman dyd dy at Horssyngdon...[352]

Now, all those alluded to by those periphrases above (chapter 1) were integrated into local society, if imperfectly. The periphrases and *aliases* attested to their acceptance within local society, even if those same forms of address represented a non-honorific status. When, however, the incumbent of Skipton registered the burial of "An ould beggar woman" in 1639, her anonymity—no local knowledge of her official name and no substituted colloquial address—reflected her non-integration into local society.[353] No name represented no social networks and no support networks. Outsiders were nameless.[354]

The anonymous—imperfectly recognized and only partially recollected in local society—consisted of two statuses, not necessarily distinct: the poor; and travelers, strangers or outsiders. Their (lack of) status is amply reflected in the entries in parish registers, most frequently the burial registers. More than an expression of linguistic register and pedantry was involved in the recording of "William *Nullus* a poore man" at his interment at Ripon in 1589.[355]

Taking migrants first, their integration into local society lacked the time necessary for the formation of dense social networks. Consequently, knowledge of and about them was imperfect. Sometimes it extended to partial knowledge: "The seconde [of October] was Buried Catharyne a poore Walshwoman noe dewes paid" or "a straunger called Clarke," the latter buried at Ripon in 1587.[356] More usually, the travelers or strangers remained anonymous and their anonymity accepted: "a certain old woman travellinge for relief died in the fields"; "a certayne travelling man dyed at Cornefourth"; "a poor man being a creepl dying in his travell was heer buryed"; and "a pegrine woeman dying at Cornforth."[357]

The extent of traveling in the North is partially revealed by the burial registers of Skipton, in which were recorded the burials of two dozen travelers or their children, mostly anonymously, between 1618 and 1639.[358] Those burials were the proverbial visible part of the iceberg. In 1620 was inscribed the burial of "an olde man that was a goer aboute his name was not knowne, he died in the howse of John Hastings of Skipton."[359] At Croston, burial registration included "a yong wench and strangere unknown," "a poore man stranger buttoner from Bretherton," "a poore beggar stranger from Byspham," "a wandering beggar," "a wandering beggars child," "O [sic] wandering Bedlamers child" and "a wandering beggard" in the decade of 1631 to 1640.[360] Brough received northern travelers, some of whom were buried in the parish: "a poore woman a stranger"; "a creple being a stranger ..."; "a poore traveller"; "Two beggars"; and "a mayde a stranger."[361] A short distance further south, the burial register of Lancaster related in 1639 the "poore wandryng woman who died in childbed in Wiersdall."[362]

Addressing now the resident poor who were not integrated into their local societies, there may appear to us now to be a measure of inappropriateness in the linguistic register employed by the incumbent of Blackburn in the early seventeenth century to register the burials of some of the poor: Jeremy *pauperculus quidem* ("Jeremy a certain little poor boy") and *Jenetta ignota pauperrima* ("Janet a very poor unknown woman").[363] In fact, in these instances, he was referring to those poor who were at least partially recognized in local society, in the way that he had discerned "one Gamble," "a child of a pipar" and *puer unius Aram* ("a child of one, Aram").[364] With some semblance of paradox, he was thus induced to contend in his burial register about another burial: "Thomas Todd an unknown poor man who died in the house of James Marseden of Tockholes."[365] More consistently, his remarks about the poor buried concentrated on their anonymity.[366]

Succumbing to the same attitude, the incumbents of Brough inserted similar entries in their register of burials about the deceased poor, some partially known, others completely unrecognized: "a power woman called Birked"; "one Jenet a poore woman"; "a poore fellow called John"; and "a poore man unknown."[367] The two cases of partial identification at Brough were complemented by two in nearby Lowther at an earlier time, 1550-4: "a poore man called Richard" and "Jenet a poore woman."[368] Two other cases can be elicited from the burials at Farnham: *Dionicia paupercula de Scotton* ("Denise a little poor girl of Scotton") and *Margeria paupercula de Farneham* ("Margery a little poor one from Farnham").[369] Importantly, the last entry confirms that not all the poor were travelers or sojourners, but were sometimes domiciled poor but who lacked dense social networks.

In particular, the burial register of Garstang contains an enormous extent of anonymity. From 1571 to 1625, fourteen burials were defined only as for "a poor man."[370] Eight burials pertained to "a poor woman" between 1595 and 1623.[371] From 1618 to 1638, the interment comprised no more detail than "a pore child" in no fewer than twenty-one instances, "a poor mans child" in another three from 1592 to 1627, "a poore child of a poore man" in 1619, and "a poor boy" in 1591.[372] The three entries reporting the burial of "a pore cripple" probably relate to cripples being conveyed through the parish.

Although many of these anonymous burial entries might have been connected to travelers in Garstang, it is questionable whether all such entries did. Indeed, when he should have had cognizance of at least the child's forename, the incumbent registered baptisms of "a poor mans child" in 1592, "a poore womans child" in 1594, and "a pore child" in 1618, with no further detail.[373] With regard again to the interments, innumerable burials additional to those above consisted of imperfect knowledge of the deceased, although many had been lodging in the parish. In 1632, a plague year, the incumbent entered the burial of "a man that clensed the housses" and "a pore fellowe called Marke."[374] Neither the incumbent nor his parishioners had made the effort to identify these marginal people.

The registers of Ormskirk divulge the same incomplete acknowledgement of poor inhabitants not integrated into local society. In 1584 was baptized "Dennis the Irishemans child."[375] Burials there included "Jenet the northeren woman" (1563) and "one Kewquicke" (1598).[376] Exogamous origins tended to produce inadequate acknowledgment of people, accounting for the burial entry in the register of Bozeat (Northants.) in 1544 of "Griffin the welchman that was the souldier."[377] Poverty no doubt induced the cryptic reference to "Gilbert a Skotish man that works at Richard Arnoldes..." in the Norwich census of the poor in 1570.[378] Difference of nationality and alien status marked out and informed the address of "Keaine the Frenchman," a victualler of Whitmore, against whom a *venire facias* was issued in 1608.[379]

Burials at Lancaster, in contrast, comprehended "a poore Cryple," "a poore wentch ..." (twice), "a poore boy ..." and "a poore man ..."[380] Unsurprisingly, the burial registers of Manchester have profuse numbers of anonymous poor, some partially identified, such as in 1591 "Jane a poore Wench that died at John Birches," but others about whom there remained ignorance, illustrated by "a poore man that died in Ardwycke" in 1592.[381] The reception of strangers and "inmates" presented one of the several social problems of the English town of the late sixteenth and early seventeenth century, against which urban authorities constantly made ordinances. It resulted in the anonymity of some newcomers, if not their *anomie*.

As indicated above, however, it was the resident poor too who were sometimes disregarded. The clerk of the parish registers of St Albans was particularly culpable of poor recognition of the resident poor, especially those who had no independent status. So he registered the burials in 1559 of Thomas servant to Wye and Helen servant to Master Ranshaw. He followed these entries in 1563 with Mary servant at Hardings, in 1568 Thomas "a boye from the Bull," in 1573 Valentine servant of John White, in 1581 Geoffrey a servant at the Lion, in 1584 Richard servant of Ed. Meadman, in 1591 Winifred "a maide from the Sarasins hed" and John a servant from The Ram, and in 1592 Margaret servant at Whitfildes.[382] Indeed, this clerk, ignorant of the full identity of one female deceased, simply recorded her as "Joane with the burnde hande" in 1559 which was no doubt how she was recognized in local society.[383]

The potential culpability of urban inhabitants in the anonymity of the poor is perhaps illustrated by events at Woodstock in 1630.

Geiven to a poore woman that would have lyen in the towne to gett her away 6d.[384]

The imperative here was not to identify the woman but to expel her so that she would not become chargeable.

Perhaps the most acute exemplification of the failure to investigate the identity of an inhabitant is the constant anonymous reference to a poor old woman who rented a house in the churchyard of Bishop's Stortford. Her landlord was the parish and the recording of the transaction was inserted in the churchwardens' accounts. In 1541-2, they acknowledged the receipt of 18d. from "le old woman" in the churchyard; then from "the old woman and her doughter"; they expended 1d. in repair of the hearth of the tenement "that the poore woman dwellith in at the cherch yarde"; and they collected the rent from "the owlde woman and her dowter."[385] Although poorly integrated into her local society and inconsequentially regarded, that old woman was not marginal in a "deviant" sense. In contrast, the lewd woman harbored by William Glover in Manchester in 1610 and who was suspected of baudry was distanced from local society, being "commonlye called the pipers wyffe."[386]

Perhaps even more marginal and deprecated were the inmates of jails and prisons, both categories of person buried in urban churchyards. "One out of the prison buried" declared the register of burials of Saint Mary, Shrewsbury, under 1588.[387] Fifteen years later, the same register vaguely alluded to the burials of "One out of the house of Correction" and "a child whose mother is in the house of Correction."[388] By no means all deceased prisoners remained anonymous—the full names of some were inscribed in the register —but sometimes their description compounds their anonymity: "a prisoner prest to deathe" and "a yong infant out of the Jayle."[389] Altogether the burials of nine prisoners maintained anonymity, simply referring to "a prisoner," between 1588 and 1631.[390] Indeed, even those from the almshouse received cursory registration: "Morris of the Allmeshouse" (1598) and "Thomas out of the Almeshouse" (1637).[391] In similar vein, a burial at Saint Mary, Reading, was registered as that of "Agnes of thalmesmonsehouse" in 1586.[392] Burials of inmates of the jail at Durham were sometimes recorded as succinctly: "One Peacocke a prisoner" (1580); "One Dodgshon a prisoner" (1586); "a prisoner" (1587 and 1589); and "another prisoner" (1631).[393] Although normally diligent in discovering and recording the names of prisoners buried in his churchyard, the incumbent of one of the Reading churches still lapsed to: "three prisoners executed, the one Thomas Puckner."[394]

Dependency, particularly but not only of women, erased the real identity of people or assumed a particular type of familiarity, resulting in the register of burials of Bishop Middleham recording "Old Margaret servant to Mr Ward" in 1590 and even "a woman servant of Henry Peirsons."[395] When the incumbent of Ripon recorded the interment of "Charles Allayne gent.," in the next entry he traduced "Gyles his man de Ryppon," as though the identity of servants emanated from their service.[396] The incumbent of Saint Mary, Shrewsbury, had a particular predilection for diminishing the status of servants by describing them in relation to their employers: "a mayd of Thomas Evans Sherman"; "a mayd of Anne Clarkes"; "a mayd of William Riders"; "a mayd of Evan Powells" (all in 1604); "a mayd of Mr Andrew Lewis" (1607); "a servant mayd of Mr Coles" (1610); and "a servant of Mr Juckes ..." (1613).[397] The compiler of the burial register of Saint Oswald, Durham, could restrict himself to "the Nursse of Mr Thomas Chaitor of Butterbie esquire," fully declaring her identity through her master's.[398]

Occasionally, the explanation for the anonymity resulted simply from no opportunity to find out from the subject. For one case of burial in 1616, then, the incumbent of Bozeat (Northants.) could exonerate himself:

A poore traveller brought from Daventrie in a Cart and dead before he was taken downe or imediatlie after not able to speake wee knowe not his name...[399]

Now, of course, it was not impossible in all these cases to ascertain names and identification. At Amwell, Thomas Hassall, the incumbent, was able to satisfy himself to some extent of the identity of a migrant who came to term in his parish:

> Elizabeth the daughter of one Margaret Walker (as shee named her selfe) who was travelling was delivered of a child in our parish at one Waltons of the Heath ...[400]

Discovery of the identity of a living person was less problematic than identifying the body at interment, but even Hassall declined this small courtesy:

> A poore travellinge woeman was delivered of a child in the churchyarde which was baptized the xxvijth of March and named Elsabeth.[401]

Such diligence seems in many cases to have deserted not only the incumbent but local society, for, even in cases of death and burial, many of the strangers were reportedly in lodging or their origins were discovered. It would seem that their anonymity was preserved by their lack of integration and inquiry.

Other characteristics — as might be anticipated — of the anonymous were their poverty, their transience, and their concentration in urban places. The register of burials for Tamworth is pervaded by anonymous entries such as "Heere was buried a stranger," "Susanna a poore child," "a pore woman," "a poore man from Fazley," "a poore wench," "a poore child caried about by Holmes," "the daughter of a poore man,""a poore old man from Merryhill" — these constituting no more than selected illustrative examples.[402] Correspondingly, the registers of Saint Oswald, Durham, were comparably replete with such entries, over three dozen between 1577 and 1624, including, for illustrative purposes: "another poore woman from Synderland that dyed in the streete"; "a poore woman died in ratten Row"; "a poor chylde from Shynklye bakehowse"; "a poore man borne in Branton in Gilsland dyed in the fields near Brome"; "a powre woman that dyed in the backhouse att Aldernedge"; "a powre man that dyed in the almossehouse his name not knowne"; and so on.[403] In 1631, a complaint was directed against John Dey in Reading for harboring "the Ragman" as an inmate. It later transpired that "the Ragman's" identity was Thomas Stone, of Kent St., London, a scavenger.[404]

The connection between distance of address and poverty is perceptible in the will of Alice Whoodd, widow of Laindon, in 1574. Although her intention was to assist the poor through legacies of 1s. or other small benefactions, she was reduced to describing the recipients as one Bacon a poor man, one Rawlynson a poor man, one Stapler a poor man, and one Cowper a poor man—thus imperfectly and distantly.[405]

Affirmation of that social exclusion (or, in some cases, self-exclusion) might be found before the justices of Somerset, "on a petition from the inhabitants of Downhead within the parish of Dowltinge..." Some—at least—of the inhabitants complained that about a year previously "one Michell, a collier" arrived in Downhead to produce charcoal in a wood—"as an unknown person for a whole year." Joined by his wife, he produced a child, and the family moved into lodging with James Weston. In 1617, these inhabitants requested the justices to order his removal.[406] Evidently, he had never been accepted into local society and the use of the term "one" intended distance and disparagement. In this context, distancing through the terms of address imputed non-acceptance.

Nonetheless, ignorance of names might also ensue from deliberate secrecy; it had polyvalency depending on context. So it was contended at episcopal visitation that Thomas Dawby "in somuche that he receyved late and kept a myssewoman called Jane and a monke with hir in a seculare manys clothing and other moo."[407] Non-disclosure of identity was deliberate here. In 1594, the rector of North Creake, Thomas Holland, sought magisterial justice over the violence employed by William Armiger to detain tithes. Armiger had procured Kentish men to prevent the tithes being taken whilst he was absent in Norwich. Reportedly, Armitage instructed the Kentish men, strangers, with "words to this effect": "Masters, I heare that warrauntes be cominge forth for you, but I knowe not your names, and therefore use your discretions."[408]

Repression of identity was involved also in the case of some whose confessional position clashed with that of local society. Amongst those who refused to take the Protestation Oath in Sussex in 1641-2 was recorded: "An olde man, whose name is not knowne, reported to be Mistress Kemps unkle."[409] Whether this constituted a case of ostracism or ignorance is unclear.

Concealment of identity then had its purpose and occasion, but the vast proportion of anonymous persons were poor and/or strangers, inadequately integrated into local society, inadvertently ill-recognized, and, in some cases, deliberately ignored and neglected as to their exact identity. Whether inhabiting local society or transient within it, they remained outsiders and marginal with the consequence that no one seemingly knew or cared for their names.

Bastardy

The assumption might be made, *a priori*, that bastards would assume the surnames of their mothers because of the biological certainties involved. The imperative for local society to maintain itself harmless, however, intervened; unmarried mothers were encouraged—not without some aggravation—to identify the putative father. The responsibility for eliciting the information belonged to midwives during labor.[410] Whether England in the late sixteenth and early seventeenth century contained a "bastardy-prone sub-society" or not, illegitimate births continued to present a persistent issue.[411] Bastardy before the middle of the sixteenth century was partly associated with the ambiguity of marriage formation.[412] After ecclesiastical sanction became the legal and only approach to marriage in the reformed English church, the closure of that ambivalence did not remove all uncertainty. Pre-marital sexual relations continued in an environment of the late age of marriage and its related social environment. The significance of names in this context is that the attribution of a surname to the illegitimate child engaged with the politics of local society, of the parish, and of personal obligations.[413]

It might be suspected that illegitimacy complicated the attribution of surnames. Usually, the extent and nature of that problem is difficult to assess. That concealment is unfortunate because bastardy existed within English society not merely because of illicit sexual relationships, but for both structured and contingent reasons. The late age of marriage and the relationship between customary and official attitudes to the *formation* of marriage induced some level of pre-marital sexual congress. Furthermore, periods of economic and social disruption resulted in unfulfilled marriage agreements and illegitimacy.[414]

The response of local society exhibited equal uncertainty. Some incumbents—perhaps reflecting the attitudes of their parishioners —attempted through the inscription of the alleged father's surname to emphasise the father's responsibility. In the registers of baptisms for the parish church of Whittington in Lancashire, from the earliest entries in 1538 through to 1548, a simple, but persuasive formula was employed for both legitimate and illegitimate offspring: *x* son or daughter of Joe Bloggs. Consequently, bastard children were for a time and in this parish associated directly and only with their putative father.[415]

Exceptionally, some insight into these issues is provided by the incumbents of at least two other Lancashire parishes in the sixteenth century. The registers of Saint Mary Magdalene at Clitheroe recorded in 1570 and between 1573 and 1606 whether children were regarded as legitimately conceived or not. Here, 4.85 percent of children baptised were remarked as illegitimate. It should be clarified that it is not only illegitimate children that are marked, but also legitimate children, so that the baptism of every child has a comment whether legitimate or illegitimate. The figures therefore are firm and unambiguous. Now, importantly, up to 1594, the incumbent made a rhetorical effort to ascribe to each illegitimate child not only a putative father, but the father's surname: thus, for example, John Preestley *filius putatus Johannis Preestley et Margarete Thorpe … illegitime procreatus* in 1573. For all twenty-four illegitimate children up to 1594 this protocol was enforced, so that each bastard child received its supposed father's surname.[416]

Remaining within Lancashire, but retreating to earlier in the sixteenth century, the registers for Prescot allow the same analysis, since each child baptized was categorized by the clergyman as either legitimate (lawfully begotten) or illegitimate (unlawfully begotten). Prescot comprised an immense parish, consisting of fifteen townships extending over fifty-eight square miles. From 1540 to c.1550, 14.2 percent of children baptized were stigmatized by the clergyman as unlawfully begotten.[417] Until 1548, the entries were rhetorically inscribed so that the child was not only affiliated to a presumed father but also received that father's surname: thus Thomas Eccleston whose putative father was Peter Eccleston. That practice was abandoned *c*.1548.

Still in Lancashire, at Chipping, the incumbent identified bastards predominantly by their father's surname, although in about nine instances he allocated the child an *alias*. Between 1602 and 1631, sixteen illegitimate children were assigned their father's surname, but only in four cases was the mother's surname attributed.[418] The practice at nearby Ormskirk was consistent.[419] From 1569, bastards were almost without exception registered with the formula: *Jaine Brookefelde filia Johannis Margeria Litherland mater*, denoting that the surname attached to the child was the alleged father's. Seventeen illegitimate children were so inscribed in the baptismal register between 1569 and 1574. The relationship was expressed even more remarkably between 1577 and 1601, when all 133 bastards were entered in the register in the manner "Margaret Barton *filia Jacobi bastarda*." Here then the mother's identity was dispensed and the child associated only with the alleged father's surname. For the incumbent so certainly to affiliate the child with the alleged father is extraordinary. It is improbable that all 133 fathers confessed their parenting of the child, so the incumbent must have accepted the allegation by the mother. Equally, however, it seems implausible that he would have taken this action on his own. He must have been influenced or supported by the churchwardens or, indeed, the whole of local society. At one point, in 1589, uncertainty was exhibited when the incumbent entered Richard Goulbron "*filius* Omfrey supposed."[420] After an interval, the incumbents recommenced this demonstrative practice, perhaps more emphatically, for they now began to mark out illegitimate children with the marginal note *spurius* or *spuria*, perhaps quickly to identify them when it was necessary.[421] Between 1626 and 1640, 103 bastards (the preponderant number) were recorded in the manner "Margrett Keele *filia Johannis*." It would seem that local society in Ormskirk was quite prepared to certify the alleged father as the real father by imposing the father's surname on the illegitimate child. The politics of poor relief —the parish exonerated from support of the child by declaring the father—determined the child's surname.[422]

Further north, in Lowther, the same formula was predominant-ly (77 percent) applied in registering the high number of baptisms of children born out of wedlock.[423] In nearby Shap, the incumbents persisted in attributing to illegitimate offspring the surnames of their reputed fathers, from at least 1569 to 1602, but occasionally revived as a practice in 1606, 1616, and 1619.[424] At Crosthwaite, the practice of registration between 1571 and 1651 was even more emphatic, for the inscription of bastards omitted the mother com-pletely and indicated only the paternal relationship, allocating the father's surname to the child.[425]

This practice and principle obtained also in the parish of Saint Oswald, Durham, in the early seventeenth century, commencing with the recording of the baptism of Thomas Stevenson illegitimate son of Ralph Stevenson in 1601 and succeeded by Alice Ellinson a bastard of Richard Ellinson in 1604.[426] In that same year (1604), the incumbent registered too Thomas Ayre bastard son of Anthony Ayre.[427] This formula of attributing to the child the father's surname and specifying the relationship only to the father was (when the father was known) consistently applied to bastards from 1604 on-wards: to over thirty illegitimate children to 1630.[428]

Ostensibly, this approach to the surname of the bastard child was characteristic of the north, but it occurred occasionally in the south too. The registers of Saint Mary, Reading, betray this predi-lection for the father's surname from 1542 to 1568, although only five illegitimacies were so recorded for that period, beginning with Richard Heywarde "base borne son of Hugh Heywarde and Annys Fullmor."[429] Before the justices of Middlesex was debated the case of the bastard son of Elizabeth Tirrell of Westminster called Thomas Swanstone after the alleged father, Christopher Swanstone.[430]

Occasionally in the later sixteenth century, some incumbents dismissed as disingenuous the disclaimer of the men involved, as at the burial of an infant at Penkridge in 1583:

> *Izabella Cotton filia Elizabethae Warde, pater fuit incertus, nam Thomas Cotton dixit non esse pater.*[431]
> [Isabel Cotton daughter of Elizabeth Warde, father was un-known, for Thomas Cotton said that he was not the father]

Intermittently also, the incumbent registered the baptized child with an *alias* to reflect both parents, explaining the registration in 1600 of Humphrey Whytte *alias* Hurst, son of Elizabeth White and Richard Hurst, single persons.[432] Presumably that same form of designation was explained by the illegitimacy of Margaret Fox *alias* Shierson, daughter of Roger Shierson and Ann Fox, buried in 1632, so that at death as well as in life, the discrimination of naming was perpetuated.

The incumbent of Eccleshall (Staffs.) also conformed to this formula of the *alias*, although inconsistently. From 1577 to 1599, nine illegitimate children were registered with an *alias*, but another twenty with only one surname.[433] One entry in 1579 recorded the father's name: Robert Gervis a bastard of one Richard Gervis; we might assume that Gervis confessed to being the father.[434] From 1600-3, the entries maintained only the relationship to the mother, but then between 1604 and 1608 eight illegitimate children were accorded an *alias* although five not (these receiving the mother's name). Thereafter, this ambiguity of surname was abandoned, although the relationship to an assumed father still alleged: for example, Catheran Watkes, a bastard, supposed daughter of John Mynshawe.[435]

More consistently, the resort to attributing an *alias* distinguished the incumbent of Ripon who adopted this practice between 1600 and 1616. The first entries constructed in this formula concerned: Jane Dybb *alias* Raughton, bastard, Richard Hewit *alias* Cravan, bastard, Mary Tomlinson *alias* Snaw, bastard, and Anthony Abbot *alias* Atkinson, bastard, all in 1600. Thereafter, another fifteen illegitimate children were entered in the register by this formula, no doubt intended to record the responsibility of both mother and father through the deployment of the alias.[436] In contrast, however, the incumbent of Norton (Derbyshire) only temporarily adopted this expedient of the *alias*, but in 1597 and 1600 at the zenith of the rate of illegitimacy: Joan Stevenson *alias* Frith reputed daughter of Richard Stevenson and Alice Frith, buried in 1597, and Robert Sheppeharde *alias* Otuwell reputed infant son of Robert Sheppeharde and Alice Otuwell, spinster, buried in 1600—neither spared the ignominy at their deaths.[437]

That this attitude was not just a conceit of the incumbent, but reflected parishioners' concerns, is confirmed by depositions before the Manchester bench about a felony committed in 1623. The informants maintained that a stolen sheep had been acquired by Mary Hobson from her bastard son, John Pursgloove. Mary, described as *alias* Hobson and a spinster, of Ashton under Lyne, declared that she had found the mutton on Ashton Moss. In his defense, John Pursgloove the younger, of Ashton under Lyne, horner, denied providing the mutton, with the alibi that he was on "Friday night last all night in the house of John Pursgloove reputed father of this Examinate..."[438] Indeed, the justices of Somerset too entertained the notion of the *alias* for bastards—although infrequently, as when, in 1617, the presentment was made of Reynold Wraye, husbandman, the reputed father of Clement Wray *alias* Hutton, conceived on the body of Lucy Hutton.[439]

At the other extreme, however, the registers of Dymock (Glos.) consistently associated the illegitimate child with the mother, rendering the father as uncertain. Some three dozen children were in this manner decided to be fatherless between 1542 and 1600.[440] Thereafter, although the primary association remained with the mother, the name of the "imputed father" was provided as well. That solution too was resolved upon by successive incumbents at Penkridge in Staffordshire between 1577 and 1633. The entries in the register explained in Latin the attribution of the name: (1577) William Reade *ex nomine materno* (from the mother's name).[441] Five baptismal registrations up to 1589 were inscribed in this way. Then in 1590 the incumbent elucidated further: Margery Jackson *ex nomine materno quia incognitus fuerat pater* (by the mother's name because the father was unknown).[442] Seven more registrations succeeded that one down to 1595. At that point, the incumbents instituted a new protocol: Mary Lattner *ex nomine materno* daughter of Alice Lattner.[443] Thereafter another thirty-three entries were recorded in this format to 1633. Now, because this method endured for well over fifty years, we have to consider whether incumbents simply followed a norm established by one cleric or whether the parishioners exerted some influence over the incumbent to conform to this establishing the child's status, perhaps through the churchwardens who certified the registration.

Confronted (elsewhere than Penkridge) with this vacillation and equivocation about the surname of the illegitimate child, it would be permissible to feel as confused as many incumbents appear to have been. Perhaps, however, a sequence can be extracted from registration and perhaps it accords with the succession exhibited in the registers of Pattingham. From 1561 to 1587, the formula observed there, although numbering only eight baptisms, involved the prior naming of the father and the assumption of the father's surname: John Foxe supposed son of John Foxe and Eleanor Pattricke.[444] In the tempestuous 1590s, nevertheless, a transformation was introduced by which mother and mother's surname became prior: Anne Bridgewood daughter of Alice Bridgewood, the supposed daughter of George Sampson (1592), being the first insertion.[445] Of course, by this formula of naming, the father was not absolved from responsibility, but would remain subject to penance (or its commutation) and most likely personally chargeable at Quarter Sessions for the maintenance of the child. Those obligations were not waived by naming.[446] What naming did perform, however, was to attach the child distinctly to the mother and to her kinship. Although common fame of bastardy could not be removed from the father, officially the child did not carry a marker of association.

It is, evidently, possible that in some baptisms of bastards, the child was the consequence of pre-marital sexual relationships, parents subsequently marrying and the incumbent making a pointed comment through surnames about that sexual incontinence. Thomas Hassall explained, perhaps with some amusement:

> Amye the abortive daughter of Bridgett Newman betrothed to one Francis Todde who should have bin married on Michaellmas daye untimely borne the daye before so turninge the marriage feast into a christeninge.[447]

That explanation will not, however, fit too many of the events.

Less charitable were those clergy who denied the full form of the ceremony to bastard children, as the rector of Capel Saint Mary refused it to the bastard daughter of Helen Kembald. As the curate was presented by his churchwarden, the intimation is that this extreme reaction did not accord with the sentiment of local society.[448]

What the ascription of surnames to bastards sometimes involved then was the imposition of a stigma for the child as well as an attribution of responsibility for maintenance. The discordance in naming marked the child out from the rest of local society, whether inadvertently or purposefully.[449] Simply the negotiation of the surname marked the child in local society—as well as, of course, the parents. Just to complicate matters, however, the attribution of an *alias* to a bastard did not always lead to ostracism from the natural parent. When Thomas Barber of Hope (Derbyshire) concluded his last will before he died in 1590, he unashamedly made a legacy to Stephen Barbar *alias* Cocke, his "base begotten son." Not content with that gesture, he also made the bastard a joint executor.[450] So the stigma attached to the *alias* of illegitimacy was not total.

Changing names

...that he has many other names which country people have given to him and he answers to and owns them and desires not to be known by his father's name.[451]

When examined before the Hertfordshire justices in 1646, Thomas Roodes, of Denham, Buckinghamshire, professed that he was a poor gentleman born at Edgworth in Middlesex, but now earned his living as a ballad singer. Whether his claims to lineage were accurate or not, he certainly admitted not only that he was known by a multitude of *alias*es, but also (and again there may be some dissembling here) that he had renounced his own family name. Another habitual migrant who proclaimed that he had changed his name for fortune's sake was Thomas Arnolde, of Cheshunt, who had pretensions to be a physician and surgeon.[452] The magistrates of the same county had interrogated him in 1589, when he announced that he had traveled throughout Europe. For eight years, he had inhabited Monmouth, but had journeyed to Cheshunt almost a year ago. From Cheshunt, he visited Ware "and ther altered his name because he wolde not have the woman which he got with child ther to follow him...," although he intended, after accumulating some means, to return to that "cuntrie" and marry her.

It thus becomes apparent that attachment to one's name was not absolute and that it suited the purposes of some people—usually men — to abrogate that identification and assume a new one. Whilst for some reasons an *alias* was appropriate, other circumstances required a complete alteration of personal identification — and there was no impediment to so doing.

Circumspectly, therefore, the investigation of itinerants in Salisbury recorded several of the vagrants as one naming herself or himself – recognizing that such wandering people were likely to vary their identification from place to place.[453] In this assumption, the interrogators were correct, for they discovered that Stephen Wood, a rogue who had a passport, insisted that he was named Thomas Wellard, which was revealed as false.[454]

Nefarious circumstances explain some temporary changes of name. Enoch Garrett visited Church's wife in High Easter, contending that her husband had sent him to collect money. Garrett had changed his name to John Wyllcocke. He had, furthermore, previously enacted the same subterfuge to extract money from Byrd's wife, declaring himself then to be named John Wawker. Reverting to John Wyllcocke, he illicitly collected rent. For another fraudulent act, he used the name John Willson. All was revealed under examination before Essex Quarter Sessions.[455] Felonies detected in Staffordshire were perpetrated in 1595 by "one Goodwyn naminge him selfe Roberte Austen."[456] To engage in illicit brewing, Robert Richardson assumed the alternative description "John Richardson of Pickeringe" in 1617, but was detected and a warrant issued against him.[457] It is at this point, of course, that the change of name becomes equivalent to an *alias*.

The alias and nicknames

Before Star Chamber in 1509, the orator, George Aynsworth, narrated that John Radclyf of Radcliffe, Lancashire, had elicited John Radclyff, son of Richard Radclyff, to collect a group of miscreants to break down the orator's barn doors and burn his hay, thus depriving his stock of feed.[458] Little effort in persuasion might have been expected of Radclyff the defendant, for the alleged perpetrator of the offence, John Radclyff son of Richard, allegedly responded to the *alias* "blak John." The *alias* thus had a purpose other than demonstrating the paternity of the bastard.

The persistence of the *alias* within English historical naming is remarkable, but, in contrast, examinations of its meaning in English anthroponymy remain negligible.[459] The *alias* consisted of two forms: a nickname *alias* such as Galloping Jacke, the alternative moniker of John Deaveny indicted for burglary in 1615; and the *alias* as an alternative formal name—whether surname, forename or both.[460] Of course, in the context of the example above, some psychologists have demonstrated an interest not only in the meaning but also the reflexive psychological influence of the *alias* in criminal situations.[461]

From the example above, the conclusion seems inescapable that the *alias* not only endured but remained the hallmark of the criminal, the ascription of the outsider, the application to the marginal in society. Whilst that association was indeed a perpetual aspect of the *alias*, it was not the exclusive use of the a.k.a. Indeed, some *alias*es appear almost benign, simply variants of a surname: Thomas Caksey *alias* Coksey *alias* Cookes, of Rowley Regis, victualler; Laurence Conway *alias* Cowley, late of Yoxall, victualler; William Cutter *alias* Cutler, late of Sedgeley, collier; and Henry Kester *alias* Christofer, of Swinford Regis, yeoman. What, however, casts some suspicion on their alternative means of identity is that all were arraigned before the Staffordshire Quarter Sessions in 1608-9 and all had outstanding against them writs of *venire facias*. Moreover, the victualler of Rowley Regis was also known as Thomas Cootes *alias* Cookes and Kester now not only by the *alias* Christofer but also that of Fraunces, now described as a labourer, had allegedly offended against the Statute of Artificers.[462] Even the apparently most benign *alias* might thus deliver a camouflage.

Any consideration of the *alias* must, nonetheless, account for some degree of polyvalency, some variety of meaning, contingent on its particular circumstance. Even so, in the preponderance of cases, it is not possible to deduce that specific meaning. Nevertheless, there are just about sufficient examples to permit an assessment of its variant meanings so that the range of its understandings can be evoked.

Now, in the attribution, assumption or adoption of *alias*es, the influences at play are in all cases both the self and the group.[463] To different extents, the self or the group will exert more or less influence. Using these respective influences as categories of analysis is, however, almost impossible. We are compelled to assume less interesting categories for discussion.

More interesting, of course, are those circumstances where the *alias* introduces a change of identity or identities or invokes new aspects of identity or identities. In medieval and early-modern local societies, an aspect of this assumption of an altered identity or transformed identities was the occasional adoption by an incoming tenant of the surname previously associated with the tenement, sometimes as a sort of nominated heir.[464] At Elsworth (Hunts.), for example, Thomas Hobbeson *alias* Fermer was admitted in 1449 to land recently held by William Hobbesson and in 1457 to tofts recently held by Alexander Fermor.[465] Profuse numbers of *aliases* of male tenants pervade admissions to tenancies of Ramsey Abbey in the early fifteenth century.[466] In this context, the *alias* accomplished a number of needs: it legitimated an entitlement to land; and it perpetuated collective memory through names in a period of disruption.

A similar association occurred in the later middle ages when an apprentice assumed the surname of his (sic) master.[467] In these cases, the *alias* reflects a life-course stage at which the self becomes complicated by new personal associations and so the *alias* represents, indeed, the continuing development of identity and identities—it confirms that identity and identities are always in the process of development, that identity and identities is and are a process or processes, a question of becoming rather than just being.[468] In these two categories, we might surmise that the *alias* is the product of attachment to a new lineage and legitimisation of that attachment.[469]

Something of the same consideration obtained in the proliferation of *aliases* in Dorchester in the late middle ages, although they are visible only in charters transferring burgage property. So, for example, in 1416 Thomas Rycheman *alias dictus* Belhous, son and heir of Walter Rycheman, deceased, conveyed to his own son, John Rycheman *alias dictus* Belhous, a burgage tenement in South Street.[470] In 1402, the meaning of the *alias* was certified more clearly: Thomas Rycheman *alio cognomine dictus Belhous* (by another name called Belhous) as grantor to his son, John Rycheman *alias* Belhous.[471] Here can be observed the adoption of the *alias* in one generation and its transmission to the next. Similar transfer of the *alias* across generations happened with the Aden *alias* Barbet kinship. In 1521, Joan Aden, widow of Robert Aden *alias* Barbet, made benefactions to her son, John Aden *alias* Barbet.[472] The binomial identification extended into the middle of the sixteenth century as Barbet *alias* Aden or Aden *alias* Barbet.[473] Another burgess with an *alias* who appeared frequently in charters was Robert Greynlef *alias dictus* Bakere. His wife's first legacy in her will of 1416 was directed to her husband, Robert Greynlef *alias dictus* Bakere.[474] Greynlef's first appearance in these charters occurred in 1396 when he was even then styled Grenelef *dictus* baker.[475] From the context of other charters in 1409 it becomes obvious that his occupation was indeed a baker.[476] Throughout his life the *alias* (in the form *alias dictus*) was attached to him, even at the point of his death *c.*1420, as styled in his will.[477]

At least thirty others involved in these transactions were also styled by an *alias*, mostly in the fifteenth century, but extending also into the sixteenth.[478] In most cases the *alias* remembered the surname of a burgess kinship—thus Hikkes *alias* Portland in the second decade of the fifteenth century. What the *alias* established here then was the remembrance of a surname in the burgage community, the relationship of that surname to burgage property during a time of discontinuity, and the legitimacy of the current owner to the burgage property.

It is interesting in these circumstances that the *alias* might persist for more than one generation, commemorating and reflecting back on the joining of the families. Accordingly, the will in 1557 of Rose Robson *alias* Gillson, a widow of South Hanningfield in Essex referred to all her four children receiving testamentary bequests by the description Robson *alias* Gilson, the *alias* transferred to the next generation too.[479] On the death of the tenant Alexander Sharples *alias* Warde in Manchester, the next heir was his son, Richard Sharples *alias* Warde in 1588.[480] So too the successor to Ralph Byrche *alias* Orcharde was his son and heir Thomas Byrche *alias* Orcharde. Thomas continued to be inscribed as Byrche *alias* Orcharde in the leet rolls until his death in 1606.[481] After the death of John Risue *alias* Clerke, his widow, self-described in her will of 1574 as Joan Risue *alias* Clerke, referred to her son John, her executor, as Risue *alias*

Clerke.[482] The *alias* did not, of course, endure indefinitely. Upon the death of Hugh Gylliam in 1593, two heirs appeared in court: John Gilliam *alias* Whitle and James Gilliam *alias* Knotte. Two years later, John Gilliam *alias* Whitle died, but his successor was simply James Gilliam, perhaps the James Gilliam *alias* Knotte.[483] That same persistence into the next generation is visible in the will of George Mason *alias* Johnson, in 1638, in which his wife, Eufemia, also disported the *alias*, but so too did at least five of his seven children benefiting from legacies, as the eldest Robert Mason *alias* Johnson.[484] That same phenomenon is visible through the will of 1580 of Emma Procter *alias* Mathewe, of Ruishton in Somerset, for she referred to her sons Thomas, Robert and Christopher all as Procter *alias* Mathewe.[485]

The ascription of an *alias* to a married woman often happened in the context where her natal family made some disposition to her. This referral back can be clearly observed when Alice Degon, widow, concluded her will in 1607. By it, she made a bequest to Margaret Degon *alias* Taton; Margaret Degon had married Roger Tatum in 1603. By this means the testator clarified the relationship.[486] The same principle might have been involved with the persistence of an *alias* across generations. Joyce Mytton *alias* Harpesfield, had died by c.1558, as a result of which her son, Edward Mytton *alias* Harpesfield, sued in Chancery about land in Rugeley in 1561.[487] It seems likely that Joyce's *alias* referred back to her natal family from whom the land had been received and that Edward also retained this identification in Chancery to establish that lineage of the land.

Now, it is possible for irony to invade this association of *alias* and attachment.

We have the famously instructive example of Agnes de Donbar who, it was reputed, was locally known as White Annays apparently because her godmother, the countess Agnes of Dunbar, might have been colloquially depicted as Black Agnes.[488] The gendered consequences of the *alias* will be visited again below. Agnes's *alias*, however, was infused not only by the relationship but also with irony and irony quite often inhered in the nickname *alias*. Irony might have obtained in the case of Litill Robin or Little Robert, for this Robert plied the trade of carpenter, contracted for repair work to the parish church in Bishop's Stortford in 1490-1500.[489] In the person of Edward Stephenson of Stoke (Notts.) were combined two aspects of the *alias*: its association with criminality for he was accused, with accomplices, of assault and robbery in 1586; and to him was attached the *alias* "Lyttell nedde," no doubt, considering his proclivity, replete with irony.[490]

So far, the personal associations which induced *aliases* have been restricted: adopted lineage and existing relationship. In many circumstances, however, the *alias* responded to the relationship of the self to a wider constituency or group of people. Much has been presumed about the presentation of the self and latterly self-fashioning.[491] Integral to that projection of the self was naming, not least the *alias*. The *alias* intimated how the self wished to be proclaimed. Advancement of the self through such an *alias* thus largely proceeded from the self and projected outwards, but did also depend on acceptance by the group—in this case, local society.

The respective roles of agency and society seem here reasonably clear. Not always was that so. Some *aliases* might superficially be regarded as actions of the group against the individual where the *alias* is ostensibly demeaning. Disparagement of an individual in response to behaviour suggests that the *alias* performed a disciplinary function. Perhaps we have this in the case of Richard Courte *alias* Clynkerdagger of Cranford, Middlesex, who alienated a messuage used as an inn in King Street, Westminster, with a third of another messuage and all his goods to acquit a debt of £100 in the late sixteenth century.[492] Yet the possibility exists that Richard revelled in the attribution and so the *alias* became an integral part of his self-projection. What is even more interesting is that his close kin also disported the *alias* and were involved in nefarious activity. Both John Courte *alias* Clinkadager of Cranford, yeoman, and Barnaby Courte *alias* Clinkadager of Bedfont, mealman, were arraigned for the theft of wheat at midnight in 1612.[493]

Such then is the wide variety of meanings of the *alias* contingently and over time. At this point, those symbolic aspects of the *alias* can be deduced and examined more concretely through more comprehensive data. The significance may, nevertheless, inhere in the symbolism of the *alias* rather than its quantity, by which is meant that the *meanings* of the *aliases* had a more profound impact than their mere numbers.

By inscribing *alias*es in the records of courts, legal authority was concerned to identify beyond any doubt to prevent misidentification.[494] Moreover, by referring to nickname *alias*es, the additional intention was to label, marginalize and proscribe.[495] The purpose was rhetorical as well as legal. In this predisposed attitude, only the suspicious would disport *alias*es and by including the *alias* in the text of the indictment and in the proceedings, the character of the accused was already defined. Furthermore, the repetition of a nickname *alias* prejudiced the accused even further through labelling and defining. It was overtly demonstrated through the *alias* that the accused belonged amongst the suspect and undignified.[496]

In contrast, however, the process of recursive allusion to the *alias*, particularly the nickname *alias*, served only to heighten the sense of belonging of the accused. The accused was confirmed through the *alias* as one of a social group and accepted within that group—the local criminal fraternity and sorority. Credentials for belonging were confirmed and self-fashioning achieved and given public recognition.[497]

We already appreciate then something of the multivocality of the *alias*, but perhaps two other categories expound the "politics" of self and society (or, more correctly, local society and group). The first category is not exclusive of some of the others, but might have obtained in the same circumstances, such as inclusion in a new lineage. The *alias* might have resulted from the negotiation about identity and identification when a newcomer entered a local society and its place. When John Awdus became a father in Howden parish in 1607, the incumbent noticed him in the register of baptisms as John Awdus *alias* Brighton John of Knedlington.[498] It might be predicated, in such cases, that the *alias* indicated one of the terms of acceptance into the local "community," whatever that term meant. Accordingly, Edward Don recorded in 1530: "to Lankeschyere Scmyth hys man for goyng to Aylysbery ijd."[499] Migrants ran the risk of being labelled by their place of origin, perhaps indicating that, although accepted, they were not really true locals. Of course, this instance is compounded by the commonness of the surname, so that some distinguishing other characteristic might be demanded; even so, to select the distant locality of origin is indicative of attitudes.

Finally, social cohesion was promoted in smaller groups by the *alias*. Here, of course, it becomes difficult to disentangle *alias* and nickname and perhaps it is too precise to attempt to do so. Perhaps what we might consider is that the nickname, after the stability of hereditary surnames, resurfaced as the *alias*. The *alias* provided an oil which lubricated small groups—a social cohesion of those small worlds.[500] It perhaps complemented or belonged to those "rituals of resistance" which consolidated groups and sub-cultures.[501] Whilst it did not—or did not necessarily—constitute an integral part of argot or cant, the *alias* was intelligible mainly within the group or sub-culture.[502] All forms of *alias*, however, defined the bearer as part of the group, so it belonged to secret, or only semi-public, language.[503] Possessing an *alias* marked one as included within the group, even if that collective was criminal. Difficulties remain, however, for in some cases we cannot be certain whether the *alias* symbolised reception into local society through familiarity or acted as a default because of lack of full knowledge of the inhabitant. For example, "Northren Robin" (interred at Ormskirk in 1590) is consistent with either of these explanations as is the record of the burial of "a child of Spotted James" in Winwick in 1604.[504] Another function performed by the *alias* in the group or sub-culture was to differentiate: that is, to provide a further means of identification when homonyms caused ambiguity.

For a variety of reasons, a minority of early-modern inhabitants received an identification involving an *alias*. In some cases, that *alias* was imposed on them, as in the instances of bastardy discussed above, and in some of the instances presented below. In other cases, the *alias* was negotiated locally between the individual and the rest of local society and in yet other situations the *alias* was assumed or accepted as a form of self-presentation. Within early-modern local societies, two particular situations occasioned an *alias*: migration from one parish to another settlement where the name could be re-negotiated; and the adoption of an *alias* for miscreants.

The two categories were not, of course, always distinct and separate. Indeed, the two combined in the activity of Thomas Dixson of Wolsingham (Durham), a laborer, otherwise called (*alias dictus*) Thomas Nixson of Wolsingham, vagabond, accused of the theft of three mares and a foal by night in 1471.[505] No doubt the *alias* acted as protective camouflage and a subterfuge. In the following year, an accusation was advanced against John Milner late of Stockton, laborer, otherwise called John Stokell, late of Stockton, for the abduction of twenty-five wethers.[506] As a perpetrator of trespass, Edward Ridley, yeoman, otherwise called Edward Henhed, of that place, yeoman, was summoned in 1511.[507] For that misdemeanor and battery, the force of the law was extended against George Johnson, of Quarry House by Durham, *alias* George Wainman, laborer, in 1556, whilst in the subsequent year William Charlton, late of Eales, *alias* William of Eales, yeoman, was arraigned for trespass and theft.[508] Those last offenses were also attributed to Robert Brown, late of Newfield, yeoman, *alias* Robert Hangershawe, late of Newfield, also in 1557.[509] In the perpetration of crime in and around Reading in 1623, one of the offenders was known only as "Hamshiere Will."[510]

The Middlesex justices of the early seventeenth century had particular experience of *alias*es and nicknames attached sporadically to those brought before them. Another appearing before the Middlesex sessions, implicated in a theft from Hadenham church in Buckinghamshire, John Pears, collected two *alias*es, Slyon and Jones.[511] They were informed that Margery Gardner, accused of railing at a minister as a knave and notorious as a common whore, was popularly known as "Scotche Mage."[512] The burglar Humming Tom or Bacon Tom, they were assured, was Thomas Bacon – his second *alias* was merely an inversion of his real name. Or was it that simple? He was also known as Thomas Baker and Thomas Mason.[513] Two geldings were presumed to have been stolen by John Garroll *alias* Lyllye *alias* Laurence *alias* Garrett.[514] Amongst the smaller number of *alias*es associated with women, Prudence Crispe was recognized as Drewrye and Wingfield, when accused of maintaining a common brothel.[515] The alleged burglar William Pleasington went by the *alias*es (incongruously) Pleasante and Cutler.[516] In what might have been a local *cause celebre*, an heiress was abducted and forced into clandestine marriage by James Billin *alias* Billingsley, Thomas Billin *alias* Billingley *alias* Holman *alias* Smythe, and George Billin *alias* Hunte *alias* Billingley *alias* Banckes.[517] A burglary perpetrated in 1614 was attributed to Thomas Griffen *alias* Roberte *alias* "Welche Tom."[518] In the following year a burglary was associated with John Deaveny who had assumed or been attributed the nickname *alias*

"Galloping Jacke."[519] In the same year, stolen goods were allegedly received by Simon Thrasher with the erudite nickname *alias* Tuquoque.[520] Commonly known by the nickname *alias* "Privie Will," William Wyatt *alias* Browne was brought before the justices for burglary alongside Thomas Poole *alias* Pooley *alias* Trunckes.[521] The horse-thief hung in the same year used the subterfuge of changing his forename: Stephen Kitchen *alias* Thomas Kitchen.[522] That tactic was also employed by William Hanson *alias* Thomas Ansone, arraigned for theft in 1613.[523]

On her burial in 1638, the incumbent of Skipton acknowledged both formal and informal address of "Ann Grange alis Nan with baggs of Skiptoun." The same incumbent, in the following year, registered the burial of "Pegg of cragend"; he had previously (1631) interred "Scotch Willie" and subsequently in 1640 Margaret the wife of John Fornas "the gay horse" and William Strickland "alis stately will."[524] Accordingly, in the burial register of Garstang in 1629, the young Grace was described as the daughter of "a poore woman called commonlye by the name of Northerne Jane."[525] Cryptically, the same register alluded to the burial in 1623 of "Megge a Myers."[526]

Would that the incumbent of Selattyn had explained why he had registered a burial as "Elin Maurice widow otherwayes the Ladye Ever" in 1626.[527] As cryptically and intriguingly, the register of burials of Saint Mary, Shrewsbury, recorded in 1621 the interment of "Orlando Furiosa son of William Cross" and two years later the burial of "Gwen of the Hole."[528] Nor did the justices at Weymouth explain the motive for the nickname of John "Hatt and feather," although it can be surmised, when he was committed to the stocks and fined for drunkenness in 1627.[529] At one of his early sojourns on his travels, the "water poet," John Taylor, described his host at Whetstone: "Exceeding fat, yet named Lean and Fen," incorporating the irony.[530] A lewd woman committed to Norwich Bridewell in 1632, although formally named Helen Wright, was also known colloquially as "beaten gold."[531] In 1613, the incumbent of Dymock suggested that the "imputed father" of a bastard was "Jacke of London."[532]

Other forms of alternative identification—and social and cultural identity—did not involve a different surname, but were constructed on the forename or a hypocorism. In 1596, then, William Armstrong, laborer, was recognized colloquially as Andrew's Will, perhaps through a previous contract of service.[533] "Mickle Will" constituted the other persona of William Hall, late of Elsdon, yeoman, implicated in burglaries, battery and even murder in 1598.[534] Having migrated across the Pennines from Cumberland, William Bell, yeoman, was more easily identified as "Will of Carlisle"; he too had perpetrated trespass and theft, at Denton (Durham) in 1598.[535] The account of larceny in Reading in 1625 could identify one of the suspects only as "Long Will."[536] Once again, City drama comes to our aid: the *dramatis persona* of "Long Meg" of Westminster alluded to her Amazonian height.[537]

Character, that criterion of reputation in criminal proceedings, became interposed in the *alias* also, so that John Nixon, late of Bewcastle in Cumberland, was arraigned before the justices for felonies in 1596, the justices having cognizance of his other moniker, Daudel John.[538] The gentleman, John Rotherforth, apparently adopted the *alias* John the Galyard, or so the justices believed in 1605.[539] Another gentleman, of Prudhoe (Northumberland), Robert Herbottell, received the *alias* Sodron ("Southern") Robert.[540] The yeoman, John Eddryngton, from Cumberland, responded to the *alias* Harbatt John (1556).[541] Although some of these alternative identifications might well have been assumed by the felons or negotiated between felon and local society, the initiative might have arisen more from local society for Percival Mautland, late of Coastley, yeoman and accused felon, was addressed also as Jock Armstrong and one of the eight notorious women expelled from the town of Manchester in 1573, Margaret Warren, had been alternatively designated "Mag o' Dents."[542] The justices at Manchester Quarter Sessions were presented with John Chorlton *alias* "threepennie John," a shoemaker, accused of trapping rabbits in 1617.[543] In Liverpool, the magistrates sentenced the petty thief and evil-disposed male, William Barcker, also known as "Long Barcker," probably because of his height.[544] When, however, Edward Don recorded a payment in his household account book to "Long Saltter"—3s. 11d. for hops—no disparagement was intended, simply following the local customary reference to Saltter's height.[545]

In some cases, the *alias* represented an attempt at self-presentation, whilst at others it must have been imposed by, or at least the initiative originated with, others. The allusion to him in the register of Saint Oswald, Durham, in 1624 specified for William Wilson the *alias* "Tom a bedlime": Tom-of-Bedlam.[546] William Robinson might have suffered from the same imposition, for Thomas Halsall without affection described him at his burial in 1628 as "a miserable poore man commonly caled Wicked Will."[547] Similarly salacious was the *alias* of Thomas Worsley—"Desperate Tom"—as he was known to the Manchester magistrates when he was presented as a common nightwalker in 1623.[548]

Disability was associated with common address as when the incumbent of Warcop inscribed the burial of Elizabeth Smyth otherwise called "Blind Besse."[549] The Norwich census of the poor in 1570 alluded to "also dombe Elizabeth, that worketh nott, but begg contynuallye."[550] Charitable concern was expressed in Essex wills for poor Stratton who received a pair of hose under the will of Philip Genno, husbandman, in 1570; another testator in that year left an old coat to "lame Stratton" and in 1567 John Pechye, a husbandman of Dagenham, had also bequeathed a leather jerkin to "lame Stretton."[551] "Lame Stretton/Stratton" was thus the recipient of several bequests and was identified by his condition and disability. The burgesses of Maidstone repeated what was commonly an attribution to one of the poor townspeople:

> It is thought fitt that blynd Awsten be allowed quarterly by the Overseers of the poore towardes his mayntenance so long as hee shall attend the free Schole every quarter xxvs.[552]

Hassall did not conceal his ambivalence towards one of his parishioners when he inscribed her burial in his register in 1632: "Elizabeth Wilkinson by byrth, Elizabeth Sheafe by marriage, Elizabeth Davis by common fame, Elizabeth Chandler by usual appellation, neither mayde wife nor widdowe, after an unquiet lyfe..."[553] Suspicion too seems inherent in the labored citation of Richard Carpenter *alias* Essex *alias* Crosby before the peculiar court of Banbury in 1635 for sexual incontinence.[554]

Another woman disporting an *alias* was also implicated in nefarious activity. Presented before the archdeaconry court of Nottingham in 1611, Elizabeth Smyth, wife of Alexander Smyth, of Lound was a notorious and active adulterer who had previously produced a bastard child by another liaison. She also ran a disordered alehouse and refused to attend communion at Easter. Elizabeth was apparently locally known by the *alias* "few clothes."[555] The object of her current adultery, Robert Barker, a vicious piece of work, was presented as a common wizard, for which he received the *alias* "Unluckye Barker."[556]

Although they escaped, John Parckhare *alias* Lysam *alias* Tyther *alias* Trayte, laborer, and his wife Margaret had been ordered to be arrested by the justices of Staffordshire, for several felonies. The justifiable inference is that the sequence of *aliases* had been adopted to cover these activities.[557] Less inventive, although suspected of burglary with violence, was Ralph Dakin who assumed the *alias* John Smyth and was implicated by examinations before the same county's justices in 1598.[558] Another suspected person mentioned in examinations about stolen clothing before the Staffordshire justices in 1600 was Black John, whose real identity was undisclosed.[559]

Amongst those most likely to invent an *alias* were itinerants, in their attempts to evade the restrictions of passes. A vagrant who confessed at Salisbury in 1601 that she traveled from fair to fair and was accompanied by four other idle companions acknowledged her names as Rebecca Wilkes *alias* Seymour *alias* Anne Wilkes. There too another idle and begging vagrant, Humphrey Saunders, adopted the *alias* Alexander Humfrey—an inversion of his name since Saunder was a hypocorism of Alexander.[560]

We might here also remark upon the use of a periphrasal affix in those (admittedly rare) cases where homonymy caused confusion. So those assessed at Cliveden in 1581 included John Nethwaye "of the marshe," John Nethway "of the myll" and John Nethway "of Chipping crose."[561]

The *alias*, although never attributed to more than a very small percentage of the population, offered nevertheless to a minority of people multiple identifications if not always identities. At a time when academic concern with social identity and identities continues to be a major concern, it is therefore surprising that the historical *alias* has not been addressed more pertinently. Perhaps a number of conclusions can be associated with the *alias*. First, the *alias* occurred mainly after the formation of hereditary surnames. Before then, people's identification could be and was negotiated through the byname or *cognomen*. Of course, after the stability of hereditary surnames and family names, it remained possible to negotiate "identity" through the forename—through hypocorisms or diminutives. It is possible that in that case the initiative derived from the individual—a mild and circumscribed extent of self-fashioning. Such a motive might have inspired the *alias* of William Vincent, a royal servant, for he disported the *alias* "Hocus Spocus." Although of London, he was a participant in gambling in Reading in 1625, an activity which might explain his alternative moniker, although at this event he lost money.[562] What the *alias* offered after the stability of family names was another, more extensive opportunity for the identification—perhaps "identity"—of a small number of individuals to be negotiated, within their peer group, local society, or more widely. The process of the *alias* was sometimes more complicated: constructed through a dialogue between the individual and others, not a simple attribution, whilst in other cases it was an ascription imposed by society to label or marginalize individuals, although the intention was not always the effect. Although it retained multiple meanings, for these reasons of negotiation about identification, it remained an important aspect of the social syntax of naming.[563]

3
Improprieties: Emotive Expressions

Friendship and love

One of the aspects that is not explored above, but about which something can be suggested here, is expressions of neighborliness and devotion which are not always direct forms of address. Interpreting those ostensible articulations of amity is a difficult process, often dependent on the context of the source. Some historians of medieval friendship have emphasized its formal, philosophical and, indeed, political content—its instrumentality.[564]

We can observe the confusion of affection with instrumentality in early-modern expectations of "friends." Vexed by William (H)ambler, an overpowering neighbor, Jenet Grene, a widow of Burstwick, resorted to the court of Star Chamber because she failed in her hope "to have founde some frende that wolde entreate the said Ambler to cease his crueltye..."[565] Expressing concern that any of his sons might turn out to be wasters or not good husbandmen, Christopher Blaides of Askrigg expected them to be "advised by his frendes for his good..." If any of his sons failed to manage his resources, he was to sell to one of his brothers "at a resonable raitt at the sight of there frendes."[566] In c. 1540, Elizabeth Smethwick committed to a letter: "I must make my frendys to do sumwhat for me."[567]

Testators sometimes, as did a Somerset will-maker in 1558, entrusted their burial to the discretion of their friends.[568] John Stodden of Selworthy in Somerset—no doubt because he was a bachelor—left the arrangements for his burial to the discretion of his friends in 1640, but several other testators depended on their friends for the formalities of their burials.[569] Christopher Collyn of Darlington also requested in his will (1600) that his friends organize the burial of his body in Darlington churchyard as near as possible to those of his father and mother.[570] We understand too the role that friends of young people were expected to play in courtship.[571] Friends were thus depended on to provide practical assistance — the instrumentality of a relationship which also, of course, involved affection. What is the concern here is the affective relationship of everyday existence in local societies.

On the other hand, some sources will be pervaded by instrumentality.[572] Is it possible, for example, to take letters simply as expressing affection, or is there not sometimes in correspondence some level of instrumentality – some artifice in the form of address intended to suit the occasion, the situation, and the author's intentions?[573] Moreover, are not many letters conceived within a context of formality or semi-formality — the very medium demands protocol, perhaps even, on occasion, dissimulation? The interpretation of letters thus requires especial care and it may well be that other sources evoke a much more affective association.[574]

"That he taketh pride of false commendations."[575] Yet, of course, commendations were the formal address in sixteenth-century correspondence. The *incipit* of letters conveyed hearty commendations. Thus, when Hugh Smyth asked Matthew Smyth in a letter for his opinion about a lease, the business was only broached after hearty commendations opening the letter.[576] Other correspondence of the Smyths exhibited the same conventional salutation.[577] When John Adams wrote to his brother-in-law, Percival Willoughby, in 1588, his valediction concluded: "And thus with our harty commendations..."[578] The conventionality of salutations and valedictions, of course, was epitomized by royal letters, commencing with the standard greeting: "trusty and right welbeloved."[579] Imitation of royal style might have encouraged a conventional form of address in correspondence.

We might detect then this element of artifice and convention in the correspondence between the Assembly of Boston and aristocratic patrons who had an interest in the borough, usually through the appointment to offices. When Lord Burghley communicated to the Mayor in 1571, he opened his letter: "Aftur my hartie commendacions...," continuing to nominate for the recordership "my verey lovyng frende Mr Stephen Thymolby," and concluding with the valediction: "Your very lovyng frende Burley."[580] Concerning the more important office of High Steward, Sir Henry Clinton also proposed his "lovyng frende" Thymolby, finishing "Your lovyng frend H Clinton," and the letter addressed "To my verie lovenge frendes the Mayor..." (also in 1571).[581]

Some degree of dissimulation or false politeness might be detected in the letter from the Earl of Sussex in 1586 "To the Commissioners of the Sewers my very loving freinds within Holland in Lincolnshire...," which he concluded "Your loving freinde H. Sussex." After his hearty commendations to the commissioners, he proceeded to a fairly vociferous complaint about a proposed drain through his lands.[582]

The connection between requests for friendship and material assistance are only too well reflected in the correspondence of the Maude family at the end of the sixteenth century. John Maude unhesitatingly wrote in 1595 to Hugh Saxey: "Syre, I moste crave your frenshippe in thes matter"—the recovery of a debt.[583] Just about a year later, Maude sent a general acknowledgement to Saxey: "with like thankes for your unfeyned frendshippe and furtherance in all and every my severall causes."[584] The next occasion on which friendship and furtherance were requested involved the purchase of lands disposed by the Crown.[585] When, shortly before and in the same year, a dispute arose over the vicarage of Ilkley, the correspondence alluded "as hitherto ye have befrended me in such like causes."[586]

In this context, then, it is interesting that by the late seventeenth century, the business letters of George Sitwell entirely observed that purpose—affairs. Like correspondents to *The Times*, he addressed his communications simply "Sir."[587] This cursory observation of a politeness and civility was far removed from the more florid address in letters of a century or so previously and earlier.

Another complication is that in past societies friendship and kinship were not necessarily differentiated or separate areas of life. Some anthropological studies, on the other hand, have maintained that strong kinship bonds exclude social relationships outside the kinship.[588] Whilst ties of kinship—including extended kinship—remained important, early-modern English local societies also depended—indeed, were predicated—on neighborliness. Whether neighborliness constituted friendship is, of course, suffused with ambiguities. Perhaps the supposition might be that it might lead to friendship and certainly to social networks, whether strong or weak. Here, then, the purpose is to explore mainly those bonds of amity which extended outside the kinship group through address as an expression of friendship. What we are seeking through language – although written – is intimacy and voluntarism as defining features of personal relationships, however difficult that may turn out to be.

In particular, such articulations occurred in wills when a testator beseeched acquaintances to act as overseer or executor. "From our friends, we hope to derive emotional support, advice and material help in times of need."[589] In a sense, then, that is an instrumental expectation, but in the situation of daily existence it is also infused with affection. At the end of life, the instrumentality is mediated or compromised: reciprocity cannot be expected from a dead person, but the affection of friendship can persist after death. In 1561, then, John Stokes, a yeoman of Fyfield (Essex) referred to two men that he desired his loving neighbors to be supervisors of his will.[590] Those requested to act as overseers or executors were described as my faithful friend, my loving friend, my trusty friend and my neighbor and friend, and well-beloved friends in the 1560s.[591] Another overseer appointed in a will of 1569 was described by the testator as his well-beloved neighbor and friend.[592] In similar manner, two supervisors (who also acted as witnesses and so were close to the testator) constituted in a will of 1567 were portrayed as the will-maker's trusty and well-beloved friends.[593] Although a co-executor of 1568 was alluded to simply as the testator's loving friend, a supervisor named in another will of that year was more fulsomely maintained as the testator's loving and trusty neighbor and friend.[594]

In 1569-70 other descriptions of supervisors represented them as my well-beloved in Christ (two wills) and more plainly my very friend.[595] The will of Robert Martin of Bury Saint Edmunds similarly referred to two men nominated as supervisors as his dearly beloved in Christ in 1636.[596] With wills, of course, we must be sensitive to the deployment of formulae from books of protocol or ascription by the writer of the will.[597] The phrase well-beloved in Christ looks suspiciously like it might fall into one of these categories, although the testators belonged to an evangelical local society in Essex.[598] On the other hand, such descriptions of overseers or supervisors and executors occurred so rarely and in a minority of wills that some meaning might be attached to them. It might be supposed that they constituted more than empty phrases or dissimulation or the expected and anticipated norm, and that they were a genuine expression of intimacy.

The nuncupative will of William Daubneye of Great Oakley in 1563 articulated this sincerity of expression well. Before his expiry, the will records, he sent for his good neighbors and friends to witness (three named men) his final wishes.[599] The end of life might well have been a time for reconciliation, but there seems no artifice about such statements. The occasional legacy in trust confirmed the relationship, as when one testator left to his faithful friend Henry Johnson a cow and three sheep to raise the testator's daughter.[600] Another will-maker appointed his especial and well-beloved friend, Davy Sampson, gent., as guardian to his son.[601] As affectively, a sole executor in 1636 was described by the testator as his well-beloved friend as his trust was in him reposed.[602] Other early-seventeenth century executors, overseers or supervisors were portrayed as the testator's loving friends, beloved friend, and well-beloved and trusty friend.[603] A smattering of Banbury wills repeated this commendation of overseers: well-beloved friends (five wills) and loving friend (one).[604] A minority of Bristol testators also commended their overseers: trusty friends; "my verye trustie Frend"; loving friends; loving and trusty friends; well-beloved friends; "my very frendes"; "my beloved in Christ"; and "my welbeloved neygbours."[605] Some Yorkshire testators concurred with this description of overseers: "my well beloved freyndes" (1558) and "trusty & welbeloved freindes."[606] A similarly small number of Somerset testators commended their overseers as "welbeloved frendes," "good Frends," "wellbeloved," "ij especiall Frinds," "loving and trustie Frinds" and "welbeloved in christe."[607] A "verye trustie Frend" was appointed executor by Anthony Goodyere, tailor of Bristol, in 1592, and another Bristol testator had recourse to a "trustie lovinge frend" to receive rents in trust in 1597.[608]

At a higher social status, the language of amity in wills attained a more florid form when it was articulated—again, though, only in a small proportion of wills. The expressions are exemplified by some Derbyshire testators whose wills were proven in the Prerogative Court of Canterbury. When Sir Godfrey Foljambe of Walton, knight, appointed the overseers in his will, he referred to them—an LCJ, two esquires, and a knight—as his right worshipful friends to reflect their dignity.[609] Nicholas Clerke, gentleman of Somersall, succumbed to the same politeness, although his two overseers were merely esquires: his right worshipful good master and friend Godfrey Foljambe of Walton, esquire, and his worshipful and dear friend Edward Berisford of Cutthorp, also esquire.[610] Joint overseers and executors in P.C.C. wills of other Derbyshire testators were more plainly established as: very good and trusty friend; trusty and well-beloved friend; my very good friend; and well-beloved friends.[611]

In the north-west of the country, John Charnocke, gentleman of Farington, proclaimed as his supervisor his "veraye assured trustye frend," Robert Charnocke, of Asteley, esquire, in 1571.[612] When Robert Entwysle appointed his supervisors in 1574, he remarked eloquently and rhetorically: "and for the frendshippe they have shewed me in theyr lyffe tyme to take the paines to se this my testament performede wyth such diligence as they wold wyshe there owne testament to be performede.."[613] Supervisors thus drawn from testators' circle of closest friends were usually thus commended by the will-maker as part of an exhortation to continue in their generosity at the end of life.

On the other hand, the language of friendship at death might have sometimes been aspiration. When one testator nominated two men as executors referring to them as his well-beloved friends, one, a gentleman, renounced the role.[614] It is thus possible that the inclusion of language of love and friendship was not only aspiration, but rhetoric—to persuade the nominated person to perform the role. The number of wills containing such expressions of affection, however, is slight and that might mitigate this argument. Most wills exhibited no affective words for executors, supervisors or overseers. That might not, however, be surprising since wills were essentially concerned with concluding the testator's affairs of the family. In arranging this business, many testators might not have given thought to expressing their attachments. Their silence in this regard did not necessarily represent lack of affection.

Other facets of testators' requests cemented the inter-relation of instrumentality and affection. When John Shaw specified the burial of his bones in the churchyard at Askrigg, he solicited that they "be honestly broght forth at the day of my death at syght of my frendes..."[615] Friends—but also neighbors—were addressed in George Parker's will in 1558 to witness the receipt of his son's child's portion.[616] In the same location, Robert Calvert invoked the "discressyon of my frends" for his burial in Askrigg churchyard in 1585.[617] A few years later another Askrigg testator designated burial in the church or churchyard "as my frendes shall thinke moste conveniente."[618] Those arrangements for a proper and honest burial constituted the greatest expectation by testators from their friends —and it is here too that the complication of friends being kin is very apposite. Testators in Yorkshire were particularly concerned that friends make proper provision for their burial, placing this request high in the order of their wills: "Also at the day of my buriall I will be broughe forthe after the mynde of my frendes of my holl goodes..."; "In primis at the tyme of my buriall I will be broughe forth of my holl goodes after the mynde of my frendes..."; "Item at the time of my buriall I will be brought forth of my holl goodes after the mynde of my frendes"; "I will be brought forth of my parte after the mynde of my frendes."[619]

Several implications issue from these solicitations. First, the importance to the testators is heightened because of the norm of the *legitim* in the northern province, whereby a married male testator's personal estate was divided into three parts: one for him; one for his wife; and one for the children. Invariably, these Yorkshire testators indicated that they wished the whole of their third part to be invested in their salvation. They did not, however, specify exactly how, but trusted in their friends to make the proper arrangements. It is likely that those "friends" to whom the role was confided were kin, by analogy with another testator's stipulation: "Also I will that my children se that I be brought forthe honestlie with dirige and messe songe and a dynner be made for my frendes."[620] Friends in this context were those intimately involved with burial arrangements, kin. In times of religious uncertainty, moreover, leaving the precise arrangements to best-trusted friends had much discretion, so that Leonard Clark of Hawton in Yorkshire in 1549 simply exhorted "my body to be buried as a Christyn man ought to be as my frendes here thinke best."[621] At issue was confidence in the proper and authorized liturgy for personal salvation—but also proper provision for status: "Also I wilbe honestlie brought forth accordinge to my degree," as enunciated by Peter Beckett of Rotherham.[622] One of the most important responsibilities committed to friends by testators, then, was to ensure proper provision for their burial and in this situation it is likely that friends constituted kin.[623]

Another concerned father expressed anxiety that any of his children as legatees of his real estate might be "a waistor or not good husband & will not be advised by his frendes."[624] Testators in "Abbotside" relied in many ways then on the continuing loyalty and affection of their friends. So too did will-makers in other locations. In the mind of Richard Langfellay of Otley in 1537 was perhaps the cementing of his relationships: "Also I bequeste xls. to be divided amonge my frendes that most nedes at the discretione of my frendes and myn executors."[625] The continuing support of friends for the deceased's family exercised the minds of testators. Anticipating the possibility—if no more—of conflict between his wife and children, Thomas Birch of Hindley Birch, gentleman, in his will of 1595 desired his "trustie frendes" (four named men) to intervene to "indevoure to make peace and quietnes amongste them."[626]

It is also in this context, however, that we encounter the ambiguity between friends and kin. It seems probable that in some cases at least the "friends" in these Askrigg wills were synonymous with kin. That implication subsists in Elizabeth Morland's will of 1598 in which she allocated to her "brethren" the education of her children "if so it be that my husband frindes in Winton be content."[627] When Michael Pratt's will of 1599 alluded to the marriage of his daughter Dorothy, he considered that she should obtain the advice of her mother and her two uncles, "hir afforesaid frendes" (i.e. the two uncles).[628] When Henry Stanley of Bickerstaffe, esquire, in 1598 entered into consideration in his will about the marital prospects of his daughters "beinge ruled by my lovinge wyff and by such other Frendes as my said wieffe shall appoynte," he was probably alluding to kin as friends.[629] Similarly, then, a testator's son, Christopher, should receive his legacy at the discretion of his mother, uncle, brother "and the rest of his nearest frendes" in 1599.[630] The "foure honest frendes" to whom Peter Metcalfe entrusted the disbursement under his will almost certainly consisted at least of his father-in-law and two Metcalfes, who also acted as his supervisors.[631]

The complication is perhaps demonstrated in Brereton *v.* Johnson in Star Chamber in 1537: "And your orator, being very nere frend and kynnesman unto the said Roger ..." implies that the two terms were synonymous.[632] The imputation that friends in some contexts were kin is contained also in the request of a Yorkshire testator in 1541: "In primis at the day of my burial I will be broughe furthe of my holl goodes after the mynd of my frendes and children."[633] The implication is perhaps there too in the bequests of another Yorkshire will-maker a year earlier, for it was desired that Elizabeth Adamson receive her child's part of ten marks "or else in goodes at the sight of my wif and the frendes of John Adamson her father..."[634]

Testamentary provisions in the north-west seem to confirm this complication. In 1598, Isabel Holland, widow of Salford, expressed a desire to be buried in Manchester parish church near her husband, her other ancestors and friends.[635] In other parts of the north, too, the imputation is present: a moiety of the testator's personal estate "to dispose for the benefecte of my sowle, the sowles of my father, mother and other freyndes."[636] When William Swift, of Rotherham, effected a trust for the marriage of his daughters in his will of 1568, the trustees were to comprise "my very loveinge freindes Mr Wortelie, Mr Rerisbie, Mr Mallorye..." whom, we know from the same will, were drawn from his wider circle of kin and in-laws, the first two nephews and the last one brother-in-law.[637] The will of William Appleton of Gateside, county Durham, gentleman, in 1579, establishes that friends might consist of in-laws: "provided that if my wife and hir frendes do by good assurance convey to myne executor all such estate as hath been granted me at the tyme of oure mariage..."[638] In all discussion of the expectations from friends, therefore, we must be conscious of the fact that friends might consist of a circle of kin.

In the Maude letters, that ambiguity of friendship and kinship seems particularly pertinent in the north of England, in the West

Riding of Yorkshire. Maude informed Saxey in 1595: "Syre, all our frendes hear in this countere his mery and in good health, my unckle Thomas with all the reaste."[639] When Saxey received a letter from William Flessher in 1595, the author sent his commendations to brother, sister, daughter "and all the rest of all our frendes at London" from the part of Flessher, his wife, children, uncle Thomas, brother Ellis and Ellis's wife "and the rest of our frendes."[640] Commendations in 1596 to brother and sister were to be communicated also to "the rest of all oure good frendes and kinsfolkes att London."[641] Throughout the discussion, therefore, remains this ambiguity whether friends were kin, particularly in expressions in wills and in the north of England.

Only a very small proportion of testators made any affectionate comment about their wives, either as legatees or executrices. It is therefore significant that some husbands did. Eleven wills of male testators in the archdeaconry of Sudbury in 1636-7—perhaps four percent or so—referred to their well-beloved wife either in making bequests or appointing executrices.[642] Ten others mentioned their loving wife and another six their beloved wife.[643] One testator appointed as his executor his loving and kind wife and another nominated his careful and loving wife.[644] One wife was commended by the testator for the faithful love and entire affection which he had always found in her, making her his sole executrix.[645] Robert Dawbeney of Hinderclay prescribed in a legacy in 1637 to his dear and loving wife and faithful yoke fellow.[646]

A similarly small proportion of Banbury wills between 1591 and 1620 included such expressions. Ten wives in wills were eulogized as well-beloved, many of whom were appointed residual legatee and executrix.[647] Two other wives who were legatees were remembered as a Banbury testator's loving wife and beloved wife.[648] A tiny proportion of wills of Derbyshire testators proved in the Prerogative Court of Canterbury before 1590 enunciated affective words for the testator's wife: faithful and true wife (joint executor); well-beloved wife (joint executor); loving wife (two); and well-beloved wife (two).[649] Some few testators in the north-west affectionately appointed their "derely beloved" and "welbeloved" wife as joint executrix in the late sixteenth century.[650] Few wills in the diocese of Worcester before 1534 revealed any sentiments for wives, except for John Moore's eulogy of his "faithful & Enteerly belovyd wife" in 1527.[651]

Nuncupative wills might particularly articulate devotion to a wife and may report the testator's actual words and emotions more directly than engrossed wills.

> I am but a poore man and all the goodes and chattles that I have I give and bequeathe unto Dorothy my wiffe and wold soe doe yf I had ten tymes as muche.[652]
> And then he said all that ever I have do I give unto my Wiffe Katheren if yt weare more.[653]

In 1602, two Bristol testators, one a joiner, the other a tailor, orally recollected the emotional debt which each owed to his wife. It is only through nuncupative wills that such devotion is visible to this extent. The compression and formalism of engrossed wills truncated such verbal gestures.

Lincolnshire wills of the early sixteenth century were singularly devoid of expressions of intimacy. The exception was the last wish of Mancer Marmyon, of Ringsdon, esquire, who, whenever he mentioned his wife, Edith, reiterated his devotion: "faythfull and hertely belovyd wyffe"; "my singuler belovyd wyff"; "my best belovyd and trusty wyff"; "hertely belovyd wyffe"; and he, accordingly, appointed her joint executrix.[654]

When an affective sentiment is manifested, then, its sincerity may perhaps be accepted. In 1582, Edward Edmundsam of Sallow, gent., bequeathed to his "right dear friend Master Benett Wilson" £6 13s. 4d. to purchase a gelding.[655] In a gesture upwards, Henry Milward of Doveridge allocated £10 in angels by his will of 1564 to his "singular good lady and mistress the Lady Pawlett."[656] These testators wished to be remembered by their friends, to continue to be regarded in death as in life as persons with social and civil honor. It is possible too that through the bequests the benefactors hoped for a continuation of the intimate relationship between legatee and the deceased's family. Such aspirations did not dilute the strength of the expression of friendship, for, as many testators openly acknowledged, the essence was trust in a respected person.

One other aspect of will-making demands comment. In some

localities, the first element in the preamble was to preserve ami-
cable relationships through the will. In some Stockport wills of
the late sixteenth century, for example, even before making provision for the soul and burial, testators expressed their concern to
maintain kin and social relationships: "meanynge that Amytie and
frendshippe shall and maye be had and contynued Amongest my
children and frends after my decease..."; "meanynge that Quyetnes
love and Frendshippe shall and maie be had and conteyned amongest my wyfe and frends after my decease..."; "to thend love and
Frendship shall and may bee hadd betwene my wyff daughter and
Frends after my decease..."[657] It may well be that these preambles,
although not exactly reiterative, represent the will formula of a local scrivener. Despite that context, their selection may also contain
the expressions actually desired by the testator. If that is so, then
the primary concern of these testators through their will-making
was to maintain social relationships after death: to prevent discord.
Another implication here, of course, might well be that friends in
this context equated with kin outside the nuclear household.

Remaining with wills, one of the obligations felt by some testators before the abandonment of Catholicism was specifically to
include friends in the provisions made by testators for prayers for
salvation after death. Illustrated in Figure 2 (page 148) are the numbers of wills through which testators remembered their friends after
death, preserving the social network of affection after life.[658] Here,
we are concerned with specific mention of friends. It should not be
ignored that the office for the dead included all Christian souls and,
indeed, a large proportion of testators recollected not only their
close kin but also all Christian souls.[659] In a sense, then, friends were
captured within that all-encompassing category. Specific mention
of friends, therefore, obtained in only a small proportion of Sussex wills. Moreover, friends were not designated by name, but by
a collective phrase: "all my good frendes soules"; "oure fryndes
sowlles"; "all our frendes soules"; "my good frendes soules"; or
"al my Fryndes sollyes."[660] Many Somerset testators also specifically included their friends in the masses for their souls.[661] A small
proportion of Buckinghamshire testators also involved friends in
masses and prayers.[662] Numerous Lincolnshire testators in 1530
made the same provision: for good friends' souls or, less frequently,

just friends' souls.[663] Moreover, the preservation of this association between the living and dead friends was maintained occasionally in other ways through the testator's will: "a convenyent dyner" at his month's mind for friends (1546); and "to cause me and my fryndes to be paide for in the bederole as I have done in tymes past" (1547).[664] Perhaps the fondest expression in a will inhered in the legacy of Guy Hill of Crewkerne in 1557 to Thomas Hawkyns "for the grete gentilnes that I have found in hym."[665]

Returning to correspondence, the letters of Thomas Knyvett to his wife defy convention in address, salutation and valediction. Thomas's letters to his wife are vividly replete with his expression of love and devotion to his wife. Even the address incorporated the words: "To his most assuered & true loving friend & wife" or "To his deerest loving wife."[666] Pervasive through his letters to Catherine were articulations of his affection: "my deerest affection to thyselfe"; "thy deerest loving husband"; "thy loving husband who loves the more than his owne life"; or "thy assuered loving husband till death."[667] His greetings were constantly of the style "sweet harte," "my deere hart," "my deerest love," "my deere sweet harte," or "sweete hart and hony bloude."[668]

His outpourings of emotion and attachment were especially strong in his special friendship with Sir Thomas Holland, illuminating, on Sir Thomas's death, the affective bonds of amity.

> We have lost the truest freinde in the worlde ... God give us patience to take these crosses patiently, for I valew the losse of a friend above all fortune in the worlde, esspeciallye such a friend as his like is not to be founde. I never looke to have such another ... I am not able to wright what I woulde, my hart is so full.[669]

Such emotion may have been intensified by his writing to his wife, from whom he had been separated for so long on business, but it undoubtedly contains too his personal fondness for Sir Thomas.

Dislike and disaffection

> *Lord Mayor* How now, what knave is this? From whence
> comest thou?
> *Firk* No knave, sir. I am Firk, the shoemaker, lusty Rog-
> er's chief lusty journey man,...
> *Lord Mayor* Stay, stay, sir knave...
> *Firk* 'Tis happy the knave is put before the shoemaker...
> *Lord Mayor* My lord, this villain calls us knaves by craft.
> *Firk* Then 'tis by the Gentle Craft, and to call one 'knave'
> gently is no harm.[670]
> *Sir Andrew* Most certain. Let our catch be Thou knave
> *Feste* Hold thy peace, thou knave, knight. I shall be con-
> strained in't to call thee knave, knight.
> *Sir Andrew* 'Tis not the first time I have constrained one
> to call me knave....[671]

Far from manipulating address in a polite fashion to expect a
similar response, occasional speech acts disregarded all sense of
propriety. Most frequently, that social interaction occurred as defamation, which has been particularly expertly explored, especially
as a form of speech act associated with women and their sexual
morality.[672] There is no intention here to re-examine that context.
What is at issue here is how males—and usually it was men—re-
jected deference in contact with authority, abusing parish officers
—churchwardens and constables—parochial clergy, and the Justices of the Peace. It is moreover the speech acts and language use of
individuals that are the concern here, not the oratory attributed to
collective social rebellion. The politics of language as social critique
in collective action is not considered here.[673] The intention is to explore the subversive speeches declaimed in the rejection of deference by individuals in public spaces against figures of authority.
The emphasis is then on the individual response in social interaction, the rejection of deference rather than dissimulation, and the
language of non-reverential address.

The conventional wisdom, and indeed apparent practice, was
that contrition before the magistrates or the ecclesiastical judge
might result in remission of the sentence. Quite contrarily, some

defendants provoked the authorities in their verbal responses. Most usually, these altercations occurred between males—male defendants rejecting authority. In many cases, moreover, the accused males were alleged to be totally disordered.

Articles against Robert Simpson scrivener sheweinge his misdemeanoure and ill cariage

1 Inprimis that he is a common alehouse haunter and diverse tymes in the night distempered

2 Item he is a common railer and reviler of honest and sober minded people

3 Item that in speciall he raileth upon Thomas Barnes thelder callinge him old drunkard and his wife an whore

4 Item that he raileth also upon Thomas Barnes the yonger calling him theife, roague, and rascall, and his wife an <old> whore

5 Item that he threatneth Robert Throope to doe him some mischeife and it being obiected that then Robert Throope would have advantage against him he answered that he would doe it privately that noe advantage should be taken

6 Item that beinge by the magistrate reproved upon complaintes he stoode in a peremptorye manner to iustifye himselfe and in the presence of Mr Maior and an other Justice of the Peace did say and bragge that he <was ready> would defend himselfe with his sworde

7 Item he useth railinge tearmes against Mr Robert Wood callinge him lame roague lame Rascall and villaine dissemblinge puritayne and hypocrite with other vile tearmes

8 Item that he raileth upon Mr Maior calling him Mr Maior Mr Horse and let him Kisse my Arse even the very Nocke of my Arse

9 Item that it is generally reported that <he> useth in the alehouses amongst his companies base and contemptious tearmes against the magistrates and many others.[674]

Simpson, presented by the constables of Nottingham in 1620, exhibited the nexus of bad habits of the generally disordered life associated with lack of reverence for authority. If increasing civility, politeness and manners were adopted at one end of society, rudeness, incivility, and provocative language persisted at the other end, where disrespect for authority was habitual, and the social proprieties and graces disregarded. The presentation of self by these miscreants remained unselfconscious, not incorporating any strategy to manipulate the response of other people. The characteristics of their address involved directness, disrespect, dissoluteness, disregard—and not a little drunkenness.[675]

The most common descriptive term for criticism of authority —and of peers—was railing. Railing should be distinguished from the gentlemanly engagement in raillery, as it developed in the late seventeenth century.[676] Railing had none of the implications of sardonic wit; it often resulted from a loss of control over emotions. The character of railing can be elicited from events at New Buckenham when Jane, wife of Francis Hayward, an excommunicate, burst into church during divine service, reprehending the minister with "many Raylinge and obbrobrious speeches," suggesting he was a "blacke sutty mowthed knave, to the greate disgrace of his callinge."[677] Such an action by a woman was less usual. More meaning is conveyed in the insulting of Master Holmes, alderman, by Robert Bold in York in 1541. Bold was adjudged to have "ralyd" at the alderman. His misdemeanor comprised seditious and slanderous words, including "fals knave and thowyng of him."[678] Another contentious event—this time in Weymouth in 1617—elucidates the context of railing. Brandishing a sword with menace, Pettin was disarmed and arrested by the constable and conducted to jail. On the way, according to the constable, Pettin persisted in "rayling," proclaiming that he "would paye him soundely, but att this time he would obay his foolish office."[679]

Aspects of the characteristics of railing are elucidated by the theater in the first decade of the seventeenth century.[680] The boy companies concentrated on "railing" productions, with an emphasis on satire, anger, invective and bitterness. The audience which appreciated such aberrant entertainment consisted of gallants and law students.[681] In this context, railing was manifestly "a mode of cynical and acerbic talking."[682] Opponents of this new form of production denounced its acrimony. So Heywood condemned its "committing their bitternesse, and liberall invectives against all estates, to the mouthes of Children, suposing their juniority to be a priviledge for any rayling, be it never so violent."[683] Middleton elucidated the meaning and context of railing in *A Trick to Catch the Old One*: "...for he rails on you [Witgood], speaks shamefully of him [Witgood's uncle, Lucre]"; "I wonder you can rail at him, sir; he comes in love to see you" [to which Dampit responded: "A louse for his love. His father was a combmaker; I have no need of his crawling love. He comes to have a longer day, the superlative rascal"]; and "'T' is ex'llent, thief rails upon the thief!"[684]

So some men might be reproved as a "common rayler."[685] Amongst such prodigal males was William Hamshire of Romford, presented in 1584 before the archdeacon's court for drunkenness, who, nonetheless, avowed that he "will continewe still in his drounckenes as he saithe in dispite of them all and saieth that he carethe not if he be presented everie weeke and raleth horiblie against the Churchwardens and Syedemen callinge them gentlemen beggerlie knaves."[686] Another common drunkard, Thomas Harrison, a laborer of Nantwich, staggered into the parish church where the ringers were announcing the burial of the Lady Lee, by his using "most base and vyle language." When approached by the churchwarden, Harrison accompanied him up and down the church, reproaching and reviling him with opprobrious and malicious words: "thou art a base fellowe, a home breed Rogue, a whyte lyverd Rascall..." When the churchwarden meant to make his escape, Harrison followed him through the churchyard, continuing the reviling. Expressing no remorse when tackled the next day by the ringers, Harrison continued his diatribe.[687]

That habitual resort to railing might have been associated with an intemperate nature, but in some cases too character was combined with conviction, not least in religious belief. Accordingly, Robert May, who exhibited heretical beliefs in the visitation of Kennington in 1511-12, commonly "raylithe ayenst prechers."[688] Probably from a similar attitude, the priest of Sibertswold was challenged by "many obprobryous and contumelyous words," not least the remonstrance: "thou preest, what doethe thou here in our churche" —with the emphasis undoubtedly on *thou* and *our*.[689]

How this denial of deference and respect resulted from the failure to manage emotions is illustrated by the response of Thomas Ince, shoemaker and councillor, at the Assembly of Chester City Council in 1619. Incensed by the taxing of alehouses, he uttered "outrageous, intemperate and irreverend speeches."[690] In similar manner, John Langton, baker, reacted to the change in baking regulations in York in 1554 "in great fury with raylyng wordes" and "with dyverse other unfyttyng and opprobriouse" words.[691] Irritated by the churchwardens' demand that he cough up the assessment of 1s. made on him in 1623, John Greaves of Nottingham, exploded in vile railing words against them.[692] The circumstances are illustrated too by the reaction of Richard Ibatson of East Retford at Easter 1596. Although excommunicate, he attended church for divine service. When the churchwarden, John Mason, asked him to depart, he railed on Mason calling him knave.[693] Whether valid or not, the excuse proffered by Anthony Bradley for railing at his vicar of North Collingham in 1625 was that the vicar, Mr Greene, was drunk in the churchyard, so Bradley's companion, Mr Samuel Shepperd (and note his status) correspondingly lambasted Greene as "rogue deboist preiste and drunken fellow," whilst Shepperd's son, in rather more youthful language, denounced the vicar as "the sonne of a bitch."[694] Reacting to the constable's attempt to muster them, John and Roger Bolton subjected him to "very evell speches" in 1596.[695] They consequently explained their words by their exasperation. In one of those unusual cases of vituperation by women, Alice Quicke, wife of John of Romford, was detected for "raylinge upon the Churchwardens...and said that if she weare a man as she is a woman she wold be revenged and said she wold not come into Corte for C^{li}."[696] Irritation was again the stimulus to this loss of control and abusive critique of authority. Such remonstrations resulted from a failure to manage emotions in social confrontation, leading to inappropriate intemperate address of others, usually others in authority or charged with some responsibility.[697]

Social and situational proprieties were ignored or not observed. Most frequently, the words were condemned as "opprobrious," as when Francis Dickins, yeoman, challenged the North Riding justices: "What a thrusting is here. I would we were att cuffes together"—scandalous words and opprobrious sayings in the opinion of the court.[698] Opprobrious became the adjective of first recourse for disapproval of critical words.[699] In defying the high bailiff of Strat-ford-upon-Avon in 1556, Richard Godwin, smith, was adjudged to have used "obprobryous woordes."[700] There too Robert Rogeres was accused the following year of "revylenge" the officers through "obprobryous wordes" (the significance of "reviling" is explored below).[701]

Office causes in the Norwich consistory court in the early six-teenth century often revolved around opprobrious words leveled against priests.[702] The bailiffs of Worcester complained in 1618 of "obprobrious wordes" directed against them.[703] In 1536 and 1539 opprobrious words were condemned in the Merchants Hall and (Common) Hall in York.[704] In the second instance, the three trades-men who pronounced against the Lord Mayor "many light and slaunderous words...maliciously and obprobriously" were impris-oned for their defiance. The magistrates of Reading suffered "op-probrious words" in 1631.[705] Those of the North Riding in 1626 punished "opprobrious and contumelious speaches."[706] The oppro-brious words leveled at the mayor of Devizes in 1575 consisted of knave (the mayor) and whore (his wife).[707] In Boston in 1561, Mr Sowthen, himself an alderman and later J.P., was reprimanded for using "certen opprobyouse wordes" against the mayor.[708]

In combination, the terms "railing" and "opprobrious" reflected the extreme indignity of the justices. Such contemptuous utterances were expected from one such as Christopher Lazenby, of White-well, immediately identified as a man of dissolute behavior. One of his offences involved "many raling and opprobrious speaches" against the established and respected justice, William Mauleverer, whom Lazenby denounced as a knave and bad judge, extending to many other vile, scandalous and lewd speeches. It was alleged, moreover, that Lazenby acted as a general browbeater.[709]

The language of abuse was also indicted as "reviling" or "to revile." An incident at Newark exemplified this manner. Some gal-lants, led by Mr James Leake, disturbed the neighborhood by il-licitly ringing the bells of the parish church, upon which one of the churchwardens, Rowland Wilson, interrogated Leake about his action. Leake's refrain was that he would continue to act in disre-gard of all churchwardens, condemning Wilson as a "busie fellow." Wilson made a presentment for "if churchwardens may be revyled

and a whole corporation so abused by such a fellow without re-
proofe...churchwardens will not be regarded, nor any their authority obeyed."[710] In one of those infrequent outbursts by a woman parishioner, Susan, wife of John Simson, reviled one of the sidesmen
who discovered her drying malt in time of divine service, alleging
he was "Rascall, Scurvy rascall, Knave, Scomme" and threatened
that if she had had notice of his arrival, she would have blinded
him.[711] The allegation of reviling was also directed against Thomas
James, "for giueing reuileing and scandalous wordes" against the
Northamptonshire justices.[712] When the constable attempted to ar-
rest William Emery's wife, Emery responded not only by impeding
the process, but also by following the constable home and reviling
him; it was alleged in court that he subjected his neighbors often
to reviling.[713] Antagonized by the decision to build a new sessions
house in 1612, Grace, the wife of the apothecary, Peter Watson, engaged in reviling speeches against Sir Baptist Hicks.[714]

Vituperation against authority was also denounced as "unseemlye" or "unfytting," as when "unseemlye and unreverent words"
were aimed at the mayor of Southampton in 1607.[715] Although
Pedley demurred in 1607, he was accused of "unseemly speaches"
against the same mayor, denouncing the mayor as "a metamor-
phized man."[716]

To return to the pronouncement of Firk in Dekker's *The Shoemaker's Holiday*, to call someone knave "gently" would, on the con-
trary, have caused offense.[717] Knave was, indeed, the most frequent
sobriquet to convey contempt. The author of the earlier *Jake Juggler*
recognized this full well, for there is a litany of use of knave as a
term of abuse in that drama.[718] Its status as the commonest insult
to males had been established during the late middle ages.[719] The
courtesy treatise *Stans puer ad mensam* (1463x1483) acknowledged
its import: "Bot oft-tymes rebukyd, and be callyd knaue."[720] Perhaps then the playwright behind *Gammer Gurton's Needle* in the
third quarter of the sixteenth century was closer to the mark:

Ech other word I was a knave, and you a hore of hores[721]

When Diccon challenged Dame Chat about the lost needle,
she, he alleged, responded with this invective: the male Diccon

condemned as a knave as the nearest equivalent of a whore without, however, the sexual accusation.[722] What offended Hodge more in this play was his denunciation by Diccon as a "shytten knave" when Hodge absconded when Diccon attempted to conjure up the devil.[723]

The rector of Bridport was thus appropriately alarmed when Walter Bayley, tailor there, whispered in his ear to denounce the rector as "a base knave, a daungerous knave, a base rogue, a daungerous rogue and sought the blood of honest people."[724] Sir Nicholas Smyth, a canon of Norwich Cathedral, was denounced in 1564 as "thou old papysshe knave" when he interrupted Jeremy Gardener, a servant, who was shooting arrows in the cathedral.[725] Even without elaboration, to be rebuked as a knave implied grave discredit. The consequence for Nicholas Banester in 1596 was his removal as an alderman for derogating George Badger in the Council Chamber of Stratford-upon-Avon as "knave and rascall" amongst other "lewde and bad speeches."[726] In one of the few instances when a woman engaged in this kind of language, Mistress Cockyng, widow, was presented for calling some of the constables in Nottingham knaves and villains in 1573.[727] Such verbal misdemeanors were more normally and normatively associated with one form of masculinity.

The connection of knave as one of the opprobrious words was made in the Monmouth Quarter Sessions in the late sixteenth century when William Bunting was arraigned for assault and brawling, during which he expressed "many opprobrious hateful and scandalous words" which seem to have revolved around his exclaiming: "Arreste yonder knave...Thou art a perjured knave ... Thou art a beggarly knave by kynde."[728] As a result of a similar invective, the mariner William Rymer, was reproved in 1657 in Liverpool; he had allegedly directed abusive and reproachful words at an alderman, Mr William Williamson: "thou art a cheating knave and I will prove thee that and more too."[729] Four years earlier, Jeanette Whitehead had denounced the bailiff, Mr Alcock, as an old arrant knave.[730]

What, of course, intensified the nature of this misdemeanor was the public announcement which demeaned the honor of persons in authority—both their personal reputation and civic honor—and thus converted the transgressive speech into subversive conduct which might incite disorder. Speech acts against those in authority could not be restricted to personal credit and honor, but had a propensity to subvert the whole social order. The offense of Robert Sympson in 1650 thus consisted as much in his openly declaring in the market that the bailiff, John Higinson, was an idle fellow and he blamed the town for electing him as in the insult.[731] So too it was the public defiance by William Mee, butcher, who cursed in open court, pointing at the jury and the mayor, heeding the devil accompany them and all their actions. The magnitude of this public demonstration was reflected in the fines imposed on him: 33s. 4d. and £5 for each offense (thus considerably more for damaging the honor of the mayor).[732] It was too emphasized that Helen Houline had not only abused the bailiff, calling him rogue, but had done so in the presence of many people.[733]

At Firk's level, it was perhaps possible to dismiss words as mere breath. Those of Firk's social standing had little to lose. The impact of speech thus depended on social context. Characterizing a person of higher social status as knave could not be as lightly dismissed as Firk suggested. In a society intimately predicated on personal honor and reputation, words had imprecations. Upwards social critique of this form—not only against personal honor, but also against order and authority—would have consequences. In an honor-based society, in which status was equated with dignity, opprobrious words were exactly that.[734] How magistrates reacted to that abuse of honor is particularly well illustrated by the submission to the justices of the North Riding in 1631.

> That whereas I was accused in open Court to have saied that Sir Thomas Gower, J.P., was an unjust Justice, and one that would sooner write his letters and mainteine whores and knaves then honester people, and that I have spoken other speaches tending both to the said Sir Thomas disreputation in particuler, as also to the dishonour of the whole Court, and that the Justices then present were satisfied by good evidence on each oath that I did speake the same, and hereupon did Order that I should make my submission.[735]

In *The Changeling*, Middleton and Rowley exhibited the potential for disdain in the designation knave.

Lollio Nay, y'are too forward there, Tony; mark my question: how many fools and knaves are here? A fool before a knave, a fool behind a knave, between every two fools a knave; how many fools, how many knaves?[736]

Priests and ministers suffered from the ignominy of being denounced as a knave, sometimes more elaborately qualified: "false knave"; "gleyed-knave"; "preciose horeson knave"; "outlandishe knave"; "scolishe knave"; "false knave"; "thereche knave"; and "rowneaway knave."[737] The rector of Caynby suffered such epithets in 1575: "foole," "doltish fool," "knave," and "doty-pole presst and a knave preest."[738] Knave had the implications of baseness and dishonorable action ("knavery"). Offended by an unwanted attempt to repay a debt in 1561, then, Narforde responded with irritation about its knavish inappropriateness.

And this examinate sayde unto hym Goodman Narforde I ded offer your servaunt Money and he ded refuse it And then the sayde Narforde sayde you had a knavisshe Labour in offering that you myght have offeryd them to some other[739]

Another dispute in Norwich—about the price of bow-staves —erupted from innocent conversation in 1571, with the alleged offensive words: "thow lyest lyke a Fake thefe, a whore master, and a False knave."[740] For the common fame that he had beaten his wife and her mother causing their deaths, John Chapman was allegedly reprehended by John Letten as a "knave" "with other revylyng woordes," reflecting the impact of "knave."[741] Still in that City, further acrimony revolved around the dishonesty connected with "knave."

The daye that my lorde of lessyter dyd Cum un to the Cetie I Chauncyd to Cum upp to se hys Comyng Inne And <stode> dyd stand in the shoppe of Andrewe Quasshe wher I dyd here a grett Controversy off wordes Ryse And spoken betwyxte John Brathwhat and Thomas Jaxson <to> And By John Brauthwhat these wordes spoken *in hec verba* Jaxson

thowe arte a false knave & a thefe for thowe dydes stele
owzte of one gowne or garment ij yerdes off Damaske And
Further thowe arte in Recorde in the shreves Corte for a
false knave & so provyd by men off thyne owne occupacion
thys ys trewe by the othe that I have taken By me Thomas
Bacon[742]

Churl had the same connotation of baseness, but in a more tech-
nical sense of a former low social status. That explanation obtained
when Thomas Luson allegedly complained: "I come not to fight nor
brawl with him, but to speak with him, but the churl will not come
forth."[743] When William Baker was arrested in Norwich for gaming
(at the height of Edwardian confiscation of religious symbols), he
could not restrain himself from exclaiming in the jailer's house, as
was alleged:

That we cannot playe for a halpeny worth of Ale at the
cardes but we are sent hither to prysone for it But there are a
sorte of Chorles that have the church goodes in their handes
that the poore can have noon And I wolbe one of them that
shall pluk it from them ...[744]

Another recollection of his proclamation repeated the term
churl in association with a denunciation of the rich:

we are sente hither to the pryson for playeng for a halpe-
nyworth of Ale and it was nott fylled <in> neyther, poore by
thus pulled, And the riche Chorles have the churche money
in their handes but pore men cannot have it though they of-
fre sewertyes; it were resonable they shulde have parte with
them And I woll have parte with them one daye ...[745]

Knave was, of course, a relatively mild accusation against a
priest in comparison with the more damning implication of sexual impropriety: "Thow art a nought priest and a horemonger";
"false horson churle"; "false hore master preiste" and "comyn hore
maister."[746] Scandalized by the declamations of Robert Long, the
archdeaconry court of Colchester in 1570 ordered him to stand two

Saturdays with a paper on his head in the open market and acknowledge his fault and on two Sundays in his parish church. The
offending words which he had advanced were "that he said that
ministers wyves were whores and their children bastardes."[747] In
similar vein, Robert Sumption, who had already forcefully criti-
cized the mayor and bailiff of Wilton, then exclaimed "very unreverent speches" against the preacher, proclaiming that "there were
many honester papists than our preacher." He too was remanded
in custody in 1609 for this excess.[748] To the dissatisfaction of the rest
of the congregation of Cuckney in 1600, John Rawlinge *alias* Johnson abused the minister with "most vile and reprochefull speches." Amongst physical threats, he declared "Avaunte thou knave &
whoremayster priest."[749] The variety of offenses of which Thomas
Jackson of Ecclesall was suspected in 1599 included "foule speches
and opprobrious wordes" including calling the vicar that most obnoxious of terms, "skurvie puritan."[750] Unusually for her gender,
Ethelred Alande, wife of Matthew Alande, of Kington (Wilts.), in
1634 cursed the magistrates and continued by railing at the vicar,
vilifying him in public with opprobrious words: "a black devill,
and a black crowe," for which she was committed to jail.[751] Now,
although the salacious terms such as whoremaster were no doubt
intended as no more than metaphors, they constituted a form of
slanderous address which dishonored the ministers concerned.[752]

In his articles against his parishioner, Henry Stan(d)ley—a rather substantial document with multiple allegations emanating from
their disagreement and contention—the vicar of Sutton Bonington
complained that Standley accused the vicar not only of "Litle bable,"
but that "he filled his arse full of Dunne." Article four, moreover,
decried: "Item also, that more to prove that his grounded spyte &
hatred generally against the ministers, for their ministery sake, he
calls them knave preistes or pild preistes, & so he hathe called his
pastor, & other preachers also." Moreover, he provided hospitality
to Thomas Burton, "continuall scoffer and derydere of the ministery," whom he had continued to shelter despite an order from the
justices, Burton having "sithens more rayled against the ministery
in more desperate maner then before."[753] Despite the rhetorical
exaggeration by the vicar, such vituperation against ministers occurred when there were arguments over religious conformity.

With even greater impudence, the servant, Edward Boston, was alleged to have denounced the bishop of Norwich as a whoremaster in 1561.[754] Accordingly not to be used to any minister was the condemnation of the vile and reproachful speeches directed by Frances Pendocke, a married parishioner of Tollerton, against her parson in 1614, although she merely caricatured him as dunce and ass.[755]

Such epithets as whoreson could, of course, be brought into service not as railing vituperation, but as appropriate vernacular —what has been termed inverted or covert prestige—for the cohesion of groups of some males, a reinforcement of a particular type of manhood.[756] So Follywit exclaimed to his roguish, "gallant" companions: "Call me your forecast, you whoresons," then going on to expound how, when they exit taverns drunk and incapable, he must implement their pranks. Concluding, he expressed his intent to "maintain a company of villains" for whom he had great affection.[757] In the same drama, Sir Bounteous portrayed his wayward son as "the whoreson boy," whom he loved, but about whom he must be circumspect.[758] In *Gammer Gurton's Needle*, both Hodge and Diccon vented the term ("horson") indiscriminately; at most, their use expressed irritation.[759] In contrast, when Thomas Corbet, although a gentleman, was alleged to have demanded of the local official: "Thou herison constable, whither go thou," the querulous intent was presumed.[760] Context and intonation as well as lexis (vocabulary) must thus be taken into account.[761]

What *is* clear, however, is that the dramatic use of the term was not confined to the stage, but the address was acted out in real encounters. It was deposed in the early sixteenth century, for example, that Robert Pownall deliberately approached the market place to grab Otwell Boothe by the clothing about his chest and exclaimed: "A horeson arte thou here to-day," mortally plunging a dagger into Otwell.[762] Although the witness might have added dramatically to this narrative, the exclamation had familiarity.[763]

One of the anxieties of Thomas Worswick, mayor of Stafford, concerned the manner in which the two bailiffs allowed themselves to be abused.

Towers suffered him selfe and his fellow to theire faces to be called knaves and fooles by John Wakeringe and yet would not bynde him to the peace or to his good abearinge beinge thereunto advised.[764]

Not infrequently, this type of verbal eruption had scatological content. Quite illustrative of this characteristic was the reaction of James Parkin of Mortomley, yeoman, at Quarter Sessions at Rotherham in 1638, when he declaimed against one of the justices, Sir Francis Wortley: "I scorne Sir Francis Wortley's proposition with my arse, and I worshipp him with my arse," euphemistically described as scandalous, malicious and contemptuous words, not only for their content, but for the dishonoring of the target and disorderly intention.[765] Some thirty years previously, the scandalous and opprobrious words emitted by Lionel Swinborne, of Gateshead, yeoman, consisted of the utterance to the constables attempting to restrain him: "Shette in the king's face and all his officers."[766] Such disobedience to the justices could induce not only scatological rejoinders, but tend also to treason, as when Roger Cooper of Malton, yeoman, exclaimed: "I care not for the Kinges lawes a fart and shite on the Kinges lawes," seditiously and scandalously.[767] Similar *lèse-majesté* was committed by John Clarke, of whom the Grand Jury found a true bill for scandalizing the constable: "Why dorst thou tell me of the Queene. A turde for the Queene."[768] Confronted by a complaint made by the Mayor's maid servant in 1606, Edmund Hewett retorted: "I care not a Turd for Mr mayor."[769]

Jonson was familiar with these scurrilous adversions. "Thy worst. I fart at thee," exclaimed Subtle, the alchemist, to his housekeeper.[770] In *Bartholomew Fair*, the playwright assigned to Humphrey Wasp, the serving man, the common exclamation: "Turd i' your teeth."[771] That motif was employed by Robert Briggs, arraigned at Worcestershire Quarter Sessions for using abusive words against the bishop of Worcester. As well as proclaiming "A pox and a plague on the Bishop and all such 'peele' Prelates," he announced: "A turd in the Bishop's teeth for anything I care for him."[772] "A pox and a vengeance" was also invoked by James Droggett on those who were responsible for the statutes against rogues and "a pox of all those that would followe her Majestie any more" because of them.[773] A turd in the teeth of the mayor of Norwich was implored by Thomas Benson, a cobbler, in 1607.[774] Disrupting divine service

Henry Perwige "disturbed and molested" the minister, denouncing him as "Vyle knave, Turd in the tethe knave..."[775] Generally disordered, John Whistons of Arley in 1602 compounded his errors by directing "most opprobrious and thretninge wordes" against the constable, imputing: "it repented him that he had not made my puddinges a praye for the [mag]pies and crowes."[776] Arrested by the watch at midnight, Timothy Pendrey recommended the constable to "kisse his taile."[777]

What heightened the repugnance at this vituperation was the intention of, for example, borough assemblies to order their proceedings. In 1612, as an example, the council of Salisbury (re-)enacted its protocol about speaking in the chamber.

> An order in what manner any speache or mocion shalbe made At this Councell yt is ordered & agreed That at suche tyme as anye speache in any Common Councell question or mocion shalbe made by anye of this Companye, That Mr Mayor may make his speache sittinge and covered And everye other of the xxiiij[tie] of this Companye shall at the firste stande uppe and then sitt downe and delyver his speache mocion or question uncovered, And everye of the xlviij shall stande and be uncovered duringe the tyme of his speache, And yf more then one of this companye offer to speake, the partie of the xxiiij[tie] to be hearde before any of the xlviij[tie] And yf more of the xxiiij[tie] or xlviij[tie] then one offer to speake att one tyme, then Mr Mayor to directe whoe shall speake firste.[778]

There remain the questions of dissimulation and reluctant deference. Forms of address constrained from inferior position to superior status were liable to dissimulation or resentment – or even overt irony. After being presented at the episcopal visitation for absence from his parish church and not receiving the sacrament, although he attended sermons, Thomas Clement riposted that he attended when sermons were preached but preferred communion at the hands of the minister of South Stoke "and laughing said to the said reverend father if it like your worship or your lordship if you will, mockingly after such time as he called him lord..."[779]

Abusive language was not confined to the lower social orders. Local rivalry within the gentry of Gloucestershire induced a petition to the Privy Council to have (Sir) Hugh Smyth removed from the bench of justices, the allegation being that he had abused Sir George Norton and Sir John Young "as tosspot beaste, a drunken knave etc..."[780]

In response to the challenge of authority, then, some (mostly men) reacted with social impropriety, ignoring the normal delicacies of social address and abandoning any notion of deference in address. The objects of this invective in address were most often the justices or the minister, whose status was denied. For some respondents, this denial of deference in address marked a temporary lapse of control over their emotions. In the case of a minority, however, the impropriety belonged to a complex of misdemeanors (like Robert Brooke's "moste Bitter and Raylinge speeches" to the justices in Staffordshire in 1601 when accused of battery against several people) or formed an habitual part of their behavior.[781]

4
Familiarity and Friction through Forenames

The poetics of pet forms

When Tom came home from labour,
Or Ciss to milking rose,
Then merrily went their tabor,
And nimbly went their toes.[782]
Meg you have a prittie child.[783]

With such address (the second quotation) did a compassionate neighbor take pity upon Margaret Ray who had recently been delivered of an illegitimate child in Theydon Bois in Essex in 1637. By using the pet form of her forename, the neighbor intended closeness. In his brief disquisition (the first citation), Richard Corbett imputed that laboring people were normally known by the short forms of their forenames. Before depending on any analysis of names conferred at baptism, we must recognize the caveat that the names provided by parents or through spiritual kinship did not necessarily relate to the later social identity of individuals in their local societies nor even, sometimes, their formal identification.[784] Hypocorisms, for example, allowed the re-negotiation of the name later in the life-course.[785] The frequency of use of hypocorisms within the speech community can be demonstrated by the absolution of a collective of thieves in the bishop of Durham's liberty in 1498. Although two were addressed by their full, formal name (George) no doubt because there was no obvious, common hypocorism, the other twelve were specified as Sandy Charelton, Crysty Milborn, Hony Milborne, Atkin Milborne, Laury Robeson, Davey Robeson,

Sandy Robeson, Gilly Dod, Rouly Dod, Barmy Dod, Sandy Dod, and Sandy Hunter.[786] Occasionally, parish registers divulge the hypocorism: *Stephanus filius Johannis alias Jenkin Fingley* baptized in 1548 at Howden.[787]

It must be emphasized again that the formal baptismal name did not necessarily persist as the informal identification of its bearer within local society or within peer social groups. It is precisely here that we encounter again the importance of the hypocorism. Use of the formal name or the hypocorism might indicate distance/formality or closeness/informality. The attribution or negotiation of a pet form of forename acted as a cement within the social network or peer group. For those very reasons, of course, the hypocoristic form rarely intruded into the written record. Trust Dekker to portray aspects of social relationships so informal that they rarely intrude into our formal documentary sources. Simon Eyre, the master shoemaker who was elevated to be Lord Mayor of London, insisted still on being Sim Eyre.

> Am I not Sim Eyre? Is not Sim Eyre Lord Mayor of London?[788]

From this exalted social and political position, he continued to address his wife by the "pet" forms of her name, even if prefixing them with the title Lady: "Lady Madgy."[789] Before his advancement, he had addressed her consistently by a couple of hypocorisms: Maggy and Madge, although we are once informed that her full forename was Margery.[790] Now, Eyre referred to and addressed his first journeyman familiarly as Hodge, his second journeyman by his surname, Firk. Firk addressed the superior journeyman as Hodge. Eyre's wife, however, renounced the hypocorism Hodge and addressed the first journeyman by his full forename, Roger.[791] Dekker revealed to us here the complex use of forename and hypocorism to indicate social relationships, closeness and distance and lower register and polite register. The males, regardless, with exception, of their occupational relationship, engaged in a lower register of address by the use of hypocorism. The differences were the upward, more formal relationship to Master Eyre to recognize his status as employer and the downward relationship from Eyre to his second journeyman, to acknowledge the relative inferiority of Firk. In contrast, Margery Eyre adopted a polite register to communicate with Roger, reflecting her social position, but a usage also informed by gender.

Middleton too reflected contemporary idiom. *A Chaste Maid in Cheapside* is pervaded by hypocoristic address. Married to Maudline, Yellowhammer called her Maud.[792] The two bastard sons maintained by Allwit were consistently called Wat and Nick. The former was, of course, named for his real father, Sir Walter Whorehound, who insisted on being godfather to his natural children. Both of Yellowhammer's children were known by their pet forms: Tim and Moll, although not without complication. Tim's existence as a gentleman commoner at Cambridge and his associated predilections led him to frown on the pet form. He remonstrated with his mother—in the company of his Cambridge tutor—to address him as *Timothius*. In return, Maudline insisted on Tim for her son.[793] Whilst the mother, Maudline, desired the intimacy of the pet form within the family, Tim preferred the distance, formality and what he pretentiously presumed to be the dignity of a much higher register. Negotiation of the use of hypocorism thus depended on context and perceived meanings. It was very much a situational propriety which required the consent of both sides. The use of the short form might be regarded as inappropriate by either.

That dramatic exposition almost mirrored the communications of the Smyth family in the third decade of the seventeenth century. At that time, the son of Sir Hugh Smyth and his wife, Elizabeth, attended Saint John's College, Oxford. His mother, in her letters, addressed him as "My deare Tom" and "Deare Tom" (1622). Two years later, Edward Gorges wrote to Sir Hugh: "if my cosin Tom doe come from Oxford..." and referred to Cousin Tom in another letter of 1626. In 1626, Elizabeth again addressed her son as dear Tom and, after her remarriage, wrote again in 1632 "Good swett Tom." When, however, Thomas Atkinson, of Saint John's, corresponded with Sir Hugh, he referred to Hugh's son as Thomas (1624 and 1626). Indeed, when the son wrote from Saint John's to his father, he signed off the letter "Thomas Smyth."[794] The social propriety of the use of pet forms was thus situational.

Hypocorisms were not then necessarily restricted to lower

social groups and avoided by those of gentle status. Lord Pou-
let, when writing to Thomas Smyth, addressed him as Tom, and
referred to his own son (John) as Jack. Thomas Gorges wrote to
inform Smyth about his "cousin Betty" (Elizabeth Phelps). When
Baynham Throckmorton corresponded with Smyth in 1640, his letter began with the salutation: "Honest Tom."[795]

It is interesting, however, that one context of the use of pet
forms in gentle families was early childhood. When compiling his
personal memoranda for his children, Sir Hugh Cholmley, remembering back to midsummer 1627, affectionately construed his first
two sons, Richard and William, then three years and one and a half
years, as "Dicke" and "Will." Baptized Elizabeth, his third child
was in her short childhood his "little girl Betty" and, after her death
and the re-use of her name for another female infant, he acknowledged her too as his "little girle Bette." When the eldest child died,
however, Sir Hugh reverted to a more formal and dignified Richard. When Sir Hugh sent his eldest surviving son, now in his early
20s, back to England to manage the estate in 1646, it was as the
adult William, not the infant "Will."[796]

Still it is interesting that hypocorisms in Nicholas Udall's *Roister
Doister* are all associated with the servants—the deployment is so-
cially downwards: Madge (Margery) Mumblecrust (former nurse),
Tibet Talkapace (maid), Dobinet Doughty, Tom Truepenny and Sym
Suresby (all servants).[797] In another context, Merygreeke referred to
the frivolous services provided in leisure time by Watkin Waster,
Davy Diceplayer, Tom Titivile, Nichol Neverthrive, and Hankyn
Hoddydodie, associating hypocorisms with the lower social orders.[798] The same meaning is attached to short forms in *Gammer Gurton's Nedle*: Gurton's servants Hodge and Tyb and Dame Chatte's
servant, Doll.[799] In this play, indeed, few characters are referenced
by their full name; instead are encountered: Diccon the Beadle; Tom
"our clarke"; Tom Tankard; the cat, Gyb; Tom Simson; Sim Glover;
and Hob Filcher.[800] Indeed, Robert Greene, who descended into the
twilight of City society in his cony-catching pamphlets, invented
with a large dose of realism the "autobiographical" characters Ned
Browne and Nan the prostitute.[801]

Moll had sexual imputations, although it was here intended as
a hypocorism of Mary, and, indeed, Maudline Yellowhammer ad-

opted that more polite register of Mary.[802] Middleton might here then have been more concerned with the dramatic device of representing the two extremes of female integrity: the virgin and the fallen woman. Chakravorty has, indeed, pressed that ambivalence further by comparing Moll Cutpurse (Mary Frith)—*The Roaring Girl* of Dekker's and Middleton's collaboration—with Moll, *The Chaste Maid of Cheapside*: the one transgressive as both cutpurse and transvestite, the other demure but constantly the subject of sexual innuendo; the one of insalubrious Bankside, the other of (then) civil Cheapside; the one caricatured for her mirth (Mad Moll, Merry Moll), the other rather sanguine.[803]

Nonetheless, pet forms comprised the familiarity of address within the family. There are two other aspects of Middleton's deployment of hypocorisms. Allwit himself was addressed as Jack by Whorehound.[804] The patron adopted a language of familiarity with his colluding cuckold. Secondly, masters used the familiar register for their servants, thus Jugg (Joan), Kix's servant. How hypocorisms could become the norm within even gentle families and friendships is illustrated by the correspondence of Thomas Knyvett. In 1625, he referred in a letter to his cousin, Edward Hunne, the attorney of South Elmham: "If my cosin Nedd Hunne wear in Towne..."[805] He constantly referred to "Jacke Holland," intending John Holland, the son of Sir Thomas.[806] Elizabeth, Sir Thomas's daughter, was known to Knyvett as "my cosin Betty Holland."[807] Indeed, Knyvett alluded to all his surviving children by pet forms of their names: Muss (his daughter, Muriel), Betty or Buss (his other daughter, Elizabeth) and Jack (his son, John).[808] Of Margaret Tollis, he committed to paper: "that foolish wench Megg."[809]

The employment of hypocorisms was thus, on the one hand, associated with familiarity.[810] In the expression of that closeness, "pet" forms solidified group cohesion. Further than that, these short and familiar forms were sometimes negotiated within the group, between individual and the group, or were, occasionally, imposed by the group as a condition of acceptance into the group. On the other hand, hypocorisms were associated with indignity as well as familiarity, so that the employment of a "pet" form might sometimes indicate lower status or idiosyncrasy.[811] Nonetheless, it would seem that some persons in local society became habitually known by all inhabitants by their hypocorism, since that form was (occasionally) inscribed in the parish registers.[812]

So, in *Bartholomew Fair*, the well-known pig-woman, Ursula, was alternately addressed by her formal name, but as frequently as Urs, illustrating her lower status.[813] The association with lower status was confirmed by Robert Graime, late of Milton, Cumberland, laborer, arraigned at Durham Quarter Sessions in 1599 for trespass and theft, for he was also recognized as Hob Graime.[814] That rhetorical association can be detected too in the description of Megge Redhem, one of two suspicious women identified in a Canterbury parish in 1511.[815] All illustrate the relationship between hypocorisms and lower social status. Now, the possibility that the truncated form might reflect idiosyncrasy was demonstrated by Middleton and Rowley in their jointly-authored *The Changeling*. In that scenario, only one character, Antonio, was attributed a "pet" form, Tony, but in demonstrably unusual circumstances.

> *Pedro* His name is Antonio; marry, we use but half to him, only Tony.
> *Lollio* Tony, Tony; 'tis a very good name for a fool; what's your name, Tony?[816]

Another distinctive social occasion for the use of hypocorisms as familiarity was masters referring to their employees or servants. In the first reference in his household book to his servant who made numerous excursions for him, Edward Don mentioned payment to Richard Furberer, for a journey to Oxford.[817] All subsequent entries for the multitudinous errands specified him, however, as Dyk Furberer, except for Richard's burial on 12 June 1534 when Don remembered him by his full forename ("Rytshearde").[818] It is worth noting, however, that he continued to refer to other Richards by their formal forename, thus, for example, Richard Scmyth of Crendon and Richard Hall.[819] The difference was the social affinity. Don reverted to a more formal register in 1532 when he employed a new servant: "Henry Cebyll dyd becum my servant at Lundun," although, as noted below, he customarily preferred the short form, Harry.[820]

Occasionally, the implementation of hypocoristic forms becomes visible in written records, intimating a much commoner usage. We should, indeed, expect that the forename Henry was rarely used in social intercourse. Consistently, in the churchwardens' accounts for Saint Mary at Hill, London, reference is to Harry, except on one revealing occasion in 1487-8 when the parishioner Vavesour was inscribed by both formal (Henry) and informal (Harry) names.[821] Contrast with this entry, however, the four men referred to as Harry and none as Henry in the list of contributors to the clerk's salary in *c.* 1485.[822] Legacies in Essex wills confirm that Harry was the norm for social intercourse, Henry infrequent.[823] Edward Don, through his household book, favored Harry when referring to any Henry close to him, so that we encounter in his memoranda Harry ap Owen, Harry Benett, Harry Schacy, Harry Welshe, Harry Pylkynton, Harry Aylwarde, Harry Brysse, Harry Hampden, Harry Fellow, Harry Wyntter, Harry Vaghan, Harry Gaden, Harry Bellys, Harry Wylkyns, Sir Harry Sclythyrst the priest, Harry Adams, Harry Rosse, Harry Horsman, and Harry Fyse the player.[824] In his later years, in the 1530s, however, Don adopted a more formal approach, espousing the full Henry, as with Henry Fellow, Henry Style, Henry Horne (the grocer who supplied spices) and others.[825]

Throughout the muster roll for the hundred of North Greenhoe in Norfolk, in *c.*1523, Harry was encountered—twenty of the mustered men—but no Henry.[826] On the other hand, it must be acknowledged that the clerks who composed the taxation of Buckinghamshire in 1524 preferred to inscribe Henry rather than Harry; the few exceptions including Harry Bruton and Harry Vaile penetrated this consistency and they were both servants assessed at the lowest amount—£1 for wages.[827] The intervention of the clerk can be epitomized further by the taxation of the Rape of Hastings in 1524 and 1525: by and large the clerk of 1524 adopted Harry whilst the writer of 1525 preserved Henry.[828] As an example of this difference, we might consider Harry a Wode assessed on wages of £1 in 1524 and his assessment on £1 10s. of wages in 1525 as Henry a Wode.[829] The dominance of Harry characterized the "census" of Coventry in 1523, in which Harry was attached to forty males listed, but Henry to merely nine—and incidentally there were no Davids, but six Davys.[830] With the exception of Sander Robenson, the clerk who compiled the listing otherwise shunned hypocorisms.[831] The clerks who compiled the military survey for Worcestershire in 1522 were equally assiduous in their avoidance of hypocorisms, although Saunder Stryngfelowe was registered.[832] With Henry, however, the attitude was different: some clerks normalized the forename as Henry, but others retained Harry.[833] The result entailed 36 percent Henry and 64 percent Harry. As significantly, those enlisted as Harry included Sir Harry Tully, parson of Doverdale, and Sir Harry Locoke, priest, indicating the general fondness for Harry.[834] What we might deduce here is that, although those taxed might have themselves had a penchant for their hypocoristic forms of forename, clerks might have occasionally subverted that predilection and committed the formal form to writing.

The intervention of clerks is interesting to the extent that it confounds colloquial exchange. At some points, the clerks of the Buckinghamshire subsidy deferred to the preference for hypocorisms: frequently Davy (as noted elsewhere); Jenkyn; Hewkyn; Bennet; and Jaket; but on the whole they seem to have been reluctant to engage too closely with pet forms.[835] In the case of Henry/Harry, we are demonstrably on firmer ground with those testators who referred to themselves in their wills, as did "me, Harry Hewbank" of Chichester in 1523.[836]

This hypocorism was not restricted to those of the lowest status. Amongst the listing in the Assembly minutes of the twelve aldermen of Boston, only two were entered with hypocorisms: Harry Fox and Harry Hoode. This situation was replicated in 1555: the long-serving Harry Fox and Harry Goode. The dignity of Fox was illuminated by his selection as mayor in 1552 and 1553. Whilst he was also mentioned as Henry, as frequently he was inscribed as Harry in the Assembly minutes.[837] When he died in 1568, he was dignified in the minutes by the full Henry.[838] When the corporation purchased a manor from the Earl of Rutland in 1557, the minutes recorded "Lord Harry Erle of Rutland."[839] Assessed on £40 and allocated the status of gentleman, Harry Hussey was listed in the taxation of Slinfold in 1524-5.[840] Perhaps more complicated is the case of Sir Harry Rither (Rider), priest, who received a legacy of 3s. 4d. from a Buckinghamshire testator in 1521 as his ghostly father and who attested several wills as the local priest.[841] Whilst the sacramental nature of the pre-Reformation priesthood invited mystery and deference, the priest's position as spiritual father also occasioned familiarity.

We can then elicit a number of points from the comparative use of the formal Henry and the hypocoristic Harry. First, some forenames tended to be more regularly understood by their pet form— Harry (and Davy) represented the two most susceptible male forenames. Even when clerks avoided hypocorisms in general, Harry (and Davy) tended to intrude into written records. Their intrusion suggests that when clerks used the formal style of the name, one of two scenarios was happening: either the clerk was suppressing the colloquial form or, when the frequency of the full form such as Henry was low, the bearer indeed preferred the formal style as a matter of dignity.

In a presentment before the archdeaconry court of Nottingham in 1599, we learn that Edward Walker responded also to the *alias* Ned Elis, Ned constituting the common short form of Edward even if the surname differed.[842] One Essex master in 1559 bequeathed to his "boy" (servant) Ned £1 on Ned's marriage.[843] Ned Painter was the recipient of 5s. from the chamberlains of Woodstock in 1620.[844] Those chamberlains collected rent from Ned Hull for his house in 1626, but the accounts subsequently referred to him as Edward Hull.[845] It is possible that this Ned was identical with the Ned the joiner who received 1s. 2d. for a day of labor in 1632.[846] In 1627, Ned Porter arranged for wine and beer in Woodstock.[847] When initially appointed in the same year as toll collector and ale taster, Ned Longe was entered in that manner, but by 1630 he was dignified as Edward Longe when making returns for his office.[848]

One suspects too that Alexander constituted too much of a mouthful for precipitate early-modern males, so that a hypocorism was usually preferred, as when Saunder Worsle received his annual wage in Saint Mary's accounts in 1491-2.[849] So also in 1531-2, Saunder the porter was remunerated with 3d. for cleaning the parish priest's chamber.[850] On his death in 1540, the bells were tolled in Henley for Saunder Grenelane.[851] Although the clerks of the Sussex lay subsidy generally refused to accept hypocorisms—apart from Harry mentioned above – Saunder crept into their listings: Saunder Fermer taxed on £5 at Barcombe; and Saunder Tutte and Saunder Haming at the other end of the scale, both on wages of £1.[852] One Essex testator referred to his son by the hypocorism of his forename as Saunder (Alexander).[853] In 1527, Edward Don recorded in his memoranda book the death of the children of Saunder Stoktun.[854] Even in the Buckinghamshire taxation of 1524, Saunder as a forename occurred sporadically: Saunder Cook and Saunder Bourne, both assessed on £1 of wages, at the lowest end of the taxation.[855]

The fuller David remained unusual in early-modern local societies, occasionally reproduced in full in written records, but even there superseded by Davy. Throughout the subsidy assessment for Buckinghamshire in 1524, Davy was predominant as the forename.[856] The latter is encountered usually in Essex wills, with only the odd occurrence of David.[857] The clerk who composed the taxation return for Carhampton Hundred in Somerset in 1581 conceded Davy.[858]

Although most frequently recorded in writing as John, the hypocoristic form Jack reflected greater familiarity in some cases. In 1519, Edward Don inserted John a Derby in his household book, assigning his half year's wage of 10s. More usually, however, Don alluded to him as Jak.[859] As interestingly, his Welsh compatriots were customarily entered as Jankin.[860] In his memoranda, Don usually alluded to Jankin Whyght, but once explained "Johan" (John) Whyght.[861] The substitution of Jenkin for John, nonetheless, was not a singularly Welsh coining. Jenkyn *alias* John Morland was designated a legatee in a Yorkshire will of 1593 and, indeed, his own will of 1597 styled him John *alias* Jenkyn Morland.[862]

In his digressive discussion of "Jack a Lent," the "water poet," John Taylor, embarked upon a lengthy enumeration of Jacks: Jack-an-Apes; Jack Daw; Jack of Newbury; Skip-Jack; Jack Drum; Jack Dog; Jack Date; Jack Fool; Jack-a-Dandy; Jack of Dover; Jack Sause; Jack Herring; Jack Sprat; Jack Straw; and Jack Cade. He attributed the origins of Jack "out of corruption of the name John...." His further implication associated Jack with baseness until recently when it had become acceptable amongst those of gentle status or those who had been elevated as Jacks to gentility, not entirely to his taste or liking, he himself remaining a John.

> And there was an old Courteous epithet attributed to John, as gentle John, but now so many Jacks are made gentles, that most Johns and Jacks make no further account of gentility than glorious titles or gaudy suits.[863]

Amongst women, Bess appeared often as a hypocorism. Entertained by the under-sheriff of Lancashire, Master Covill, Taylor, the "water poet," alluded to Covill's "modest daughter Bess."[864] A post-bed, other household stuff and ten marks were bequeathed by Edward Popley, clerk, in 1559 to Bess Poplye.[865] Another Bess —Barkar – received a legacy of 1s. in 1561.[866] A recipient of a legacy in 1563 was another Bess, child of the testator.[867] William Heigham, a butcher, was a benefactor through his will to his maid, Bess, in 1564.[868] Most interestingly of all, a testator in 1564 was described by her full name, Elizabeth [Masson, of Stock, widow] and she ordained legacies of a kercher each to her namesakes, Bess Comes, Bess Stokes and household utensils to Bess Reddall.[869] A younger recipient of a legacy in 1564 was little Bess Sawman.[870] In 1607, Bess Green of Banbury was acknowledged in the same way.[871] Rather enigmatically, another Banbury will in 1594 contained a bequest to the little girl at John Baule's house "which wee call Besse Baule."[872] Amongst the debts of one testatrix were the wages of her servant, Bess Cutler.[873] Once, in his household book, Edward Don rather formally referred to "my dowghter Elyzabeth," but in all other entries more familiarly inscribed her as Besse.[874] He also commemorated in his journal the death of the daughter of Besse Brytere in 1527.[875]

In 1570, Catte Lewis, widow, attended on a testator shortly before his death, witnessing his will.[876] Another Cate—Cate Skyllington—was presented before the archdeaconry court of Leicester for being "a busye bodie of her tong," causing dissension between the vicar, for whom she was employed as housekeeper, and his flock.[877] The Katherine with her child harbored by John Todd was more commonly known as "Little Kate."[878] Edward Don purchased "cullys" from Kate Hunte.[879] In 1620, Cate Meaddowes was buried in Woodstock.[880]

Milicent is encountered only occasionally, but a testator's daughter in Essex was acknowledged in the will as Mille Sammond.[881] Apparently Frissy was a hypocorism of Frideswide, for Frissy *alias* Friswith Wilkinson was accused of stealing two napkins in 1613.[882] In *Roister Doister*, the eponymous Ralph Roister Doister ultimately descended to calling Christian Custance Kit(te), but adopted this moniker when his love for her had turned to hatred, which rather inverts the normal association of pet forms.[883]

It is apparent too that Petronilla had stabilized in its short form, Parnel, illustrated by legacies to Parnels in 1561, one by father to daughter.[884] Other fathers made benefactions to daughters called Parnel in 1569 and 1571.[885] Presumably Parnel had become disassociated from the connotation of prostitution with which it had been tainted in the later middle ages.[886]

What these examples illustrate is that there was no gender bar on hypocorisms. Women were as likely to be addressed by short forms of their forenames as men. As further examples, the chamberlains of Woodstock recorded payments for the burial of Nann Cox in 1619 and for Megg Hamond's assistance to the cook in 1620.[887] In this context, then, women did not preserve a more prestige form of language use, by contrast with the negotiation of naming between Dame Eyre and Roger (Hodge) recited above.

One rather surprising aspect of Essex usage was that Bennet was assigned as a male forename, not just a female forename as it was predominantly in some other areas.[888] For example, in 1559, a younger son named Bennet received a legacy of £2.[889] The son of another testator, another Bennet by forename, acquired 13s. 4d. by a bequest.[890] Other male Bennets featured in other testamentary bequests.[891] In particular, the explanation of Bennet is expounded by the appearance of Bennet Blaknall in the assessment to the lay subsidy of Buckinghamshire, once as *Benedictus* and once as Bennet (by his hypocorism assessed at £26).[892] Similarly Benedict Painter who became chamberlain of Woodstock was entered in his accounts as both Benedict and Benet in 1635, but subsequently—and perhaps self-consciously as these were his accounts—as Benet.[893] This particular hypocorism was, however, applied to both gender. Of particular concern in Staffordshire, for example, was Bennet Hazelton, a widow, and a "perverted and obstinate recusant," presented for her non-attendance at church in 1613.[894] Deflowered in her mistress's garden in Norwich at night in 1563, another Bennet was confined to prison.[895]

Occasionally, there is ambivalence whether we are confronted by a hypocorism or a genuine alias. In 1631, a widow was accused of appropriating the goods of a stranger who died at her house, although she was dismissed by the court. Her presentment described her as Magdalen *alias* Mary Bentley.[896]

It will be evident from some of the citations from wills above that hypocorisms were not the preserve of childhood or adolescence. Short forms of names adhered throughout the life-course. For the most part, they expressed familiarity and closeness. Pet forms were not, however, without their ambiguities in this respect. Some hypocorisms—especially Harry—were consistently substituted for the formal name, whatever the nature of the relationship; these hypocorisms assumed a standard and conventional position. In other cases, what had been at earlier times a hypocorism developed more or less as a separate baptismal name. Such might have occurred with Bennett and Austin, which became disassociated from Benedict(a) and Augustine.

Poetics of conferment: confessionalism?

In terms of the poetic—the imaginary and symbolic—allusion and metonymy in forenames continued in the Protestant nation, perhaps not on the scale of late-medieval Catholic England, but significantly enough.[897] Some forenames imported values which indicated a continuing attempt to associate with sanctity and holiness, if of a different kind from "traditional" religion. The fact that the vast quantity of forenames exhibited conformity to a common corpus should not obscure the significance of naming at the margins.

Although Puritan "hortatory" or grace forenames have been consigned to a marginal position, both quantitatively and in their regional incidence submerged by the preponderance of "nondescript" common forenames, a question remains about their symbolic importance.[898] Tyacke has conclusively demonstrated that "Puritan" forenames were concentrated in one particular locality in Sussex. He conceded, however, that these names were conferred sporadically elsewhere, but as isolated incidences. So, for example, we encounter as early as 1581 in the taxation of Nettlecomb Covenant Thorne assessed for goods and at East Quantockshead Covenant Sulley whose goods amounted to £5 8s. 4d.[899] Their continuation indicates a persistent objective to consort and associate with the holy, not with saints in the traditional manner, but with holiness and the emulation of the devout and righteous.[900] Middleton perhaps depicted Puritan gentry through Sir Bounteous Progress and the oxymoronic Penitent Brothel in *A Mad World, My Masters*.[901]

Their existence, moreover, had some impact, since they were satirized on the stage. The theatrical panegyric of Jonson's *Bartholomew Fair* and his "Banbury man," Zeal-of-the-Land Busy, is familiar. As described below, it was female rather than male forenames which in Banbury had the intimation of grace and certainly by 1641 those compounded male grace names did not exist in Banbury. Those who subscribed to the Protestation Oath in Banbury exhibited a fairly familiar pattern of forenames, headed by forty-nine Johns, thirty-seven Williams and thirty-two Thomases, the whole male population producing the forename statistics below. Amongst the 230 males, perhaps thirty or so disported "Biblical" names such as Jobe, Zachary and Nathaniel[902] (See Table 4.1, page 149. Descriptive statistics of male forenames in Banbury in 1641-2).

The dramatization of Puritan grace names nonetheless insinuated into popular imagination. The discourse established was as important as their numerical insignificance. Although sparse, such names proclaimed a sanctimonious marking off which compelled a reaction.

Amongst again a minority of the population, there appears to have been an attempt to associate the child with a saint, but not one of the restricted number of saints allowed in the reformed calendar, nor the traditional saints of late-medieval England, but with saints which might be considered non-"Roman" and of "English" identity. In one sense, these saints were neutral; in another they confirmed a sense of English identity; and in another they maintained local identity. Two examples can be isolated: Cuthbert in the north, particularly around the patronal seat of Durham, and Frideswide near Oxford. Honoring these saints permitted an association with the holy within the new *ecclesia anglicana*, although they were not authorized saints of that new church[903] (See Figure 3, page 150. Cuthbert in co. Durham: Protestation Oath, 1641-2; and Figure 4, page 151. Durham Quarter Sessions, 1511-1624: actors called Cuthbert).

Although Frideswide too belonged to only a tiny proportion of female children baptized, some symbolic significance can be perceived in its adoption in Banbury in the vicinity of the saint's patronal district (based on Oxford). Between 1558 and 1599, just under forty female children were christened with this name.[904] Now, the adoption of that name might have been a precursor to the deployment of grace names for female children in Banbury between 1610 and 1652, for Hopestill (almost exclusively conferred on females) accounted for over a dozen chrism daughters, Temperance for ten, Obedience for two, Patience for nine, Justice for one, Prudence for two, Makepeace for one, and Silence for one, in the absence of grace names for male offspring.[905] Within this Puritan-influenced urban center, therefore, religious affiliation was expressed through grace forenames, but especially through the names of females, which tends to confirm the potential for creativity in female names.[906] In this instance, then, Ben Jonson was guilty of misrepresentation through dramatic license in *Bartholomew Fair*. Zeal-of-the-Land Busy, "a Banbury man," was an entirely fictitious caricature, for it was females who received grace names in Banbury, not males.

Evocative too, perhaps, is the number of male infants baptized as Edmund in the parish of Marsham (Norfolk) between 1538 and 1552, eleven out of sixty-three males.[907] Nor did the name disappear thereafter, but recurred at intervals, a further eighteen males receiving it at baptism over the next century.[908] The Chadd (*Cedda*) Harvie of Bromley, selected as a juror for Pirhill Hundred in Staffordshire in the 1590s, commemorated in his name the local insular saint (the dedication of Lichfield cathedral).[909] In the same county, another saint with local associations was remembered in the person of Modwyn, daughter of Helen Tompson *alias* Cooke of Burton-on-Trent, widow, whose marriage was celebrated at nearby Yoxall in 1561, perhaps establishing her birth during the unresolved religious climate of the later years of Henry VIII.[910]

Whilst naming in northern areas generally conformed to the wider pattern of the relative insignificance of "biblical" names, some inhabitants of Bingley had a greater propensity to use these names. Females there named Epiphany (two), Martha (forty-one), and Rebecca (six) do not constitute incontrovertible evidence of the acquisition of biblical names. On the other hand, male baptismal names emphatically reveal this acceptance in the early seventeenth century, particularly the 1620s and 1630s, illustrated by the thirty-nine Abrahams and twenty-seven Samuels, as well as seven Josephs, eleven Isaacs, nine Joshuas, four Nathaniels, five Jonathans, and ten Jeremiahs. One kinship group in particular contributed to this religious zeal in naming: Abraham Threapland of Culling-worth (d. 1650) consigned to his children the names Mary (1609), Joshua (1611), Martha (1614), Hester (1616, d. 1630), Phoebe (1619), Jonathan (1622) and only on his last son the patrilinear, but biblical, name of Abraham (1625).[911]

As is inherent in the names Cuthbert and Frideswide, poetics could not be separated from politics; the saints' names had to be acceptable politically – in terms of nation-building.[912] Conversely, recusants were marginalized and their process of name-giving compromised.

> Also yt is learned that about Michaelmas last a childe of the same Martyns is said to be christianed by a midwief named Mother Man alias West....'[913]

Like other magistrates, Nathaniel Bacon was required to moni-tor the attendance of recusants at church and that surveillance extended to baptism. Traditionally, midwives were permitted to baptize children *in extremis*, but recusants resorted to routine chris-tening by midwives avoiding the celebration of Christian initiation and incorporation through the rites of the reformed church. Martin was not singular in this recourse and aversion, for others came to the attention of Bacon.[914] It is possible, therefore, that we lack cog-nizance of naming predilections of non-conforming recusants and to what extent they retained traditional names symbolic of their confessional allegiance—and that might have serious consequences in Lancashire.[915] Indeed, some of the reformed persuasion might have resisted baptism by an incumbent who exercised the rites in a manner to which they objected. The issues here, of course, sur-rounded the sign of the cross and the wearing of the surplice. In many cases of presentments for non-baptism of children we simply cannot deduce the reasons, as when, for example, the churchwar-dens of Weedon Bec (Northants.) in 1595 presented "that William Rodhouse hath a child or two to be baptised being two or three years of age."[916]

Confessional influence on name selection has recently been

largely discounted at the national level.[917] That conclusion was mainly germane for "Puritan" or godly names.[918] Smith-Bannister allowed the sporadic and fairly isolated incidence of such names throughout the country and that phenomenon has been confirmed above.[919] It has occasionally, however, been claimed that there was a relationship between some names and Catholic allegiance—particular recusant names. As noted by both Smith-Bannister and Tyacke, the conferment of a baptismal name reveals only the inclination of the giver of the name, not the child. With recusants, however, there is a presumption that confessional adherence ran in families over generations. We might then be able to use presentments of adult recusants (aged over sixteen) to establish whether there were indeed any distinctively recusant names (See Table 4.2, page 152. Descriptive statistics of recusants' names [920]).

In the North Riding in 1614, three forenames comprehended 44 percent of the total number of male recusants: John (sixty-six), William (sixty-two) and Thomas (fifty-three), whilst seven names accounted for 65 percent (additionally George and Robert each with twenty-three, Christopher with twenty and Francis with seventeen). There was nothing inordinate about any of these male names. Nor was the situation for female names any different. Some 59 percent of female recusants were encompassed by six names: (Elizabeth 101, Jane seventy-five, Ann seventy-three, Margaret fifty-nine, Isabel and Mary forty-four). Whilst both Mary and Ann—principal members of the Holy Family—might have continued to have a symbolic significance, their occurrence was no more pronounced amongst recusants than in the population as a whole. If we add the secondary tranche of female names—Dorothy with thirty-one down to Helen with nineteen—then 77 percent of females were accounted, but few names in this secondary tier had religious connotations (perhaps only Catherine). Forenames of male recusants displayed a similar pattern in county Durham in 1606. Here, well over half the males were represented by four forenames (John thirty-four, William sixteen, Thomas fourteen, and Robert thirteen). Cuthbert pertained to only three males. In the same county then, four female forenames accounted for half the female recusants: Margaret (thirty-two); Elizabeth (twenty-five); Ann (twenty); and Jane (fifteen), all of which belonged to the mainstream of English early-modern naming. The recusant roll of 1593-4, moreover, reveals no deviation from the normative naming pattern, containing no Cuthberts, but one Frideswide (at Haseley in Oxfordshire), and Alban Draycott, a gentleman of Wolstanton in Staffordshire.[921] It has been suggested that Cuthbert became associated with recusancy, but such a connection had not been established before 1640. The relationship was between Cuthbert and northern England, as demonstrated above.

What these marginal confessional names allowed was the self-presentation—or self-fashioning, if you will—of parents through the names which they conferred on their children. Whilst attempting to socialize their offspring through the name imposed, parents also attempted to establish their own credentials through the process. Although quantitatively insignificant, the names provided the important function of widening the active name stock and furnishing the means of self-definition, if not identity.

Poetics of conferment: forms of femininity

There are several reasons for expanding the analysis of female names. Firstly, Smith-Bannister's exposition, although comprising both gender, tended to concentrate on male name forms. It is, however, acknowledged that female name forms have tended at some times in the past to contain a wider corpus of different names, including more exotic forms.[922] Finally, at least one name—Mary—resonated with religious significance which was associated with confessional allegiance. Following on from the intention of confessional association, a corpus of female forenames presented a means of socializing the female child, for some names had an implicit lexical and emotive content.

Amongst this last category, Prudence accounted for fifty-five and Philippa for fifty-four baptisms, whilst Priscilla was conferred on forty-two female children, in early-modern Plymouth (Devon). At the margins in that port, some of the exceptional forenames contained an inherently rhetorical content: Honor (twenty-eight female infants); Faith; Charity; Florence; Obedience; Comfort; Prudence itself; Temperance; Felix; Patience; Argent; Orange; Flower; Placencia; Triphena; Clemence; and Modestie—although Lucrecia (three daughters, 1622, 1628, 1629) and Sallome (1628) cause some hesitation.[923] Whilst not conferred on numerous children, these exotic names reflected the openness and receptiveness of Plymouth to external influences. Those exogenous intrusions, however, did not disguise localized characteristics, perhaps best represented by the relative profusion of Thomasine, which featured throughout the south-west.[924]

Contained within the regional analysis is an indication of the rhetorical content of some female names which apparently escaped male names. That characteristic is apparent in parishes throughout the southern half of England. To cite one of the earlier early-modern illustrations, the daughter of Robert Giles was christened Temperance in 1554 in Norwich St Giles. In 1600 and 1603, other female offspring in the parish received the names Prudence and Patience.[925] At Aldenham (Herts.), a female child was baptized Plesance in 1571, as were two successors in 1584 and 1585.[926] Registered there in the early seventeenth century were daughters designated Angel (1602), another Plesance (1603), Faith (1604), Mercy (1615), Silence (1618), another Angel (1619), Victoria (1620), another Faith (1623), and a Constance (1633).[927] A married couple with nondescript names, John and Joan Veysey, John a tailor of Bristol who died in 1597, decided upon the names Joyce, Goodlove and Pascae for their three daughters.[928]

Whilst names might not have been associated linguistically (in their phonemes as gendered constructs) with femininity, there might well have been a female resonance of some names in an almost lexical manner.[929] This aspect can be illustrated further by the naming at baptism of some females at Chislet in Kent: Mercy (1564, 1579, 1583, 1606); Angelica (1574); Fortune (1584, 1596, 1603, 1624); Pleasance (1593, 1612, 1613, 1623, 1626); and Charity (1604).[930] Until the "hortatory" Puritan names, few male names exhibited the same attributes. Although the number of females baptized with such names remained small, the names retained a symbolic importance in the gendered aspect of naming—forenames which had an implicit meaning, possibly conferred to socialize the child or represent the infant's character.

It is very interesting in this respect that at Chislet developed a somewhat hortatory name in the late sixteenth century which was entirely attached to female offspring whilst grace names did not feature at all for males—with the exception of the solitary Repent, son of Anthony Maye, baptized in 1621.[931] The first daughter recorded as baptized with the name Godly was christened in 1567.[932] This name was conferred on female offspring in 1569, 1570, 1581 (2), 1586, 1590, 1603.[933]

Quite remarkably, a similar phenomenon developed in Chesterfield (Derbyshire), where a particular grace name—Troth (Truth) —established a frequency from the beginning of the first extant register in 1559. Between 1559 and 1632, seventy-eight female children received this name at their baptism in Chesterfield parish church.[934] This name was adopted by parents of different social levels. For example, it was conferred by George Foljambe of Brimmington, esquire, and his wife, Ursula, on one of their daughters. Equally, the Chesterfield mercer, Thomas Boulsover, and his wife, Lucy, bestowed the name on their eldest daughter (and Lucy's name on the second daughter).[935] Although quite affluent, William Shawe of Chesterfield was designated yeoman in his will and he too had an eldest daughter Troth.[936] During the same time, moreover, Faith was conferred on thirty-three, Constance on twenty-three, Fortune on three, Prudence on two, Philadelphia on seven, and Charity on three.

Although there was not a total absence of grace names in the more northerly regions, such names remained unusual in northern rural parishes—by contrast with, perhaps, in urban centers. A pattern therefore existed in which grace names had a more prolific existence in the south, were evident in northern urban centers, but had a diminished presence in northern rural parishes. For example, the only grace name occurring in Thirsk—a significant market town in the north of Yorkshire—was Faith, conferred on only two females between 1556 and 1640.[937] At Pontefract, on the other hand, female grace names were interspersed at baptism: from Prudence in 1589 and Faith in 1594, through Honor and Truth, to Angelory in 1619 and Patience in 1628.[938] Similarly at Berwick female grace names interceded: Charity, Grace, Constance, Florentine, Florence, Fortune, Patience, and Faith, intermingled with other more exotic flowerings such as Priscilla, Cassandra, Eufemia, and Philadelphia.[939]

By the very end of the sixteenth century, a few more grace

names were adopted in some northern parishes, but not in any proliferation. An exceptional parish was Bingley where biblical names were appropriated for boys in the late sixteenth century (as above), but comparably fewer grace names on girls. From its first incidence in 1610, Mercy was conferred on seven female children.[940] In 1597, another female received the forename Prudence.[941] Most explicitly, one female child was baptized Righteous in 1625.[942] These more exotic names were accompanied by a sprinkling of Edens (seven), which achieved a minor position locally for female children.[943]

We can therefore differentiate parishes in those areas where these female grace names were introduced from those where they did not obtain or remained in relative paucity. What results from this comparison is a vague demarcation between northern and southern zones, grace names continuing to be relatively unusual in the north by comparison with the Midlands and south. Moreover, those grace names which were adopted from the middle and late sixteenth century were almost exclusively names for females, especially in the North. Perhaps they should be considered a re-adoption as some had featured intermittently in antiquity and the middle ages.

What can be remarked upon further is that in southern England the introduction and constancy of these grace forenames was associated with gender—they were characteristic more of female children than male. Parents thus conceived of female forenames in some cases with a greater sense of creativity, flexibility, and emotion. In some cases daughters received names which, presumably it was hoped, would socialize them and reflect their character. In a single nuclear family, we can observe this difference of naming by gender. By his wife, Julian, William Addams, of Bridgwater, feltmaker—and thus of no high status—had issue three sons, John, William and Robert—frequent male forenames, including the patrilinear forename. Whilst three of his surviving daughters received the names Mary, Abigail and Sarah (which might conceivably have had religious connotations), three others bore the resonant forenames Virtue, Grace and Patience. The selection of forenames by William and Julian was more adventurous and emotive for daughters.[944]

Defining deviance: bastardy

The question then arises whether more exotic names were associated with not only females, but those of marginal status. Something of this social phenomenon can be observed at Arksey where, on his burial in 1580, it was revealed that one *filius populi vel spurius* had been baptized Ismael Huscrofte. [We might interpret *filius populi* — literally "son of the populace" — as an indication that local society would have to support the child rather than the (unknown) father). The interment of the son of Jane Wycham, another bastard, in Arksey in 1584 referred to him as Absalon, whilst Zephora Wilbore, *filia populi vel spuria*, received burial there in 1593.[945] Rosamund, still sparsely employed in the early seventeenth century, was conferred on a bastard in Bingley in 1601.[946] Such idiosyncratic forenames, outside the normal repertory of names in local society, constituted marked names. So occasionally, bastards received more "florid" rather than "mundane" names.[947] Two illegitimate females at Chislet were accordingly named Fortune (1603) and Charity (1604).[948] So too was encountered Charity—*filia spuria*—at Howden in 1584.[949] With more resonance, bastards—especially females—were consigned names which correlated to their status: at Chislet again, merely for example, Creature, the base daughter of Sander Hadds and Elizabeth Huntsmell, in 1638, and, three years previously Peregrine [sic] *filia populi*.[950] In the last case, external interference in the naming seems obvious, but in the case of Creature some or all of the parishioners may also have intervened to impose a disciplinary name on the parents and child. The intervention of (some of) the parishioners is more demonstrable at Gnosall in 1607 in the naming of "a boy of unknown parents," an orphan from birth, "Fabian called Foundling" (with obvious, and poetic, alliteration).[951] This intervention of the parishioners might also have compelled the baptism of a bastard as William Wee, for his mother was Abigail Dillworthe and the alleged father Roman Bolton.[952] *Tychicus* was the name conferred on a new-born boy abandoned in the window of Cuthbert Smith in Coniscliffe in 1603.[953] In some case, then, if not numerous, there was direct intervention of the "community" in naming.

As elaborated below, Thomasine, although present in northern parishes, remained an infrequent female name by comparison with its relative popularity in southern areas. This forename occurred only once in Bingley before the middle of the sixteenth century, significantly conferred on a bastard child in 1622.[954] Another bastard, in Ormskirk in 1615, was marked out by this name infrequent in northern areas.[955]   Accordingly, several bastards in Ormskirk (Lancs.) between 1602 and 1623 had imposed on them names rather exotic within the "community": Griffin; Silvester; Jeffrey; Alexander; Peregrina (intimating, of course, vagrancy); Thomasine (as above); Clarice; Sarah; Evan; and Nicholas.[956] Now, although some of these forenames do not appear to us unusual, they were nonetheless infrequent in Ormskirk then. So also in Howden in 1578 the infant boy of a poor girl (*filius pauperculae*—and thus presumably another bastard as well as associated with poverty) was named Bartholomew—not exotic in our eyes, but exceptional in the "community" at the time.[957] In Thirsk, bastards received the names Percival in 1568 and Daniel in 1617.[958] Whilst only a small proportion of bastards received these kinds of names, the conferral of such a name might have sometimes constituted one way of marking off illegitimate children and disciplining their parents.

In such a way, a name might have been imposed on the parent and child by local society as a marker and label of deviance, uncivil behavior, and disordered character of the parent(s). Whether the child carried that stigma forward cannot be discovered, but shame and humiliation were extended at baptism, when the ritual of incorporation became a rite of exclusion.[959] Unusual at it was, the shaming of naming is visible at Tamworth. There, the daughter of Alice Hutchenson was christened Transgression in 1604. Since the incumbent never signified illegitimacy in the register, we might suppose that Transgression fell into the category of bastard.[960] The same fate awaited Alice Bickerton whose daughter in 1607 was also designated Transgression at baptism.[961] Perhaps we might assume therefore that that poor Transgression christened as the daughter of Francis (sic) Richardson in 1600 actually had a mother, Frances.[962] That consequence obtained too to Boler Hulda spurious son of Hulda Hensley wife of John Hemsley as it is supposed by Edward Boler" when he was baptized in November 1604 in Chesterfield. It must probably be imagined that this identification was oppressively ordained rather by the "community" than as an act of commemoration by the parents.[963] Perhaps another "community" strategy for distinguishing bastards was adopted in Howden in 1619-20, for here two bastard sons, identified only by their association to their mothers in the registers, were yet given the forenames Williamson and Richardson, as if to identify and humiliate the fathers and, whether inadvertently or not, as a stigma to be borne through life.[964] When the incumbent of that parish in 1636 inscribed in his register "Uncertaine" the son of Alice Storie—and thus by implication a bastard—it is uncertain whether Uncertain constituted his name or the incumbent's ignorance.[965]

How this might eventuate *in extremis* is perhaps indicated by the naming of an orphan whose burial was registered at Cantley (Yorks. W. R.) in 1600:

> Charitie Orfelyne which was found nye Besacle and nursed
> at the charges of the whole parish.[966]

Although intentions were undoubtedly benign, the parishioners imposed on the poor child a name which marked her out as the recipient of charity and relief, segregated her from the rest of the parishioners, and labeled her according to her singular social position. Referring to another aspect of marginality, the burial of Solomon, a black man owned by Master William Hayman, was recorded at Saint Augustine the Less in Bristol in 1632—the name was an unusual, if not entirely unheard, one.[967]

It was equally apparent, however, that the adoption of unusual names operated at the other end of the social scale, the top end of the "middling sort" concerned to fashion their cultural identities. As much can be suspected when Charles Hutton, town clerk of Berwick, conferred on his twin sons the names Pelham and Anthony in 1631.[968] In Pontefract, Master Henry Tindall and Master Matthew Thomson in 1637 and 1639 assigned to their respective sons the names Bradwardine and Maximilian.[969] Nevertheless, even amongst this social cadre, uniformity and consensus in naming seems to have been important. We can, nonetheless, suggest that access to unusual names was available to both the lower and upper margins of local society, although for different reasons.[970]

Conclusion

Much recent attention has been directed to social and cultural transformations such as the ordering of society, the impulse towards state formation, and the development of civility.[971] To some extent (if unacknowledged), the last two engage with Norbert Elias's notions of the *Civilizing Process*.[972] Elias's "civilizing process," although realized through self-reflection and self-restraint, depended somewhat on a model of downwards diffusion—from "court society." It was figurational in that the imperative for self-restraint also derived from the interdependency of social beings. On the other hand, there were also higher, exogenous influences outside unimpeded social interaction. Without wishing to deny the importance of these higher-level influences and the fascinating, absorbing and convincing recent research into them—without obeisance to Elias—the concentration here has been on how social interaction related to social ordering without considering that external interference.

Excluding those phenomena remains, of course, artificial. On the other hand, it allows us some possibility of discovering how ordinary people in their day-to-day social transactions perceived their social relationships and how those interactions connected to *their* wider notions of social ordering. We are permitted to move away from immediately hierarchical and rhetorical depiction of social organization. Representations of social ordering by early-modern contemporaries issued from those with social or cultural authority. Dominant discourses of social organization were maintained by those with social and cultural dominion. Those representations and ideologies did indeed interact with and had an impact on social action in the *real* social world. Nonetheless, in their everyday activities ordinary people did not consciously acknowledge those forces, nor were they deluded into an entire false consciousness, nor did they imbibe or assimilate entirely those influences. Their casual, non-reflexive, unselfconscious doings meandered, were inconsistent, eluded and inadvertently subverted.[973] It is then perhaps not satisfactory to accept descriptions of social ordering without looking first at social interaction and what that meant for social ordering.

One of the other important paradigms elucidated by recent research is the impact and power of speech and language in an honor-based society, excavated from depositions in courts, in particular in cases of defamation, in which honor was directly impugned.[974] We can also perceive the impact of speech acts directly in the social interaction of how people address each other or refer to others. The recovery of that direct speech is, of course, fraught with difficulty—at best, it is a hermeneutic process, a refined interpretative analysis.

One of the resources mined here is drama, in particular the metropolitan comedies. Objections might be leveled against this approach: dramaturgy belongs to the realm of discourse, the representation of the world rather than being in the real world. In exoneration, we might respond in a number of ways. First, we have the epistemological issue. Whence does discourse come or arise? It does not exist in an intellectual vacuum. Its context is reflection on the real world by many. In the case of the metropolitan playwrights, who constructed these representations, they lived intimately and closely in that real world. They either empathized with some of it (such as Dekker's admiration for aspects of civic life) or were critics of it, as in the implied criticisms of Middleton or the more vocal denunciations of Jonson. They were, nonetheless, engaged in it, not divorced or separate from it. They suffered its travails and experienced its quotidian situations. Their discourse, moreover, impacted on a wide sector of City society, confirming and reinforcing prejudices or being appropriated for particular interests. Drama came out of and fed into the real world.

What much of this City comedy reflected on was the vicissitude of social transformations taking place between 1540 and 1640. At the heart of much of the performance was the disruption caused by commercial enterprise: the equation of everything to a commercial value, the social world as market. Traditional ideas of social organization were under stress.

The fracturing of social organization had an influence on forms of social address. The demand for gentle status in urban and commercial society led to the appropriation and wider dissemination of the form of address as Master or M(a)istress. On the other side of the balance sheet, the form of address as Goodman and Goodwife was ultimately a casualty. Whilst the discourse of society as a commonwealth endured, these forms of address flourished and held their own. During the seventeenth century, however, they declined into residual use. Goodmen and Goodwives were symbols of commonwealth, hospitality, and traditional social values, but were being displaced by new commercial culture. From the late seventeenth century, the development of "polite" or "civil" culture associated with a "middling sort" of commercial means confirmed the expansion of titles of gentility identifying the reflexive self (Master) rather than titles reflecting one's contribution to a common purpose (Goodman/Goodwife).

So forms of address were associated with structural changes in larger social worlds. Even so, they also reveal much about the way people interacted in their local societies in those intimate small worlds of social interaction. The use of language here was connected with social distance and closeness, exclusion and inclusion, solicitation and demurrer, devotion and dissimulation. These exchanges were the speech acts of individuals, but formed patterns of social interaction, informed by convention and the rejection of convention, social compliance and the rejection of deference. One of the characteristics of early-modern England is the opportunity for us to see social interaction as a real process not concealed beneath ideological and hierarchical social descriptions. Real social processes come alive: "sorts" of people in negotiation; "chief inhabitants" intent on leading (and manipulating) local societies; and the solicitation of gentle status associated with the decline of goodies. All co-existed in this transformative age when social processes were bared and made naked by profound social transformations. We have a sight of the complementary but different perceptions of both large and local societies in action, working through as process, refracted through social practice, in confusion and confounded, but there and visible nonetheless.

Appendix: abuse and defamation

The last section of chapter 3 explored abusive language, particularly against those in authority. There is a distinction to be made here between abuse and defamation, although both actions threatened to have the same result: causing disharmony. The distinction has been succinctly shown by Richard Helmholz.[975] To encourage harmonious resolution of disputes about words, the ecclesiastical courts, following the common law courts, at this time introduced favor for *mitior sensus*—a lesser interpretation of the words as abusive rather than defamatory. Whilst the concern of chapter 3 has been with vituperation rather than defamation, it might be useful here to elaborate further on Helmholz's keen insight.

In instance causes—those between individuals rather than office causes brought by the archdeacon—in the court of the archdeaconry of Nottingham, this idea of *mitior sensus* was introduced in practice although its introduction was not formally pronounced. The practical application can be discerned in the interrogatories for witnesses who deposed in defamation causes. Four of the interrogatories inquired of the witness (that is, demanded an opinion) the following questions. (i) Did the plaintiff have a reputation for honesty before the alleged words? (ii) What was the meaning and intent of the words? (iii) Were the words spoken in anger and malice? (iv) Have the words hurt the credit and reputation of the plaintiff?. By these questions, the officials were attempting to define whether there was real defamation or whether a lesser construction could be placed on the words. The extracts below suggest that, in the court of the archdeaconry of Nottingham, these questions had become a standard part of the interrogatories for witnesses by the first decade of the seventeenth century.

The intention was no doubt to dampen hostility and animosity in local societies and to restore harmony as quickly as possible by mitigating the impact of the words—the *mitior sensus*. The effectiveness of that intent, in the light of these extracts, must be tempered, however, since the responses to the interrogatories to do not seem inclined to support a lesser interpretation of the words. In short, the strategy became appropriated, it would seem, as a way of confirming the worst impact of the words. The witnesses always opined that the words had been highly slanderous and hurtful to the status, credit and honor of the plaintiff. Only occasionally did a witness suggest that the person had not been harmed by the words. We can suspect then that witnesses attended court *ex parte*. Although the interrogatories attempted to find out if witnesses had been influenced by the parties, the witnesses almost always maintained that they appeared independently. Their statement should, however, be viewed with some skepticism. If this court and these few causes are any guide, we might assume that the courts implemented the rule of *mitior sensus*, but its application did not make any real impression other than in procedure. The adoption of the rule does confirm, nonetheless, a distinction between abuse and defamation.

[1] Rooker *c.* Cawdwell (Laxton)[976]

Alleged words: "a pawltrie prieste" and an habitual frequenter of alehouses, a drunkard.

"spoken in malice, anger, and in a skornefull & an upbreadinge maner and in such like sort, as the said Edward Cawdwell uttered and spake the same to, of, or by the said William Rooke clerk in <common> comon sence and understanding and use of speeche within the Towne & Parish of Egmanton aforesaide and other places adioynenge, did, & doe importe asmuche as if the said Edward Cawdwell had said that the said William Rooke clerk, was & is a man of lewde Life and conversation ... a fellowe not fit for the Clergye, or to take <him> upon him any ecclesiasticall function or office. And in that sence & meaninge, and to that effect, did they, who were presente & hard the same wordes, uttered, and spoken by the said Edward Cawdwell, the time & place aforesaid, take interprett & understande theim"

[2] Prynne *c.* ? (Nottingham, 1576)[977]

Alleged words: "a whore" etc.

Response of Robert Carston, of Nottingham, to interrogatories three and four:

"That in deede by reason of this slaunder beinge spreade abroad the libellate Anne Prynne is wors thought of amongst her neighbours & that he this iurate hath hard some say that they misliked her the more therfore."

[3] Parties not named (East Bridgford, 1601)

Alleged words: "whoremaster" (alleged that he slept with another man's wife)

[to the 5th article] "that it is commonlie thoughte that the good name of the articulate Gabriel...is greatelie hurte by meanes of the wordes before by him deposed of"[978]

[to the same] "that the good name of the said Gabriel is greatelie hurte by meanes of the wordes deposed of because yf somme doe not beleeve the saide sclaunderous wordes to be true yeete others doe beleeve them to be true...."[979]

[4] Sudbury c. Bothomley (Sutton on Trent, 1603)[980]

Alleged words: "thou art a burnt arsed queane"

[the words] "are worse then if she had in plaine termes called her whore & so did this deponent as she sayeth, take and understand theime & so they are commonly taken in Sutton articulate...."

'which were <worst> as ill (sayes this deponent) as if shee had called her whore in plaine termes, & so this deponent did then take theim...."

[5] Mee c. Thorneley (Nottingham, 1604)[981]

Alleged words: "arrant whore" (slept with a man other than her husband)

[to the 5th article] "the good name of the said Jane Mee articulate is greatlie hurte as she this deponent thincketh"

[6] Lascelles c. Swigget (Sturton, 1605)[982]

"in common sense it had binne as much as yf <she had said that> he the articulate Sir George Lassels had attempted the chastitie of the woman to whome he had spoken such wordes & so he thincketh the same wordes to be commonlie understoode in Stretton articulate...."

[7] Bigges c. Lascelles (Sturton, 1605)[983]

"that the words before by this deponent deposed of in the 3d article doe importe signifie & meane as much as yf the articulate Sir

George had said that George Bigges articulate had attempted the chastitie of the articulate Anne Swigget in this deponents iudgement & further saithe that theie are <so generallie> understoode to be of the same sence & meaninge in the parishe of Sturton."

[the words] "doe importe signifie & meane as muche as yf <the said> Sir George Lassels articulate had said that the articulate George Bigges had attempted the chastitie or unlawfullie soughte to have the use & carnall knowledge of the bodie of Anne Swigget libellate & that the same wordes were to be taken construed & <meaninge> understood in that sense & meaninge & none other in this deponents iudgement & further sayeth that the same wordes are taken in the same sense by the most parte of the parishioners of Sturton articulate...."

"that he hathe hearde Peter Bose & Robert Shacklocke <understande the> saye that the same words before by this deponent deposed of in the thirde article did importe & meane as muche as is before by this deponent deposed of...."

[to the 6th article] "that by reason of the speakinge of the words before by this deponent deposed of in the third article the good fame & name of the articulate George Bigges is greatelie hurte as he this deponent thincketh"

[8] Lascelles *c.* Bigges (Sturton, 1605)[984]

[the words] "doe importe & meane as much as yf the said George Bigges had said that Sir George Lassels would have had carnall knowledge of his maides bodye ... that he this deponent hathe hearde that the same wordes did importe so muche in the parishe of Stretton but of whome he heard it he doth not remember."

[9] Same cause.[985]

"that the wordes...beinge spoken in suche sorte as theie weere did in this deponents understandinge signifie & meane that the partie to whome theie weere spoken attempted the chastitie of the woman or unlawfullye to have the use & carnall knowledge of her bodye and that theie doe importe & meane as much as yf the articulate George Bigges had charged the articulate Sir George Lassels to be a gentleman of an incontinent and adulterous liefe and further saieth that he verilie beleeveth that theie that weere present & did heere the wordes spoken did understande them to be spoken in the same sence."

[10] Walker *c.* Calton (Nottingham, 1605)

Alleged words: "Thou arte a baggage iade & a cowe and not fitte to keepe anye honest woman companye"

"he this deponent thincketh that the words before by him deposed <in> the article nexte afore goinge doe signifie & meane as much as yf the articulate Margaret Calton had called the articulate Marie Walker whore & so thincketh the same wordes to be commonlie reputed & taken in the parishe articulate."

[11] Bowes *c.* Stother (Clipstone, 1606)[986]

Alleged words: "Go like a pockie Jade, or go like a pockie arsed Jade, or go like a pockie burned arsed iade"

"...in and by the common use of speache in Clipson and Edwinstowe aforesaid and other places therabouts, by the space of 10 yeres last paste before the suite began, ended and paste, and more did & do import signifie and meane as much, as though the same speaker had charged and infamed the same woman to be naught of her bodie, & to be <an> unchaste and incontinent person, and so the wordes of the said Stother geven to the said Joice Bower, as it appeareth by the said deposicions, did & do in and by the commune use of speache aforesaid, importe, signifie and mean as much, as if the same Stother had called, or affirmed her the said Joice, to be naught of her bodie, or to be an unchaste and incontinent person, and a whore, and that the same wordes were in that sense & none other by the bearers construed and understoode, when as they were spoken;..."

[12] Barker *c.* Reade (South Collingham, but the words uttered at Quarter Sessions in Newark, 1606)[987]

Alleged words: "I am an honester man then thou arte. Thou doest live of other mennes goodes. Thou art maynteyned by other mennes wives. Thou waste taken in bed with Britteyns wyfe and the neighbours of Collingham will speake it."

[to the 4th article: "that as he this deponent verilie beleeveeth the wordes videlicet And keepest two or three besides thie wyfe, or to saye to anye maried man that he keepeth two or three besides his owne wyfe, beinge spoken in anger displeasure & upbraydinge manner in & by the common sense & understandinge & use of speece in Newarke aforesaid & other places there aboutes did & doe importe signifie & meane as much as thoughe the speaker thereof shoulde saye that he to whome he or she soe speaketh was & is a man of an incontinent unchaste & adulterous lyfe & that in that sence & none other weere & are such wordes to be taken and understanded, and this deponent dothe understand wordes spoken to the same effecte to be of the same sence and none other...."

[the words should be construed to mean] "...a man of an incontinent unchaste and adulterous lyfe ... in common sence and understandinge & use of speech in Newarke aforesaid & other places thereaboutes did and do importe and meane as muche as thoughe the said John Reade had called the said Barker whore Maister and had said that he kepte whores...."

Figures

Table 1.1 Widows in the Hearth Tax for seven southern and Midland counties, 1664-1674[154]

No. of hearths	Widows C	Widows NC	Other females C	Other females NC
1	1906	5326	449	958
2	1122	960	308	175
3	689	73	212	12
4	413	27	161	11
5	176	5	123	1
6	113	4	84	1
>7	124	0	246	0

Notes to Table 1.1 In this and subsequent tables, Widows represents the formula of address Widow + surname; C= chargeable; NC = not chargeable (exempt, certified); other females connotes other forms of address (forename and surname, Mistress and surname, Madam and surname).

Table 1.2 Widows in the Shropshire Hearth Tax, 1672[155]

No. of hearths	Widows C	Widows NC	Other females C	Other females NC
1	407	413	230	473
2	148	0	71	0
3	83	0	40	0
4	34	0	21	0
5	17	0	17	0
6	11	0	14	0
>7	14	0	42	0

Table 1.3 Widows in the Oxfordshire Hearth Tax, 1665[159]

No. of hearths	Widows C	Widows NC	Other females C	Other females NC
1	62	19	41	12
2	43	36	31	20
3	85	0	45	0
4	28	0	20	0
5	18	0	10	0
6	5	0	5	0
>7	12	0	14	0

Table 1.4 Widows in the Dorset Hearth Tax, 1662-4[160]

No. of hearths	Widows C	Widows NC	Other females C	Other females NC
1	282	60	286	45
2	234	16	223	6
3	147	0	137	0
4	59	1	53	0
5	28	0	25	0
6	11	0	16	0
>7	18	0	23	0

Table 1.5 Widows in the Hearth Tax for some urban places[162]

No. of hearths	Widows C	Widows NC	Other females C	Other females NC
1	150	141[1]	84	72
2	157	27	69	18
3	77	0	37	0
4	53	0	34	0
5	24	0	17	0
6	24	0	22	0
>7	30	0	34	0

Table 1.6 Women in the hearth tax exemption listings in Norwich, Kings Lynn and Great Yarmouth 1673-4

No. of hearths	Widow and surname	Some other description Usually forename and surname
1	900	198
2	208	25

Table 1.7 Occurrences of the titles good/goody/goodwife/goodman in the Norwich hearth tax, 1671-4[310]

Parish	Total hearth taxpayers	Good/goody/good wife/goodman
St Andrew	39	11
St Augustine	86	1
St Benedict	68	10
St Clement	42	5
St Edmund	38	0
St Ethelreda	26	0
St George Colegate	84	14
St George Tombland	27	1
St Giles	78	4
St Gregory	61	3
St Helen	30	4
St James	74	1
St John de Sepulchre	120	4
St John Maddermarket	33	1
St John Timberhill	109	8
St Julian	95	1 .
St Lawrence	103	11
St Margaret	91	5
St Martin at Oak	186	10
St Martin at Palace	112	6
St Mary Coslany	147	100[2]
St Michael at Plea	29	1
St Michael at Thorn	156	11
St Michael Coslany	141	33
St Paul	147	6
St Peter Hungate	10	0
St Peter Mangate	104	8
St Peter Parmentergate	266	8
St Peter Southgate	108	3
St Saviour	48	8
St Simon and Jude	28	5
St Stephen	164	11
St Swithin	63	8
Trowse Millgate	53	7

Figure 1 Goodies in some Hearth Tax assessments

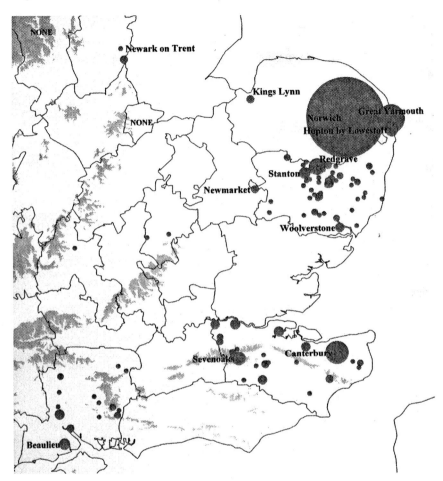

Table 1.8 Rank order of goodies by hearths in Suffolk in 1674

Number of hearths	Number of goodies
1	33
2	42
3	12
4	8
5	5
7	1

Table 1.9 Rank order of goodies by hearths in Kent and Hampshire in 1664-5[316]

Number of hearths	Number of good/goody/goodman /goodwife (chargeable)	Number of good/goody/goodman /goodwife (not chargeable)
1	21	64
2	16	21
3	6	1
4	4	0
5	3	0
6	1	0

Table 1.10 Titles of address in rates for Cambridge, St Mary, 1620-4[326]

Date	Mr	Goodman	Father	None (male)	Widow	Goodwife	Mistress	Mother	None (female)
1620	63	29	1	55	15	3	8	2	4
1621	54	27	0	62	12	3	5	1	6
1622	63	26	1	62	10	3	10	0	2
1623	44	25	1	95	14	1	8	0	2
1624	56	25	2	76	17	0	10	8	4

Figure 2

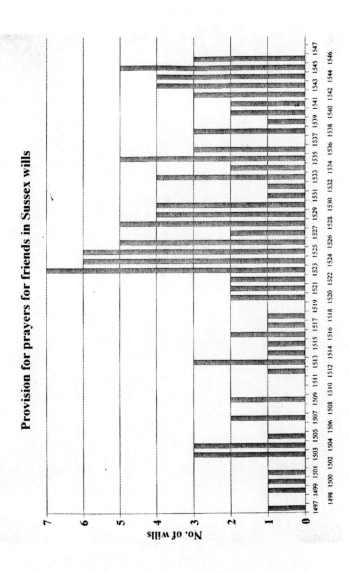

Provision for prayers for friends in Sussex wills

Table 4.1 Descriptive statistics of male forenames in Banbury in 1641-2

No. of different forenames	Mean of oathtakers per forename	Standard deviation	Median of oathtakers per forename	First quartile	Third quartile	Min.	Max.
41	5.61	10.38	2	1	4	1	49

Figure 3 Cuthbert in co. Durham: Protestation Oath, 1641-2

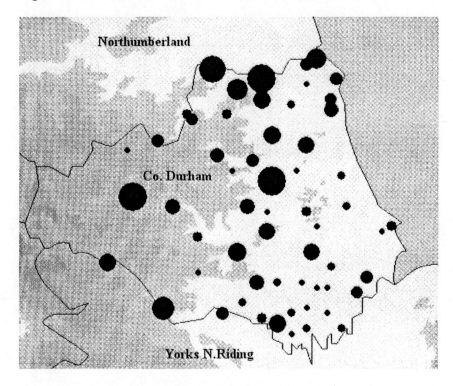

Figure 4 Durham Quarter Sessions, 1511-1624: actors called Cuthbert

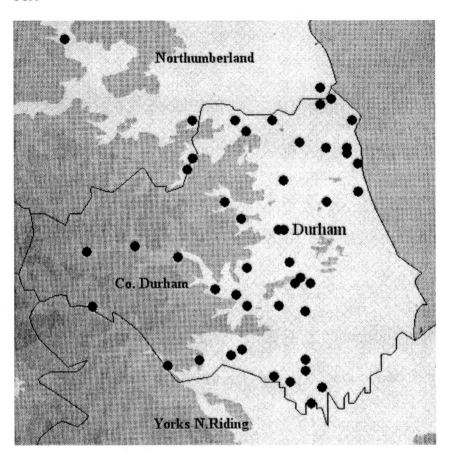

Table 4.2 Descriptive statistics of recusants' names [920]

Location/ date/ category	Number of different names	Mean	Standard deviation	Median	First quartile	Third quartile
North Riding 1614 males	52	7.79	14.54	2	1	5.75
North Riding 1614 females	52	12.94	21.7	4	1	13.5
County Durham 1607 males	31	4.39	6.88	1	1	5
County Durham 1607 females	31	6.94	7.81	4	1	10

Note: The statistics relate to the number of persons per forename.

Notes

Acknowledgments

¹ Kate Holland, ed., *Mender of Disorders. Court and Community in the Archdeaconry of Nottingham, 1560-1756* (Nottingham: University of Nottingham, 2004), describes the project and its location (URL) on the World-Wide Web.

Introduction

² E. R. Brinkworth, ed., *The Archdeacon's Court. Liber Actorum, 1581,* I, ORS vol. 23 (1942), 12.

³ J. H. Baker, ed., *Reports of Cases by John Caryll Part II 1501-1522,* Selden Society vol. 116 (London, 2000 for 1999), 571.

⁴ Erving Goffman, *The Presentation of Self in Everyday Life* (New York: Anchor Books, 1959), 26.

⁵ The approach here is stimulated by Goffman, *Presentation of Self;* and idem, *Behavior in Public Places. Notes on the Social Organization of Gatherings* (New York: Free Press, 1963). The intention here is to examine empirical data about social interaction in context. For that reason, I eschew the "symbolic interactionism" of Mead and Blumer, but appreciate the relating of micro-sociology to macro-sociology presented in Sheldon Stryker, *Symbolic Interactionism. A Social Structural Version* (Menlo Park, Calif.: Benjamin/Cummings Publishing, 1980) through inter-relating social interaction to social structure. On the other hand, there is much to be said for an approach which dissolves social structure and starts afresh from social relations: John Scott, *Social Network Analysis. A Handbook* (London: Sage Publications, 1991) (sociology) and Per Hage and Frank Harary, *Structural Models in Anthropology* (Cambridge: Cambridge University Press, 1983). For figurational sociology—predicated on social interdependence and group dynamic: Steven Loyal and Stephen Quilley, eds., *The Sociology of Norbert Elias* (Cambridge: Cambridge University Press, 2004). From Goffman, I especially respect his notion of "situational propriety" and the primary influence of the social process. Those who suspect Goffman of cynicism are referred again to Anthony Giddens, "Erving Goffman as a Systemic Social Theorist," in idem, *Social Theory and Modern Sociology* (Stanford,

Calif.: Stanford University Press,1987), 109-39, a reference which I owe to William I. Miller, *Faking It* (Cambridge, 2003), 244-5, n. 9. Throughout, I prefer self-presentation to the fashionable New Historicist notion of self-fashioning, because I adhere to Goffman's (and Mead's) epistemology of the social process contributing to the formation and development of self. Without inferring any direct parallels or comparisons, my thinking has been much stimulated by Simon J. Charlesworth, *A Phenomenology of Working Class Experience* (Cambridge: Cambridge University Press, 2000). I also owe a great debt of gratitude to my Leicester colleagues, Barbara Misztal [*Informality. Social Theory and Contemporary Practice* (London and New York: Routledge, 2000)] and Eric Dunning (his patient conversation).

[6] The context is discussed fully by Henry French, "Social Status, Localism and the Middling Sort of People in England, 1620-1750," *Past and Present* 166 (2000): 66-99, so the arguments are not recapitulated here; for the proposition of "sorts" and "degrees" of people, Keith Wrightson, *English Society 1580-1680* rev. ed. (London: Routledge, 2003), 25-46 and idem, "'Sorts of people' in Tudor and Stuart England," in *The Middling Sort of People. Culture, Society and Politics in England, 1550-1800*, ed. Jonathan Barry and Christopher Brooks (Basingstoke: The Macmillan Press, 1994), 28-51.

[7] W. LeHardy, ed., *Calendar to the Sessions Books and Sessions Minute Books ... County of Hertford 1619 to 1657*, Hertfordshire County Records vol. V (Hertford, 1928), 69.

[8] Victor Morgan, J. Key and B. Taylor, eds., *The Papers of Nathaniel Bacon of Stiffkey volume IV 1596-1602*, NRS vol. 64 (2000), 10.

[9] A. Hassell Smith and G. M. Baker, *The Papers of Nathaniel Bacon of Stiffkey volume III 1586-1595*, NRS vol. 53 (1987-8), 11.

[10] NNRO NCR case 16 shelf c no. 5, fol. 279v (assembly minute book, Norwich City Council, 1604).

[11] NRO NBR 3/1, p.599 (Northampton assembly minutes about measures for the prevention of the dissemination of plague).

[12] Wrightson, "'Sorts of People'," 31.

[13] Wrightson, "'Sorts of People'," 38: "It was needed ... to express both the immediate social tensions and the longer-term reconstructions of social identities ... of the sixteenth and earlier seventeenth centuries."

[14] Wrightson, "'Sorts of People'."

[15] Wrightson, "'Sorts of People'," 39.

[16] French, "Social Status, Localism and the Middling sort."

[17] The implications of the excellent Andy Wood, "'Poore men woll speke one daye': Plebeian Languages of Deference and Defiance in England c.1520-1640," in *The Politics of the Excluded*, c.1500-1850, ed. Tim Harris (Basingstoke: The Macmillan Press, 2001), 67-98, should, however, not be ignored.

[18] Steve Hindle, "The Political Culture of the Middling Sort in English Rural Communities," in *Politics of the Excluded*, ed. Harris, 125-52.

[19] J. H. Baker, ed., *Reports of Cases from the Time of King Henry VIII* vol. I, Selden Society vol.120 (London, 2003), 41 (23). So, for example: "Nicholas Reynoldes, called a gent, but of noe trade nor callinge: his father dwelleth at Norton in Hartfordsheare" (1632): J. M. Guilding, ed., *Reading Records. Diary of the Corporation*, 4 vols. (London: Reading Corporation, 1892-6), 3:115.

[20] Goffman, *Presentation of Self*, thus contains an extensive chapter 1 on "Performances" (pp. 28-82).

[21] The question of the origins of discourse and its interaction with the material world is discussed further in the "Conclusion."

[22] The general context of early-modern theatre is succinctly described by the contributions to Arthur F. Kinney, ed., *A Companion to Renaissance Drama* (Oxford: Blackwell Publishing, 2002).

[23] R. Dutton, A. Findlay, and R. Wilson, eds., *Region, Religion and Patronage. Lancastrian Shakespeare* (Manchester: Manchester University Press, 2003); Siobhan Keenan, *Travelling Players in Shakespeare's England* (Basingstoke: Palgrave/Macmillan 2002).

[24] Act I, scene i, ll. 62-3.

[25] Act I, scene iv, ll. 29-30, 65. *Dampit* also resonated with the implications of hell, of course.

[26] Act II, scene i, ll. 271-2.

[27] Act I, scene iv, l. 34 (with also the imprecation of the Devil, "old Harry").

[28] Act II, scene i, l. 174.

[29] For example, in Act V, scene ii, at l. 99, Lucre denounced his nephew, Witgood, as a knave, face-to-face. For male honor and character, Alexandra Shepard, *The Meanings of Manhood in Early Modern England* (Oxford: Oxford University Press, 2003). For the repetitive use of "knave," David Underdown, *Fire from Heaven. Life in an English Town in the Seventeenth Century* rev. ed. (London: Pimlico, 2003), 77.

[30] Kathleen L. McLuskie, *Dekker and Heywood* (Basingstoke: The Macmillan Press, 1994), 14; for Dekker's indulgence in "pamphlet urbanism" reflecting the realism of his "heterocosm" of the City, Lawrence Manley, *Literature and Culture in Early Modern London* (Cambridge: Cambridge University Press, 1995), 355-71. Paul Seaver and David Bevington have discussed Dekker's "artisanal world" and "theatre as holiday" in *The Theatrical City. Theatre and Politics in London, 1576-1649* ed. D. Smith, R. Strier and Bevington (Cambridge: Cambridge University Press, 1995), 87-100 (chap. 3: "Thomas Dekker's *The Shoemakers Holiday*").

[31] Blair Worden, "Ben Jonson among the Historians," in *Culture and Politics in Early Stuart England*, ed. Kevin Sharpe and Peter Lake (Basingstoke: The Macmillan Press, 1994), 67-89: Worden's conclusion asserts Jonson's moderate position, but David Norbrook, *Poetry and Politics in the English Renaissance*, rev. ed. (Oxford: Oxford University Press, 2002), 135-72 ("Jonson and the Jacobean Peace, 1603-1616") concentrates on the political ideology of Jonson.

[32] Summarized by David Riggs, *Ben Jonson. A Life* (Cambridge, Mass.: Harvard University Press, 1989), 3.

[33] S. Chakravorty, *Society and Politics in the Plays of Thomas Middleton* (Oxford: Oxford University Press, 1996), 17-19.

[34] McLuskie, *Dekker and Heywood*, 2-3.

[35] See most recently Subha Mukherji, "Women, Law and Dramatic Realism in Early Modern England," *English Literary Renaissance* 35 (2005): 248-72.

[36] Guilding, *Reading*, 3:208.

[37] Guilding, *Reading*, 3:258.

[38] Levi Fox, ed., *Minutes and Accounts of the Corporation of Stratford-upon-Avon and Other Records Volume V 1593-1598*, DS 35 (1990), 6.

[39] Laura Gowing, *Domestic Dangers. Women, Words, and Sex in Early Modern London* (Oxford: Oxford University Press, 1996), chap. 7 ("Narratives of Litigation"); W. J. T. Mitchell, ed., *On Narrative* (Chicago: Chicago University Press, 1981).

[40] W. K. Boyd, "Chancery proceedings *temp*. Elizabeth A.D. 1560 to A.D. 1570," *CHS* n.s. 9 (1906), 79.

[41] Boyd, "Chancery Proceedings," 41.

[42] C. Phillips and J. Smith, eds., *Stockport Probate Records 1578-1619*, RSLC 124 (1985), 16.

[43] There is much in Phil Withington, *The Politics of Commonwealth. Citizens and Freemen in Early Modern England* (Cambridge: Cambridge University Press, 2005), which it has not been possible to integrate into this discussion.

[44] N. Fairclough, *Language and Power*, 2nd. ed., (Harlow: Longman, 2001), 54-61.

[45] *Early Prose and Poetical Works of John Taylor the Water Poet (1580-1653)* (London, 1888), 9, and "The Penniless Pilgrimage" therein, passim.

[46] H. Littlehales, ed., *The Medieval Records of a London City Church (St Mary at Hill) A.D. 1420-1559*, EETS Extra Series 125, 128 (1905), 129.

[47] Littlehales, *Medieval Records of a London City Church*, at, for example, pp. 244, 246, 260-1.

[48] Littlehales, *Medieval Records of a London City Church*, 142.

[49] Littlehales, *Medieval Records of a London City Church*, 23.

[50] Littlehales, *Medieval Records of a London City Church*, 257.

[51] Littlehales, *Medieval Records of a London City Church*, 185, 241.

[52] Littlehales, *Medieval Records of a London City Church*, 127, 182, 193, 205, 206, 209.

[53] Littlehales, *Medieval Records of a London City Church*, 138-9.

[54] Littlehales, *Medieval Records of a London City Church*, 199.

[55] Ralph A. Griffiths, ed., *The Household Book (1510-1551) of Sir Edward Don: an Anglo-Welsh Knight and his Circle*, BucksRS 33 (2004).

[56] Griffiths, *Household Book*, 123, 135, 172, 176, 179, 183, 255, 270, 346 and passim.

[57] Griffiths, *Household Book*, 80, 93, 108, 128, 159, 170, 196, 264, 265, 266, 267 and passim.

[58] Griffiths, *Household Book*, 98, 99, and passim.

[59] Griffiths, *Household Book*, 134, 137, 140, 141, 143, 151, 152, 153, 155, 156, 157, 163, 165, 167, 169, 174, 175, 181, 183, 207, and passim.

[60] Griffiths, *Household Book*, 33 and 34 are examples, but for a fuller description, see below.

[61] *Report of the Manuscripts of Lord Middleton*, Historical Manuscripts Commission, (London, 1911), 410.

[62] G. D. Lumb, ed., *Testamenta Leodiensia*, ThS 19 (1913), 123.

[63] I owe an immense debt here to Barbara Rosenwein, "Worrying about Emotions in History," *American Historical Review* 107 (2002): 821-45.

[64] F. J. Furnivall, ed., *Books of Courtesy*, EETS Extra Series 8 (1869), 53 (wise man).

[65] Furnivall, *Books of Courtesy*, 45 (good wife).

[66] Scott Smith-Bannister, *Names and Naming Patterns in England 1538-1700* (Oxford: Oxford University Press, 1997). More detailed references to this and other

research into naming appear in chap. 4.

[67] The facet is brilliantly explained by Misztal, *Informality*, 29. For the implications for "time," Michel de Certeau, *The Writing of History* trans. Tom Conley (New York: Columbia University Press, 1988), 88-9.

[68] For a satirical exposition of the "gallants," Ben Jonson, *Every Man in His Humour* (London, 1616), epitomized by Captain Bobadil.

Chapter 1

[69] William Shakespeare, *Much Ado About Nothing*, Act III, scene 5, ll. 9-12.

[70] The wider implications of naming are now beautifully conceptualized by Anthony Cohen, *Self Consciousness. An Alternative Anthropology of Identity* (London: Routledge, 1994), 71-9.

[71] N. W. Tildesley, ed., *Penkridge Parish Register*, SPRS (1945-6), 144.

[72] Tildesley, *Penkridge Parish Register*, 132.

[73] Margaret Pelling, "Old Age, Poverty, and Disability in Early Modern Norwich: Work, Remarriage, and Other Expedients," in *Life, Death and the Elderly. Historical Perspectives*, ed. eadem and Richard M. Smith (London: Routledge, 1991), 74-101; Shepard, *Meanings of Manhood*, 214-45.

[74] The most recent, and compelling, exposition of the experience of old age is Susannah Ottaway, *The Decline of Life. Old Age in Eighteenth-century England* (Cambridge: Cambridge University Press, 2004); for female ageing, Lynn Botelho and Pat Thane, eds., *Women and Ageing in British Society since 1500* (Harlow: Longman, 2001).

[75] Cambridge University Library Ely Diocesan Records D/2/2 fol. 25r.

[76] H. Brierley, ed., *The Registers of the Parish Church of Blackburn in the County of Lancaster 1600-1660*, LPRS vol. 41 (1911), 36.

[77] Brierley, *Registers of the Parish Church of Blackburn*, 186 (1630).

[78] W. Preston and J. Rowe, eds., *A Transcript of the Early Registers of the Parish of Guiseley* (Bradford: Lund, Humphries, 1913).

[79] H. Brierley, ed., *The Registers of the Parish Church of Chipping*, LPRS vol. 14 (1903), 93.

[80] E. L. Guilford, "Extracts from the records of the borough of Nottingham," *Transactions of the Thoroton Society* 30 (1926), 126.

[81] William Rowley, Thomas Dekker and John Ford, *The Witch of Edmonton* ed. P. Corbin and D. Sedge (Manchester: Manchester University Press, 1999), 38-49.

[82] F. G. Emmison, *Wills of the County of Essex (England) Volume III 1571-1577* (Boston: New England Historic Genealogical Society, 1986), 269 (633).

[83] H. Brierley, ed., *The Parish Registers of Garstang Church* vol. I, LPRS vol. 63 (1925), 148-9, 153, 155-6, 160-5, 174-5, 177-8, 181, 183-4, 188-9, 193, 197-8, 202, 204.

[84] *Leeds Parish Church Registers*, ThS vol.1 (1891), 107, 122, 123, 135, 298, 307-8, 310-11, 315, 326, 360 (1578-1607).

[85] A. W. Headlam, ed., *The Parish Registers of St Oswald's, Durham* (Durham: T. Caldcleugh, 1891), 155-6, 161-2, 171-2, 174, 193, 208, 220, 228.

[86] J. G. and F. Clifford, eds., *Eyam Parish Register 1630-1700*, DRS vol. 21 (1993).

[87] A. H. Smith, ed., *The Papers of Nathaniel Bacon of Stiffkey Volume II 1578-1585*,

NRS 49 (1982-3), 209.

[88] Smith and Baker, *Papers of Nathaniel Bacon Volume III*, 49.

[89] WSRO G23/1/3, fol. 51v: "At this assemblye hit is concluded that olde mother grafton shall hold the howse that she nowe dwelleth in Didles streat during hir lyfe payeinge yerly xs...." For the meaning of "mother," see below.

[90] Peter and Jenny Clark, eds., *The Boston Assembly Minutes 1545-1575*, LRS vol. 77 (1987), 15 (131).

[91] S. G. Doree, *The Parish Registers and Tithing Book of Thomas Hassall of Amwell*, HRS 5 (1989), 95.

[92] Doree, *Parish Registers and Tithing Book*, 92.

[93] Doree, *Parish Registers and Tithing Book*, 181.

[94] The Rt. Rev. Bishop Hobhouse, ed., *Churchwardens' Accounts of Croscombe, Pilton, Patton, Tintinhall, Morebath and St Michael's Bath*, SRS vol. 4 (1890), 222.

[95] *Records of Maidstone* (Maidstone: [Maidstone Corporation], 1926), 66 – and he continued with other information.

[96] E. H. Bates, ed., *Quarter Sessions Records* vol. I, SRS 23 (1907), 6 (63).

[97] A. Sabin, ed., *The Registers of the Church of St Augustine the Less, Bristol*, Bristol & Gloucestershire Archaeological Society Record Series vol. 3 (Gloucester, 1956), 75 (1639).

[98] G. P. Crawfurd, ed., *The Registers of the Parish of St Mary, Reading, Berkshire* II (Reading: Bradley, 1842), 107-9 (1617-23).

[99] S. G. Doree, ed., *The Early Churchwardens' Accounts of Bishop's Stortford 1431-1558*, HRS vol. 10,(1994), 289.

[100] W. C. Renshaw, ed., *The Parish Registers of Cuckfield, Sussex, 1598-1699*, SxRS vol. 13 (1911), 130-44.

[101] Renshaw, *Parish Registers of Cuckfield*, 135, 136, 139, 141.

[102] H. D. Roberts, ed., *The Parish Registers of Brighton, 1558-1701* (Brighton: Brighton Public Library, 1932), 183.

[103] Margaret Statham, ed., *Accounts of the Feoffees of the Town Lands of Bury St Edmunds 1569-1622*, SfRS vol. 46 (2003), 150, 165, 363.

[104] Statham, *Accounts of the Feoffees*, 278.

[105] F. G. Emmison, ed., *Wills of the County of Essex (England) Volume I 1558-1565* (Washington D.C.: New England Historic Genealogical Society,1982), 1 (1).

[106] Emmison, *Wills of the County of Essex* I: 73 (232), 134 (434).

[107] M. Siraut and A. J. Monday, eds., *Somerset Wills*, SRS vol. 89 (2003), 27, 92.

[108] Emmison, *Wills of the County of Essex* I: 179 (582).

[109] Emmison, ed., *Wills of the County of Essex (England) Volume II 1565-1571* (Boston: New England Historic Genealogical Society, 1983), 98 (363).

[110] "A Register of Stafford and other Local Wills," *CHS* (1928 for 1926), 52 (71).

[111] UN AN/PB 326/2/15.

[112] R. Dickinson, ed., *The Register of Winwick Parish Church Part II 1621-1660*, LPRS vol. 113 (1974), 117.

[113] J. Pound, P. Seaman and R. Smith, eds., *Norfolk Hearth Tax*, NRS vol. 65 (2001), 42-3, 55-6, 60-4, 73, 97, 104, 105, 117, 118, 119

[114] *Suffolk in 1674*, Suffolk Green Books no. xi, vol. 13 (Ipswich, 1905), 167, 267; W. Watkins-Pitchford, ed., *The Shropshire Hearth Tax Roll of 1672*, SPRS (1949), 43; Duncan Harrington, Sarah Pearson, and Susan Rose, eds., *Kent Hearth Tax Assess-*

ment Lady Day 1664, KR vol. 29 (2000), 48, 62.

[115] Emmison, *Wills of the County of Essex* I: 48 (147).

[116] Emmison, *Wills of the County of Essex* III: 31 (79).

[117] Emmison, *Wills of the County of Essex* II: 122 (446).

[118] Emmison, *Wills of the County of Essex* II: 157 (560).

[119] Emmison, *Wills of the County of Essex* II:190 (677).

[120] Emmison, *Wills of the County of Essex* II: 202 (710).

[121] M. Maslen, ed., *Woodstock Chamberlains' Accounts 1609-50*, ORS vol. 58 (1993), 208, 234. For confirmation of the use of old in these accounts, the payments requested by the mayor for "ould Lowe" and "ould Dissell" at p. 85 (in 1620).

[122] Emmison, *Wills of the County of Essex* I: 183 (595), 187 (610).

[123] E. R. C. Brinkworth and J. S. W. Gibson, *Banbury Wills and Inventories Part 1 1591-1620*, BHS vol.13 (1985), 196 (98).

[124] F. W. Weaver, ed., *Somerset Wills (1501-1530)*, SRS vol. 19 (1903), 283; idem, ed., *Somerset Medieval Wills (Third Series) 1531-1558*, SRS vol. 30 (1905), 155.

[125] *The Registers of Bishop Middleham*, DNPRS vol. 13 (1906), 144.

[126] E. Axon, ed., *The Registers of the Cathedral Church of Manchester*, LPRS vol. 31 (1908), 321.

[127] W. J. Stavert, ed., *The Parish Registers of Skipton-in-Craven* (Skipton: Craven Herald, 1894-6), 33.

[128] Brierley, *Registers of the Parish Church of Blackburn*, 174.

[129] J. W. Penfold, *The Parish Registers of Haslemere*, SuPRS vol. 8 (1910), 70.

[130] *Tamworth Parish Registers* I, SPRS (1917), 42, 126.

[131] Headlam, *Parish Registers of St Oswald's, Durham*, 34.

[132] A. C. Chibnall & A. V. Woodman, eds., *Subsidy Roll for the County of Buckinghamshire Anno 1524*, BucksRS vol. 8 (1950), 29, 51, 87.

[133] J. H. Bettey, ed., *Calendar of the Correspondence of the Smyth Family of Ashton Court, 1548-1642*, BrisRS vol. 35 (1982), 56 (114)

[134] A. Hassell Smith, ed., *The Papers of Nathaniel Bacon of Stiffkey Volume II 1578-1585*, NRS vol. 49 (1982-3), 19.

[135] W. L. Sachse, ed., *Minutes of the Norwich Court of Mayoralty 1632-1635*, NRS vol. 36 (1967), 14.

[136] Sachse, *Minutes of the Norwich Court of Mayoralty*, 28.

[137] Sachse, *Minutes of the Norwich Court of Mayoralty*, 53.

[138] J. Webb, ed., *The Town Finances of Elizabethan Ipswich*, SfRS vol. 38 (1996), 40-1, 44, 52, 59.

[139] Webb, *Town Finances*, 42, 43, 50, 54, 55, 56, 59, 61, 81, 88.

[140] J. A. Twemlow, ed., *Liverpool Town Books* vol. 1 (Liverpool: University of Liverpool, 1918), 266.

[141] For personal naming at this time, Smith-Bannister, *Names and Naming Patterns*.

[142] Morgan, Key and Taylor, *Papers of Nathaniel Bacon IV*, 11.

[143] Brierley, *Registers of the Parish Church of Chipping*, 82-93.

[144] *Registers of St Mary's, Shrewsbury*, 24-6, 28-9, 32-5, 37-8, 53.

[145] Headlam, *Parish Registers of St Oswald's, Durham*, 8, 11, 25-7, 29, 32-3, 37-8, 40-3

[146] Crawfurd, *Registers of the Parish of St Mary, Reading*, II: 98 et ff.

[147] C. W. Foster, ed., *The Parish Registers of Gainsborough*, LRS vol. 6 (1916), 151-2, 154, 164-5, 172, 176-7, 181-2, 204-5, 208, 212, 214, 216, 225-6, 229, 232.

[148] C. W. Foster, ed., *The Parish Registers of Grantham*, LRS P.R. Section vol. 4 (1916).

[149] J. C. C. Smith, ed., *The Parish Registers of Richmond*, SuPRS vol. 50 (1903), 161-96.

[150] D. M. Nolan, W. J. Watkinson and P. Riden, eds., *Chesterfield Parish Register 1601-35*, DRS vol. 15 (1990).

[151] D. Shorrocks, ed., *Bishop Still's Visitation 1594*, SRS vol. 84 (1998), 98-9.

[152] Morgan, Key and Taylor, *Papers of Nathaniel Bacon IV*, 174.

[153] J. S. W. Gibson and E. R. C. Brinkworth, eds., *Banbury Corporation Records: Tudor and Stuart*, BHS vol. 15 (1977), 145-6.

[154] "Hearth tax return 1671," *Bedfordshire Historical Record Society* vol. 16 (1934); D. G. Edwards, ed., *Derbyshire Hearth Tax Assessments 1662-1670*, DRS vol. 7 (1982). The numbers are low because only parts of Derbyshire allow the collection of such data. Derby is separated off for a table on urban widows, below. Elizabeth Hughes and Philippa White, eds., *The Hampshire Hearth Tax Assessment, 1665*, Hampshire Record Society vol. 11 (Winchester, 1991). Southampton, Portsmouth and Winchester are separated off for a table on urban widows, below. Harrington, *Kent Hearth Tax Assessment*; W. F. Webster, ed., *Nottinghamshire Hearth Tax 1664:1674*, Thoroton Society Record Series vol. 37 (Nottingham, 1988). J. Bourne and A.Goode, eds., *Rutland Hearth Tax 1665*, Rutland Record Society (Oakham, 1991). *Suffolk in 1674*. The figures are only an approximate representation because of the nature of the edition.

[155] Watkins-Pitchford, *Shropshire Hearth Tax Roll*: excluding Shrewsbury which occurs below in the urban statistics; the widows throughout are described in two forms, as Widow Jones and as Joan Jones widow, in approximately equal numbers; the numbers in the table are approximate because of tears in the roll; the lists of exemptions do not specify the number of hearths, so they have all been attributed one hearth by default for the purposes of the tabulation.

[156] The data for Skyrack Wapentake, including Leeds, in the West Riding are not considered as the information for non-chargeable hearths is not specific in the printed edition: J. Stansfield, ed., "Return of the Hearth-Tax for the Wapentake of Skyrack part II," *Miscellanea*, ThS vol. 4 (1895). The problem with the Northwich Hundred hearth tax returns is that they seem to under-record widows who may be represented here by their forename and surname: G. Lawton, ed., *Northwich Hundred. Poll Tax 1660 and Hearth Tax 1664*, RSLC vol. 119 (1979). If, for example, we simply consider those listed for 1 hearth, we have twelve widows chargeable, nine widows not chargeable, 152 other women chargeable, and 244 other women not chargeable, the preponderance in the last two categories (other women chargeable and not chargeable) identified by their forename and surname.

[157] The normative nature of this distribution can be indicated in another way. If we tabulate the number of widows with one hearth chargeable, one hearth not chargeable and the total hearths, in Bedfordshire, Hampshire, Nottinghamshire, Rutland and Suffolk, and calculate chi-square, the probability (p) of an association is 0.000 with a value of 403.282 with 10 degrees of freedom. The figures for the total population of hearths are derived from *Cambridgeshire*, viii.

[158] M. M. B. Weinstock, ed., *Hearth Tax Returns, 1665*, ORS vol. 21 (1940), 73.

[159] Weinstock, *Hearth Tax Returns, 1665*, excluding Oxford, which is presented below for urban widows.

[160] C. A. F. Meekings, ed., *Dorset Hearth Tax Assessments 1662-1664* (Dorchester, 1951).

[161] Figures collected together in C. A. F. Meekings, S. Porter and I. Roy, eds., *The Hearth Tax Collectors' Book for Worcester 1678-1680*, WHS n.s. vol. 11 (1983), 39.

[162] Combined figures for Southampton, Portsmouth, Winchester, Derby, Oxford, Shrewsbury, and Cambridge. For Cambridge, Nesta Evans, ed., *Cambridgeshire Hearth Tax Returns Michaelmas 1664*, CRS vol. 15 (2000), 1-39. The information for Nottingham in 1674 does not differentiate non-chargeable hearths, so we have a distribution of chargeable hearths of widows as follows: one hearth = 28 widows; two = 24; three = 17; four = 11; five = 3; six = 3; and nine = 1; almost all are listed as Widow and surname.

[163] Watkins-Pitchford, *Shropshire Hearth Tax Roll*, 1-28; 1 and 27 for the examples.

[164] One or two hearths = 7 widows (only one of whom had a single hearth); three or four hearths = 12 widows; five or six hearths = 7 widows; seven or more hearths = 5 widows.

[165] One or two hearths = 94 widows (equally divided); three or four hearths = 25 widows; five or six hearths = 6 widows; seven hearths = 2 widows.

[166] H. Hartopp, ed., *Leicester and its Inhabitants in 1664* (Leicester: Clarke & Satchell, 1912).

[167] Meekings, Porter and Roy, *Hearth Tax Collectors' Book for Worcester*.

[168] For the use of forms of address rather than names to separate off familiarity and respect – but in an entirely different context – Cohen, *Self-Consciousness*, 74-5; for social distance, I. Thomas, *Meaning in Interaction. An Introduction to Pragmatics* (Harlow: Longman, 1995), 128-30.

[169] Doree, *Parish Registers and Tithing Book*, 84.

[170] W. H. Stevenson, ed., *Records of the Borough of Nottingham* IV (Nottingham: Nottingham Corporation, 1889), 221.

[171] Foster, *Parish Registers of Gainsborough*, 152, 155, 161, 163.

[172] R. P. Crawford, ed., *The Parish Registers of East Grinstead, Sussex, 1558-1661*, SxRS vol. 24 (1917), 135-6, 138-9, 145, 147-50, 155-6.

[173] J. H. Parry, ed., *The Registers of Bishop's Cannings* (Devizes: Gazette Printing Works, 1906), 2-4, 6.

[174] *Shotely Registers*, Suffolk Green Books vol. 16 pt. 1 (Bury Saint Edmunds, 1911), 108-9, 113, 115, 118, 120, 146.

[175] H. Gibbs, ed., *The Parish Registers of Hunsden, co. Hertford, 1546-1837* (London: Saint Catherine's Press, 1915), 65, 73, 74, 75, 76, 77, 80.

[176] Gibbs, *Parish Registers of Hunsden*, 65, 75, 77.

[177] Crawfurd, *Registers of the Parish of St Mary, Reading, Berkshire* II: 95, 97, 103-4, 106-7.

[178] Penfold, *Parish Registers of Haslemere*, 83. Mother Steere had been buried there in 1587: p. 66.

[179] W. Holland and J. J. Raven, eds., *Cratfield. A Transcript of the Accounts of the Parish from A.D. 1490 to A.D. 1642* (London: Jarrold, [1895]), 104, 123 (1578, 1596).

[180] Richard Savage, ed., *Minutes and Accounts of the Corporation of Stratford-upon-Avon & Other Records 1553-1620 Volume I 1563-1566*, DS vol. 1 (1921), 120.

[181] Savage, *Minutes and Accounts* I: 127.

[182] Richard Savage, ed., *Minutes and Accounts of the Corporation of Stratford-upon-Avon & Other Records 1553-1620 Volume II 1566-1577*, DS vol. 3 (1924), 67, 74.

[183] Richard Savage, ed., *Minutes and Accounts of the Corporation of Stratford-upon-Avon & Other Records 1553-1620 Volume III 1577-1586*, DS vol. 5 (1926), 133; Fox, *Minutes and Accounts of the Corporation of Stratford-upon-Avon V*, 5, 18.

[184] Fox, *Minutes and Accounts of the Corporation of Stratford-upon-Avon V*, 95.

[185] Littlehales, *Medieval Records of a London City Church*, 398, 407 (1554-7).

[186] Doree, *Early Churchwardens' Accounts of Bishop's Stortford*, 163, 176, 181, 193, 198.

[187] J. Webb, ed., *Poor Relief in Elizabethan Ipswich*, SfRS vol. 9 (1966), 127, 135-6; we might also note in the context of 'old' above, Old Frize, impotent, aged 80, formerly a cobbler, whose wife was aged 60: p. 124.

[188] Webb, *Poor Relief in Elizabethan Ipswich*, 23.

[189] Webb, *Poor Relief in Elizabethan Ipswich*, 37, 49, 102-4.

[190] H. Falvey and S. Hindle, eds., *"This Little Commonwealth." Layston Parish Memoranda Book, 1607-c.1650 and 1704-c.1747*, HRS vol. 19 (2003), 30-8, 41-3.

[191] Emmison, ed., *Wills of the County of Essex*, I: 27 (79), 37 (111); idem, *Wills of the County of Essex*, II: 85 (316).

[192] Emmison, *Wills of the County of Essex*, I: 42 (128).

[193] Emmison, *Wills of the County of Essex*, I: 179 (582).

[194] Emmison, *Wills of the County of Essex*, I: 79 (250).

[195] Emmison, *Wills of the County of Essex*, I: 84 (266), 86 (276).

[196] Emmison, *Wills of the County of Essex*, I: 118-19; this William Evartson made provision for four widows as well.

[197] Emmison, *Wills of the County of Essex* I: 173 (563), 175 (568).

[198] F. G. Emmison, ed., *Wills of the County of Essex (England) Volume III 1571-1577* (Boston: New England Historic Genealogical Society, 1986), 8 (18).

[199] Emmison, *Wills of the County of Essex*, II: 214 (749).

[200] Emmison, *Wills of the County of Essex*, II: 152 (549).

[201] Emmison, *Wills of the County of Essex*, II: 198 (689); Father Pigion and old Father Banke benefited from another will, each to the tune of 2s.: idem, *Wills of the County of Essex*, II: 163 (582) (1567).

[202] Emmison, *Wills of the County of Essex*, III: 347 (816).

[203] Emmison, *Wills of the County of Essex*, III: 256 (603).

[204] Emmison, *Wills of the County of Essex*, III: 386 (902).

[205] Emmison, *Wills of the County of Essex*, III: 5 (10).

[206] Emmison, *Wills of the County of Essex*, II: 198 (689). Father Pigion and old Father Banke also benefited from a will, receiving 2s. each: idem, *Wills of the County of Essex*, II: 163 (582) (1567).

[207] Emmison, *Wills of the County of Essex*, I: 114 (370).

[208] Emmison, *Wills of the County of* Essex, I: 235.

[209] Emmison, *Wills of the County of Essex*, I: 130-2 (325).

[210] Emmison, *Wills of the County of Essex*, I: 118 (381).

[211] Emmison, *Wills of the County of Essex*, I: 57 (174).

[212] Holland and Raven, *Cratfield*, 127, 130.

[213] W. H. Turner, ed., *Selections from the Records of the City of Oxford* (Oxford: Oxford University Press, 1880), 105.

[214] Holland and Raven, *Cratfield*, 152. Another Mother, Mother Swaine, died in Cratfield in 1599: p. 128.

[215] A. Finn, ed., *Records of Lydd* (no place of publication: s.n., 1911), 363.

[216] A. Palmer, ed., *Tudor Churchwardens' Accounts*, HRS vol. 1 (1985), 112, 116, 119, 124, 160. Mother Gray was also described as Widow Gray and Goodwife Gray, revealing overlapping categories: pp. 147, 158, 159,162.

[217] Statham, *Accounts of the Feoffees*.

[218] Statham, *Accounts of the Feoffees*, 115, 119, 127-8, 165, 240, 278.

[219] Statham, *Accounts of the Feoffees*, pp. 96, 98, 248, 253, 257, 278

[220] W. Rye, ed., *Depositions Taken before the Mayor and Aldermen of Norwich 1549-1567* (Norwich: Norfolk and Norwich Archaeological Society, 1905), 85.

[221] F. Collins, ed., *The Registers of St Michael le Belfry, York*, YPRS vol. 1 (1899), 21, 25.

[222] NNRO NCR Case 12a/1c, fol. 86r.

[223] Bettey, *Correspondence of the Smyth Family*, 113 (248).

[224] *The Witch of Edmonton* (Corbin and Sedge), 61, Act 2, scene i.

[225] John F. Pound, ed., *The Norwich Census of the Poor 1570*, NRS vol. 4 (1971), 77, 34.

[226] C. W. Foster, ed., *The Parish Registers of St Margaret in the Close of Lincoln, 1538-1837*, LRS P. R. Section vol. 2 (1915), 58.

[227] J. E. Foster, ed., *Churchwardens' Accounts of St. Mary the Great, Cambridge, from 1504 to 1635*, Cambridge Antiquarian Society (Cambridge, 1905), 340-1.

[228] P. Northeast, ed., *Boxford Churchwardens' Accounts 1530-1561*, SfRS vol. 23 (1982), 52-3, 63, 65.

[229] Statham, *Accounts of the Feoffees*, 104.

[230] Statham, *Accounts of the Feoffees*, 72.

[231] Statham, *Accounts of the Feoffees*, 179.

[232] Statham, *Accounts of the Feoffees*, 179.

[233] W. Stephenson, *Gammer Gurton's Needle* (1562x1575), Act II, scene i, l. 281 (Mother), Act IV, scene ii, ll. 814, 856 (Mother), Act V, scene ii, ll. 1146, 1222, 1268 (Goodwife).

[234] For honor of both men and women inter-relatedly, Shepard, *Meanings of Manhood*, 186-213.

[235] Foster, *Parish Registers of Gainsborough*, 156.

[236] Crawfurd, *Registers of the Parish of St Mary, Reading*, 97, 106.

[237] G. W. Marshall, ed., *The Registers of Worksop* (Guildford: Billing, 1894), 109.

[238] Smith, *Parish Registers of Richmond*, 161-2.

[239] Holland and Raven, *Cratfield*, 105.

[240] Finn, *Records of Lydd*, 354.

[241] *Registers of St Mary's, Shrewsbury*, 31, 33, 49, 55.

[242] Littlehales, *Medieval Records of a London City Church*, 360.

[243] Headlam, *Registers of St Oswald's, Durham*, 53.

[244] Headlam, *Registers of St Oswald's, Durham*, 29, 33, 49, 55, and further examples of the relationship at pp. 56-7, 63, 71, 81.

[245] *Jacke Jugler*, ll. 142-3.

[246] Emmison, *Wills of the County of Essex*, I: 48 (147).

[247] Emmison, *Wills of the County of Essex*, I: 78 (248).

[248] Emmison, *Wills of the County of Essex*, I: 178 (581).

[249] Emmison, *Wills of the County of Essex*, I: 299.

[250] Emmison, *Wills of the County of Essex*, II: 96 (357).

[251] Emmison, *Wills of the County of Essex*, II: 189 (671).

[252] NNRO NCR Case 12a/1c, fol. 53r.

[253] In one of his letters, indeed, Sir Thomas Gorges referred to his wife as "my old Dame": Bettey, *Correspondence of the Smyth Family*, 112 (246).

[254] Thomas Dekker, *The Shoemaker's Holiday*, scene x, ll. 21-3.

[255] *Registers of St Mary, Shrewsbury*, 49, 55 (1614).

[256] Crawfurd, *Registers of the Parish of St Mary, Reading*, 98, 100.

[257] Guilding, ed., *Reading Records*, III: 70.

[258] Crawfurd, *Registers of the Parish of St Mary, Reading*, 105, 106, 107.

[259] Headlam, *Registers of St Oswald's, Durham*, 77, 81.

[260] Turner, *Selections from the Records of the City of Oxford*, 189-90.

[261] Stephenson, *Records of the Borough of Nottingham* IV: 202-10 correlated with pp. 419-20.

[262] Savage, *Minutes and Accounts I*, 130-2, 135-7, 141-7; Savage, *Minutes and Accounts II*, 1-2, 4, 28, 32, 37-8, 88; Savage, *Minutes and Accounts III*, 34-5.

[263] Anthony Nott and Joan Hasler, eds., *Wells Convocation Acts Books 1589-1665. Part I: 1589-1629*, SRS vol. 90 (2004), 225, 231.

[264] Nott and Hasler, *Wells Convocation Acts Books*, 308-11.

[265] J. P. Earwaker, ed., *The Court Leet Records of the Manor of Manchester* II (Manchester: Blacklock, 1885), 61, 67, 232, 258, 260, 269, 278, 290, 300, 302, 309, 325; III (Manchester: Blacklock, 1886), 14, 22, 42, 51, 56, 65, 68, 76, 82, 96, 112, 118, 127, 133, 140, for example.

[266] N. Udall, *Roister Doister* (1566), Act III, scene iii, ll. 922, 1044; Act IV, scene vii, ll. 1726, 1744; Act V, scene vi, ll. 1962, 1993.

[267] Smith and Baker, *Papers of Nathaniel Bacon III*, 311.

[268] Doree, *Parish Registers and Tithing Book*, 116.

[269] Doree, *Parish Registers and Tithing Book*, 79.

[270] Collins, *Registers of St Michael le Belfry*, 84-170

[271] *The Witch of Edmonton* Act 1 scene ii (Corbin and Sedge, pp. 38-9).

[272] Nott and Hasler, *Wells Convocation Acts Books*, 167; S. Bond, ed., *The Chamber Order Book of Worcester 1602-1650*, WHS n.s. vol. 8 (1974), 170.

[273] Sir Thomas Smith, *De Republica Anglorum* ed. M. Dewar (Cambridge: Cambridge University Press, 1982), 74.

[274] G. Chapman, B. Jonson and J. Marston, *Eastward Ho!* Act 1, scene i, ll. 90-2.

[275] W. H. Godfrey (and R. G. Rice), ed., *Transcripts of Sussex Wills* III, SxRS vol. 43 (1938), 8.

[276] But note, however, in the burial registers for Richmond (Surrey) were included twelve females styled as Goodwife, although only two men considered as Goodman: Smith, *Parish Registers of Richmond*, 161-96 – for example, pp. 161, 163.

[277] Holland and Raven, *Cratfield*, 101.

[278] Holland and Raven, *Cratfield*, 60.

[279] Holland and Raven, *Cratfield*, 123, 125-7.

[280] J. E. Stocks *et al.*, eds., *Market Harborough Parish Records* (London: Elliott Stock, 1926), 54, 59.

[281] Stocks, *Market Harborough Parish Records*, 63, 78.

[282] Stocks, *Market Harborough Parish Records*, 64. Note also the payments to Goodwife Cutler, Goodman Alsop's man, Goodman Wright, and Goodman Horne: pp. 53, 63-4, 83.

[283] Foster, *Churchwardens' Accounts of St. Mary the Great*, 337-41.

[284] Smith and Baker, *Papers of Nathaniel Bacon III*, 138.

[285] F. W. Weaver and G. N. Clark, eds., *Churchwardens' Accounts of Marston, Spelsbury, Pyrton*, ORS vol. 6 (1925), 70, 76.

[286] Weaver and Clark, *Churchwardens' Accounts of Marston*, 83.

[287] Finn, *Records of Lydd*, 341, 343, 367.

[288] Finn, *Records of Lydd*, 361.

[289] Finn, *Records of Lydd*, 343.

[290] Littlehales, *Medieval Records of a London City Church*, 259-60.

[291] Littlehales, *Medieval Records of a London City Church*, 278.

[292] Littlehales, *Medieval Records of a London City Church*, 359.

[293] Littlehales, *Medieval Records of a London City Church*, 301, 303, 306, 310, 370, 395.

[294] C. Burgess, ed., *The Church Records of St Andrew Hubbard Cheapside c.1450-c.1570*, London Record Society vol. 34 (London,1999), 125, 130, 160, 168-9.

[295] Emmison, *Wills of the County of Essex*, I: 6 (17).

[296] Emmison, *Wills of the County of Essex*, I: 4 (10).

[297] Emmison, *Wills of the County of Essex*, I: 41 (126).

[298] Emmison, *Wills of the County of Essex*, I:. 73 (230), 79 (250), 118 (379), 134 (434), 166 (534), 170 (550); II: 150 (544).

[299] Emmison, *Wills of the County of Essex*, II: 72 (261) (1569), 167 (596).

[300] Emmison, *Wills of the County of Essex*, II: 136 (497).

[301] Emmison, *Wills of the County of Essex*, I: 149 (477).

[302] Emmison, *Wills of the County of Essex*, I: 70 (218).

[303] Emmison, *Wills of the County of Essex*, I: 89 (285).

[304] Emmison, *Wills of the County of Essex*, I: 192 (630).

[305] C. Jackson, ed., *Newbury Kendrick Workhouse Records, 1627-1641*, BerksRS vol. 8 (2004), passim.

[306] Nesta Evans, ed., *Wills of the Archdeaconry of Sudbury*, SfRS vol. 35 (1993), 70 (157).

[307] H. J. Moule, ed., *Descriptive Catalogue of the Charters, Minute Books and other Documents of the Borough of Weymouth and Melcombe Regis* (Weymouth: Sherren, 1883), 65.

[308] Guilding, *Reading Records*, III: 315, 348 438, 447.

[309] This point was made to me by Henry French at the Economic History Society annual conference in Leicester in April 2005.

[310] Pound *et al.*, *Norfolk Hearth Tax Exemption Certificates*, 1-159.

[311] Pound *et al.*, *Norfolk Hearth Tax Exemption Certificates*, 166-93. There were merely two occurrences in King's Lynn: pp. 216, 230.

[312] Nesta Evans, ed., *Cambridgeshire Hearth Tax Returns Michaelmas 1664*, CRS vol.

15 (2000), 181.

[313] *Suffolk in 1674*, Suffolk Green Books vol. 13, no. xi, (1905), vi (estimated heads of household), 2, 8, 9, 10, 32, 38, 44, 46, 50, 65, 104, 79, 101, 104, 105, 107, 110, 111, 124, 132, 133, 142, 150, 151, 155, 163, 172, 184, 206, 209, 216, 222, 223, 225, 229, 237, 238, 239, 240, 245, 258, 265, 266, 267, 268, 271, 281, 282, 286, 299, 301, 303, 304, 305, 309, 311, 314, 317, 321.

[314] This figure is derived by dividing the estimated number of households by the estimated total hearths: *Suffolk in 1674*, p. vi.

[315] *Suffolk in 1674*, 151, 236, 258.

[316] Harrington, *Kent Hearth Tax Assessment*, 5, 11, 13, 14, 35, 39, 43, 44, 49, 61, 63, 66, 80, 85, 95, 125, 128, 134, 143, 151, 172, 173, 231, 248, 278, 293, 320, 321, 364, 371, 378, 380, 381, 382, 405, 406, 408, 414, 421, 422; Hughes and White, *Hampshire Hearth Tax Assessment, 1665*, 45, 98, 103, 112, 116, 121, 124, 130, 153.

[317] Edwards, *Derbyshire Hearth Tax Assessments 1662-1670*; Bourne and Goode, *Rutland Hearth Tax 1665* (Goodlad at p. 17 looks like a forename); Meekings, *Dorset Hearth Tax*; the returns for the City of Worcester are also devoid of the titles: C. A. F. Meekings, S. Porter and I. Roy, eds., *The Hearth Tax Collectors' Book for Worcester 1678-1680* WHS n.s. vol. 11 (1983); Watkins-Pitchford, *Shropshire Hearth Tax Roll*,

[318] Webster, *Nottinghamshire Hearth Tax*, 15, 21.

[319] "Hearth tax return 1671," *Bedfordshire Historical Record Society* vol. 16 (Bedford, 1934), 65, 98 at pp. 96, 102.

[320] Weinstock, *Hearth Tax Returns, 1665*, 128.

[321] For Widow and surname, see above.

[322] At p. 4.

[323] W. Rye, ed., *The Norwich Rate Book* (London, 1903).

[324] Rye, *Norwich Rate Book*, 16.

[325] Foster, *Churchwardens' Accounts of St. Mary the Great*.

[326] Foster, *Churchwardens' Accounts of St. Mary the Great*, 363-96: a purposive sample of continuous accounts.

[327] H. R. Plomer, ed., *The Churchwardens' Accounts of St Nicholas, Strood*, KR vol. 5 (1915), pp. xiv, 6, 19, 46-7, 51.

[328] Plomer, *Churchwardens' Accounts of ... Strood*, pp. xiv, 27-9.

[329] Plomer, *Churchwardens' Accounts of ... Strood*, 31.

[330] Plomer, *Churchwardens' Accounts of ... Strood*, 83-4.

[331] F. Besant, ed., *The Parish Registers of Boston*, LRS P. R. Section vol. 1 (1914), pp. x, 127, 131, 132, 134, 135.

[332] Smith, *Parish Registers of Richmond* 1: 161-7.

[333] NRO 50P/1.

[334] Savage, *Minutes and Accounts of the Corporation of Stratford-upon-Avon II*, 104; Savage, *Minutes and Accounts of the Corporation of Stratford-upon-Avon III*, 41, 77-8, 133, 135; Fox, *Minutes and Accounts of the Corporation of Stratford-upon-Avon V*, 4, 7.

[335] Savage, *Minutes and Accounts of the Corporation of Stratford-upon-Avon II*, 119.

[336] Savage, *Minutes and Accounts of the Corporation of Stratford-upon-Avon III*, 15, 17, 27, 43.

[337] Savage, *Minutes and Accounts of the Corporation of Stratford-upon-Avon III*, 28.

[338] Savage, *Minutes and Accounts of the Corporation of Stratford-upon-Avon III*, 117.

[339] Savage, *Minutes and Accounts of the Corporation of Stratford-upon-Avon III*, 135.

[340] Fox, *Minutes and Accounts of the Corporation of Stratford-upon-Avon V*, 17 and n. 2.

[341] W. J. Connor, ed., *The Southampton Mayor's Book of 1606-8*, SoRS vol. 21 (1978), 89 (175).

[342] Guilding, *Reading Records*, III: 268, 272, 276, 315.

[343] This social transformation is discussed more fully in the "Conclusion."

Chapter 2

[344] Wrightson, "'Sorts of People'."

[345] At this point, the temptation was resisted to appropriate Michel de Certeau's concept of the "unnamable" by which he intended the "shroud of silence" around death: *The Practice of Everyday Life* trans. Steven Rendall (London: University of California Press, 1988), 191.

[346] *The Register of Munslow*, ShPRS (n.d.), 90 (burial 1649).

[347] Llewellyn Lloyd Simpson, *The Parish Registers of St James' Church, Norton* (Derby, 1908), 386 (the text has been normalized by Simpson): burial, 1594.

[348] I. Gray & J. E. Gethyn-Jones, eds., *The Registers of the Church of St Mary, Dymock*, Bristol & Gloucestershire Archaeological Society Record Series vol. 4 (Gloucester, 1960), 4-5, 8, 10-11, 13-17, 28-9, 45, 48, 53-4, 56-7, 59, 63-5, 81 (burial, 1612).

[349] Gray &Gethyn-Jones, *Registers of St Mary, Dymock*, 86 (burial, 1616).

[350] *Tamworth Parish Registers* I, SPRS (1917), 4 (baptism, 1566).

[351] *Rocester Parish Registers*, SPRS (1906), 30. The most comprehensive account of vagrants is still A. L. Beier, *Masterless Men. The Vagrancy Problem in England, 1560-1640* (London: Methuen, 1985).

[352] Griffiths, *Household Book*, 413 (1547).

[353] *Parish Registers of Skipton-in-Craven*, 161.

[354] Howard S. Becker, *Outsiders. Studies in Sociology of Deviance*, rev. ed. (London: Simon and Schuster, 1996) – the revised edn. is important for Becker's response to his critics; here it is not so much the labeling as the ignorance of and failure to investigate names that confirms the status of actual and figurative outsiders – and the apparently untroubled acceptance of their anonymity.

[355] W. J. Kaye, ed., *The Parish Registers of Ripon* I, YPRS vol. 80 (1926), 36.

[356] *Parish Registers of Skipton-in-Craven*, 38 (1604); Kaye, *Parish Registers of Ripon* I: 31.

[357] *The Registers of Bishop Middleham*, 146, 147, 153, 155 (1597, 1624, 1632).

[358] *Parish Registers of Skipton-in-Craven*, 131-64.

[359] *Parish Registers of Skipton-in-Craven*, 134.

[360] H. Fishwick, ed., *Registers of the Parish Church of Croston*, LPRS vol. 6 (1900), 202, 208-10, 212, 219-20.

[361] H. Brierley, *The Registers of Brough under Stainmore* I, CWPRS (1923), 149, 156, 158 (1587-1600).

[362] H. Brierley, ed., *The Registers of the Parish Church of Lancaster*, LPRS vol. 32 (1908), 238.

[363] Brierley, *Registers of the Parish Church of Blackburn*, 170, 210, 213.

[364] Brierley, *Registers of the Parish Church of Blackburn*, 186, 193, 210.

[365] Brierley, *Registers of the Parish Church of Blackburn*, 172 (*Thomas Todd ignotus pauper qui moriebatur in domo Jacobi Marseden de Tockehoales* – "Thomas Todd an unknown poor man who died in the house of James Marseden of Tockholes") (1624).

[366] Brierley, *Registers of the Parish Church of Blackburn*, 162-5, 169, 171, 182: *ignota quaedam mulier pauperima ...; ignota quaedam paupercula ...; ignotus pauperculus ...; pauperculus ignotus ...; ignotus pauper ...; mulier quaedam decrepita et ignota...* (1623-8). The employment of *ignotus/ignota* might suggest that some were travelers, but compare the earlier entries for "a poore man that was killed" and "a poore woman," cryptically entered in 1614 and 1616 in the vernacular: pp. 144, 147.

[367] Brierley, *Registers of Brough*, 139, 140, 141, 156. (1569-97).

[368] J. F. Harwell, ed., *The Registers of Lowther*, CWPRS (1933), 128-9.

[369] F. Collins, ed., *Registers of Farnham*, LPRS vol. 56 (1905), 67, 73.

[370] H. Brierley, ed., *Parish Registers of Garstang Church 1567-1658*, LPRS vol. 63 (1925), 116, 130. 137, 142, 144, 151-3, 166, 182.

[371] Brierley, *Parish Registers of Garstang Church*, I: 149-50, 153, 181-3.

[372] Brierley, *Parish Registers of Garstang Church*, I: 137, 142, 151-2, 154, 156, 165, 176-8,180-4,196-7.

[373] Brierley, *Parish Registers of Garstang Church*, I: 30, 33, 56.

[374] Brierley, *Parish Registers of Garstang Church*, I: 190.

[375] J. Arrowsmith, *The Registers of the Parish of Ormskirk 1557-1626*, LPRS vol. 13 (1902), 43.

[376] Arrowsmith, *Registers of the Parish of Ormskirk*, 140, 196.

[377] NRO 46P-204 (not foliated or paginated: 15 November).

[378] Pound, *Norwich Census of the Poor*, 77.

[379] D. H. G. Salt, ed., *Staffordshire Quarter Sessions Rolls Easter 1608-Trinity 1609* CHS (1950 for 1948-9), 9.

[380] Brierley, *Registers of the Parish Church of Lancaster*, 183, 208-10.

[381] E. Axon, ed., *Registers of the Cathedral Church of Manchester*, LPRS vol. 31 (1908), 281 and 287. For other poor men and poor women, some specifically aged, others explicitly crippled, pp. 231, 249, 252, 260-1, 281, 287, 292-3, 311-13, 317 (to 1598).

[382] W. Brigg, ed., *The Parish Registers of St Albans Abbey 1558-1689* (Harpenden: William Brigg, 1897), 178, 180, 181, 183, 188, 189, 190, 191.

[383] Brigg, *Parish Registers of St Albans*, 178.

[384] Maslen, *Woodstock Chamberlains' Accounts*, 135.

[385] Doree, *Early Churchwardens' Accounts of Bishop's Stortford*, 263, 278, 289, 310, 315.

[386] Earwaker, *Court Leet Records of Manchester* II, 257: perhaps with sexual innuendo.

[387] *Registers of St Mary's, Shrewsbury*, 7.

[388] *Register of St Mary's, Shrewsbury*, 32.

[389] *Register of St Mary's, Shrewsbury*, 75, 59 (1628 and 1631): one perhaps subjected to the *peine forte et dure* and the child a consequence of a plea of the belly. For plea of belly, Cynthia Herrup, *The Common Peace. Participation and the Criminal Law in Seventeenth-century England* (Cambridge: Cambridge University Press, 1987), 143 n. 16.

[390] *Registers of St Mary's, Shrewsbury*, 7, 18, 40, 75, 79.

[391] *Registers of St Mary's, Shrewsbury*, 24, 89.

[392] Crawfurd, *Registers of the Parish of St Mary, Reading*, 97.

[393] H. M. Wood, ed., *Registers of St Mary-le-Bow*, DNPRS vol. 27 (1912), 119-21, 125, 130.

[394] Crawfurd, *Registers of the Parish of St Mary, Reading*, p. 106.

[395] Peacock, *Registers of Bishop Middleham*, 145, 148.

[396] Kaye, *Parish Registers of Ripon*, I: 41.

[397] *Registers of St Mary's, Shrewsbury*, 33, 39, 44, 47. See also the burial of "Joane a maide" in 1638: *The Register of Selattyn*, ShPRS (n.d.), 115.

[398] W. Headlam, *Parish Registers of St Oswald's, Durham*, 46.

[399] NRO 46P-204 (not foliated or paginated – 20 December).

[400] Doree, *Parish Registers and Tithing Book*, 35, 46 (1634), although he himself succumbed to the anonymous recording of strangers: pp. 4, 9, 12, 14, but early in his incumbency.

[401] Doree, *Parish Registers and Tithing Book*, 16; see also the similar entries at pp. 15, 16, 18 (1609-1612).

[402] *Tamworth Parish Registers*, I: 2, 15, 16, 31, 94, 96, 107, 111, 118, 122, 125, 128, 129, 130-2, 136, 138, 141, 161, 163-4, 177, 213, 227, 238, for the full proliferation of entries – over three dozen between 1560 and 1614.

[403] Headlam, *Parish Registers of St Oswald's, Durham*, 23, 28, 30, 33, 38, 41, 51, 56, 66-9.

[404] Guilding, *Reading Records*, III: 56, 95.

[405] Emmison, *Wills of the County of Essex*, III: 150 (367).

[406] E. H. Bates, ed., *Quarter Sessions Records for the County of Somerset Volume 1*, SRS vol. 23 (1907), 216 (6).

[407] Kathleen L. Wood-Legh, ed., *Kentish Visitations of Archbishop Warham and his Deputies 1511-12*, KR vol. 24 (1984), 105.

[408] Smith and Baker, *The Papers of Nathaniel Bacon III*, 285.

[409] R. G. Rice, ed., *West Sussex Protestation Returns 1641-2*, SxRS vol. 5 (1906 for 1905), 187.

[410] The episode of childbirth and designating the father is explored by Laura Gowing, *Common Bodies. Women, Touch and Power in Seventeenth-century England* (New Haven: Yale University Press, 2003), 158-67. For midwives extracting the name of a father: "she did charge Ellen in the name of God to declare who was the father of her child" (1640): *Quarter Sessions Records, with Other Records of the Justices of the Peace for the County Palatine of Chester, 1559-1760* ... compiled and edited by J. H. E. Bennett and J. C. Dewhurst, RSLC vol. 94 (1940), 99; "Symon the base sonne of Symon Clare gent. as the midwief sayth upon the confession of the Mother" (1567): *The Registers of Munslow*, ShPRS (n.d.), 37; also at p. 17 in Latin *Simon spurius (ut ostetrix ex affirmacione matris eius asseruit) Simonis Clare* ("Simon a bastard son of Simon Clare as the midwife asserts from his mother's infirmation") (1567).

[411] Gowing, *Common Bodies*, 175 ff. refers to the lowering of the rate of illegitimacy as the seventeenth century progressed; the level had been higher in the late sixteenth and very early seventeenth century: Peter Laslett, Karla Oosterveen and Richard M. Smith, eds., *Bastardy and its Comparative History. Studies in the History of Illegitimacy and Marital Nonconformism in Britain, France, Germany, Sweden, North America, Jamaica and Japan* (London: Edward Arnold, 1980), 1-247 is still the most

170   Notes to Chapter 2

comprehensive analysis; at pp. 217-39, Peter Laslett, "The bastardy prone sub-society"; with reference to this present examination, Hawkshead and Rochdale, both in Lancashire, were considered at pp. 94-120 and 185-6.

[412] Richard M. Smith, "Marriage Processes in the English Past: Some Continuities," in *The World We Have Gained*, ed. Lloyd Bonfield, Smith and Keith Wrightson (Oxford: Blackwell Publishing, 1986), 43-99.

[413] Generally, Keith Wrightson, "The Politics of the Parish in Early Modern England," in *The Experience of Authority in Early Modern England*, ed. Paul Griffiths, Adam Fox and Steve Hindle (Basingstoke: The Macmillan Press, 1996), 10-46.

[414] Generally now, Richard Adair, *Courtship, Illegitimacy and Marriage in Early Modern England* (Manchester: Manchester University Press, 1996).

[415] A. Wrigley & T. H. Winder, eds., *The Registers of the Parish Church of Whittington*, LPRS vol. 3 (1899), 2, 4, 6, 8-9, 11, 13-14, 18-19, 21-22, 24-26, and 28 (twenty-one baptisms); the change occurs to a more neutral protocol at p. 31: *x* son or daughter of Joe Bloggs and Jane Doe.

[416] J. Perkins, ed., *The Registers of St Mary Magdalene, Clitheroe, 1570-1680*, LPRS vol. 144 (1998), at p. 2 for Preestley. It is apparent that rates of illegitimacy differed locally; at Aughton, for example, eleven percent of children baptised were illegitimate, that is, fifty-five out of 505: F. Taylor, ed., *The Parish Registers of Aughton*, LPRS vol. 81 (1942).

[417] J. Perkins, *The Register of the Parish of Prescot*, LPRS vol. 137 (1995).

[418] Taylor, *Parish Registers of Aughton*, 28-52; cases have been discounted where an *alias* was employed but the child not specified as illegitimate, so the rate for *alias*es might be slightly higher.

[419] J. Arrowsmith, ed., *The Registers of the Parish of Ormskirk*, Pt. 1, LPRS vol. 13 (1902), 6-84 for the following information.

[420] Arrowsmith, *The Registers of the Parish of Ormskirk*, 1: 52.

[421] T. Williams, ed., *The Registers of the Parish Church of Ormskirk* Pt. II *1626-1678*, LPRS vol. 98 (1960), 1-59.

[422] For the politics of poor relief, see now Steve Hindle, *On the Parish? The Micropolitics of Poor Relief in Rural England c.1550-1750* (Oxford: Oxford University Press, 2004).

[423] J. F. Haswell, ed., *The Registers of Lowther*, CWPRS (1933),

[424] M. E. Noble, ed., *The Registers of the Parish of Shap* (Kendal: Titus Wilson, 1912), 18, 19, 20, 22, 36, 37, 39, 40, 45, 46, 53, 143, 144, 148.

[425] J. F. Haswell, ed., *Registers of Crosthwaite-cum-Lyth* (Penrith: Herald Printing Co., 1935), 6, 7, 9, 11, 14, 15, 16, 19, 27, 30.

[426] Headlam, *Parish Registers of St Oswald's, Durham*, 40, 42.

[427] Headlam, *Parish Registers of St Oswald's, Durham*, 42.

[428] Headlam, *Parish Registers of St Oswald's, Durham*, 42-4, 46, 49-53, 55, 61-2, 64, 66, 71, 74-5, 79, 87, 90, 92-3.

[429] Crawfurd, *Registers of the Parish of St Mary, Reading* II: 4, 9, 14, 27-8.

[430] LeHardy, *Calendar of Middlesex Quarter Sessions*, I: 263 (1615).

[431] N. W. Tildesley, ed., *Penkridge Parish Register*, SPRS (1945-6), 103.

[432] P. W. L. Adams, ed., *Gnosall Parish Register*, SPRS (1922), 47.

[433] F. J. Wrottesley, ed., *Eccleshall Parish Registers* vol. 1, SPRS (1907).

[434] *Eccleshall Parish Registers*, 8.

[435] *Eccleshall Parish Registers*, 51, except for one *alias* in 1610 and another in 1612: pp. 54, and (a burial) 131.

[436] Kaye, *Parish Registers of Ripon*, I: 51-3, 57, 62, 64, 67-9, 119, 122, 124.

[437] Simpson, *Parish Registers of St James' Church, Norton*, 389, 391.

[438] E. Axon, *Manchester Sessions* I, RSLC vol. 20 (1901), 180-1.

[439] Bates, *Quarter Sessions Records*, I: 218 (16).

[440] Gray & Gethyn-Jones, *Registers of the Church of St Mary, Dymock*, 4-5, 8, 10-11, 13-17, 28-9, 45, 48, 53-4, 56-7, 59, 63-5.

[441] Tildesley, *Penkridge Parish Register*, 6.

[442] Tildesley, *Penkridge Parish Register*, 14.

[443] Tildesley, *Penkridge Parish Register*, 21.

[444] H. R. Thomas, *Pattingham Parish Regsters*, SPRS (1934), 31-4, 36-7, 40.

[445] Thomas, *Pattingham Parish Registers*, 42.

[446] One complication is the occasional pressure brought to bear on young women not to name a father or to mislead about the father's identity: Morgan, Key and Taylor, *Papers of Nathaniel Bacon Volume IV*, 70 is an example.

[447] Doree, *Parish Registers and Tithing Book*, 46 (1634).

[448] J. F. Williams, ed., *Bishop Redman's Visitation 1597. Presentments in the Archdeaconries of Norwich, Norfolk and Suffolk*, NRS vol. 18 (1946), 151.

[449] Goffman is again valuable: Erving Goffman, *Stigma. Notes on the Management of Spoiled Identity* (New Jersey: Prentice-Hall Inc., 1963), spoiled identity being a fabulous description in these cases of bastardy.

[450] D. G. Edwards, ed., *Derbyshire Wills Proved in the Prerogative Court of Canterbury 1575-1601*, DRS vol. 31 (2003), 107 (177).

[451] W. T. LeHardy, ed., *Hertford County Records Sessions Rolls 1581-1698* vol. 1 (Hertford: Hertfordshire County Council, 1905), 87.

[452] LeHardy, *Hertford County Records Sessions Rolls*, 1: 2-3.

[453] P. Slack, ed., *Poverty in Early-Stuart Salisbury*, WRS vol. 31 (1975), 37, for example.

[454] Slack, *Poverty in Early-Stuart Salisbury*, 29.

[455] ERO Q/SR 101/49, 49a.

[456] S. Burne, ed., *The Staffordshire Quarter Sessions Rolls* volume III *1594-1597* CHS (1933 for 1932), 101.

[457] J. C. Atkinson, ed., *Quarter Sessions Records* vol. III, NRRS vol. 3 (1885), 115.

[458] R. Stewart-Brown, ed., *Lancashire and Cheshire Cases in the Star Chamber Part 1*, RSLC vol. 21 (1916), 17.

[459] S. Wilson, *The Means of Naming. A Social and Cultural History of Personal Naming in the West* (London: UCL Press, 1998) addresses the *alias* sporadically and insubstantially at pp. 249, 258, 282 and 311.

[460] W. T. LeHardy, ed., *Calendar of Middlesex Quarter Sessions* n.s. II, *1614-1615* (Hertford: Hertfordshire County Council, 1936), 304. My principle here is whether the original document uses the term *alias* to denote the alternative surname or the nickname. In general, see also Goffman, *Stigma*, 77. How the two might be associated in a linguistic sense can be deduced from George Lakoff & Mark Johnson, *Metaphors We Live By* (Chicago and London: University of Chicago Press, 1980), chap. 8 ("Metonymy").

[461] A. A. Hartman, "Criminal Aliases: a Psychological Study," *Journal of Psychol-*

ogy 32 (1951): 49-56 (in this more contemporary research, *aliases* were much more extensive than the historical sources divulge); David Hey, *Family Names and Family History* (London: Hambledon, 2000), 87-8 citing the work of George Redmonds; Redmonds, *Surnames and Genealogy. A New Approach* (Boston, Mass.: New England Historic Genealogical Society, 1997) concentrates on the evidence of *aliases* for linkages between kinship groups.

[462] D. H. G. Salt, ed., *Staffordshire Quarter Sessions Rolls Easter 1608-Trinity 1609 CHS* (1950 for 1948-9), 8, 11, 13, 14, 43.

[463] Here, I use the "self" in a non-technical sense by comparison with the definition in C. Taylor, *Sources of the Self. The Making of Modern Identity* (Cambridge: Cambridge University Press, 1989), 32-6. For the sociology of the problem of the self, Anthony Elliott, *Concepts of the Self* (Cambridge: Polity, 2001).

[464] Edwin Brezette DeWindt, *The Liber Gersumarum of Ramsey Abbey: a Calendar and Index of B.L. Harley MS 445* (Subsidia Mediaevalia 7, Toronto: Toronto University Press, 1976).

[465] DeWindt, *Liber Gersumarum*, 333 (3953), 369 (4331).

[466] DeWindt, *Liber Gersumarum*, passim (well over one hundred instances).

[467] Margery M. Rowe & Andrew M. Jackson, eds., *Exeter Freemen 1266-1967*, Devon & Cornwall Record Society Extra Series vol. 1 (Exeter, 1973), contains numerous examples of apprentices with the same surname as their masters; in many cases these were presumably father and son, but in a few cases the apprentice has an *alias* equivalent to the master's surname.

[468] Philosophically, Judith Butler, *Gender Trouble. Feminism and the Subversion of Identity* (London: Routledge, 1990).

[469] Whilst I ought here to consider questions of subordination, there is insufficient space, but that situational consideration is important for a wider appreciation.

[470] C. H. Mayo, ed., *The Municipal Records of the Borough of Dorchester, Dorset* (Exeter: Pollard, 1908), 210 (266).

[471] Mayo, *Municipal Records of the Borough of Dorchester*, 151 (93).

[472] Mayo, *Municipal Records of the Borough of Dorchester*, 325 (586-7).

[473] Mayo, *Municipal Records of the Borough of Dorchester*, 350-2 (643-6) (1554-60).

[474] Mayo, *Municipal Records of the Borough of Dorchester*, 211 (268).

[475] Mayo, *Municipal Records of the Borough of Dorchester*, 120 (10, 11).

[476] Mayo, *Municipal Records of the Borough of Dorchester*, 184 (194, 195).

[477] Mayo, *Municipal Records of the Borough of Dorchester*, 243 (364). For other references to him: pp. 212-14 (269, 273-5), 224 (306), 225 (308, 309).

[478] Mayo, *Municipal Records of the Borough of Dorchester*, 160 (122), 161 (124), 170 (151), 171 (155), 178 (176), 179 (180), 182 (190), 197 (232), 197 (233), 199 (239), 212 (269), 213 (273), 214 (274), 216 (282), 217 (283), 221 (295), 222 (299), 223-6 (301-3, 306, 308-10), 227 (312), 248 (376), 249 (379), 254 (392), 256 (396), 259 (405-6), 260-1 (409-10), 262 (416), 266 (424), 268 (432), 280 (467), 293 (501), 297 (513), 300 (519), 303 (527), 306 (541), 310 (549), 345 (634), 350-2 (643-6), 355 (654).

[479] Emmison, *Wills of the County of Essex*, I: 51 (155).

[480] J. P. Earwaker, ed., *The Court Leet Records of the Manor of Manchester* II, 29, 33.

[481] Earwaker, *Court Leet Records*, II: 69, 76, 120, 215.

[482] Emmison, *Wills of the County of Essex*, III: 412 (960).

[483] Earwaker, *Court Leet Records*, II: 77, 91.

[484] John M. Bestall and DudleyV. Fowkes, eds., *Chesterfield Wills and Inventories 1604-1650*, DRS vol. 28 (2001), 346 (434).

[485] M. Siraut and A. J. Monday, eds., *Somerset Wills*, SRS vol. 89 (2003), 189.

[486] Brinkworth and Gibson, *Banbury Wills Part 1*, 99 (197).

[487] "Elizabethan Chancery Proceedings, Series II, 1558-1579," *CHS* (1933 for 1931), 201.

[488] Dorothy M. Owen, "White Annays and Others," in *Medieval Women* ed. Derek Baker (Oxford: Blackwell Publishing, 1978), 332 and n. 4. An *alias* was thus not the preserve of males: see further below.

[489] Doree, *Early Churchwardens' Accounts of Bishop's Stortford*, 42, 78, 86.

[490] S. A. H. Burne, ed., *The Staffordshire Quarter Sessions Rolls Volume I 1581-1589*, *CHS* (1931), 115.

[491] One assumes of course, the origin of this concern with Goffman, *Presentation of Self*, preceding the New Historicist contemplation of S. Greenblatt, *Renaissance Self-fashioning: from More to Shakespeare* (Chicago and London: University of Chicago Press, 1980); the issue ensuing from Greenblatt and Charles Taylor (above) for the medievalist, therefore, is what kind of "self" and "consciousness" is being considered. Dignity is employed here merely to denote relative status.

[492] *Calendar of Ancient Deeds* vol. 1 (London: HMSO, 1890), 165.

[493] W. Le Hardy, ed., *Calendar to the Sessions Records 1612-1614*, Middlesex Records n.s. vol. 1 (London, 1935), 36.

[494] For the pressures on the clerk who compiled the bills of accusation, John Beattie, *Crime and the Courts in England, 1660-1800* (Oxford: Oxford University Press, 1986), 333.

[495] Becker, *Outsiders* – in later editions Becker explained how his "labeling" theory has been misconstrued in terms of action/performance.

[496] The most impressive explanation of the context at this time is still Beattie, *Crime and the Courts*, but also more recently the same author's *Policing and Punishment in London, 1660-1750: Urban Crime and the Limits of Terror* (Oxford: Oxford University Press, 2001).

[497] For how this might work, see, most recently, Paul Griffiths, "Overlapping Circles: Imagining Criminal Communities in London, 1545-1645," in *Communities in Early Modern England* ed. Alexandra Shepard and Phil Withington (Manchester: Manchester University Press, 2000): 115-33.

[498] G. E. Weddall, ed., *The Registers of the Parish of Howden Volume I*, YPRS vol. 21 (1904), 196; repeated in 1610 at p. 204.

[499] Griffiths, *Household Book*, 207.

[500] For how language use lubricates the cohesion of social groups, Charlesworth, *Phenomenology of Working Class Experience*, 219-20, especially through forms of initial address or greeting.

[501] Stuart Hall & Tony Jefferson, eds., *Resistance through Rituals. Youth Subcultures in Post-War Britain* (London: Hutchinson, 1975), passim, but especially pp. 13-14 for the definition of sub-cultures and addressing briefly the question of their historical existence, and pp. 54 and 56 for the relationship between argot and "style" through which sub-cultures cohere and are expressed . Although their principal concern is youth sub-cultures, the contributions and the introduction do approach

also the general criteria of sub-cultures.

[502] For a phenomenological and somatic explanation of the language of class, Charlesworth, *Phenomenology of Working Class Experience*, 213-20, 226-7 – language use is unreflexive in this case; by contrast, language use could be reflexively and purposely used to be intelligible only to insiders of marginal groups: R. Jütte, *Poverty and Deviance in Early Modern Europe* (Cambridge: Cambridge University Press, 1994), 178-85; A. L. (Lee) Beier, "Anti-language or Jargon? Canting in the English Underworld in the Sixteenth and Seventeenth Centuries" in *Languages and Jargons. Contributions to a Social History of Language*, ed. Peter Burke and Roy Porter (Cambridge: Polity, 1995), 64-101.

[503] For the semi-public, Goffman, *Behavior in Public Places*; in this sense, an *alias* is a "situational propriety" rather than "situational impropriety" in Goffman's taxonomy, since it conforms to the conventions or norms of the group in contact.

[504] Arrowsmith, *Registers of the Parish of Ormskirk* volume 1, 178; R. Dickinson, ed., *The Register of Winwick Parish Church Part I*, LPRS vol. 109 (1930), 127.

[505] C. M. Fraser, ed., *Durham Quarter Sessions Rolls 1471-1625*, SS vol. 199 (1991), 40.

[506] Fraser, *Durham Quarter Sessions*, 55.

[507] Fraser, *Durham Quarter Sessions*, 71.

[508] Fraser, *Durham Quarter Sessions*, 91, 96.

[509] Fraser, *Durham Quarter Sessions*, 96.

[510] Guilding, *Reading Records*, III: 147-8, 150, 156.

[511] Jeaffreson, *Middlesex County Records*, I: 30.

[512] W. Le Hardy, ed., *Calendar to the Sessions Records New Series* I, 225 (1613).

[513] Le Hardy, *Calendar to the Sessions Records New Series* I: 294, 296.

[514] Jeaffreson, *Middlesex County Records*, I: 203.

[515] Jeaffreson, *Middlesex County Records*, I: 235.

[516] Jeaffreson, *Middlesex County Records*, I: 282.

[517] W. Le Hardy, ed., *Calendar to the Sessions Records New Series* II: 111.

[518] Le Hardy, *Calendar New Series*, II: 159.

[519] Le Hardy, *Calendar New Series*, II: 304.

[520] Le Hardy, *Calendar New Series*, II: 304.

[521] Le Hardy, *Calendar New Series*, I: 389.

[522] Le Hardy, *Calendar New Series*, II: 202.

[523] Le Hardy, *Calendar New Series*, I: 297.

[524] Stavert, *Parish Registers of Skipton*, 151, 160, 161, 163, 164.

[525] Brierley, *Parish Registers of Garstang Church*, I: 69.

[526] Brierley, *Parish Registers of Garstang Church*, I: 182.

[527] *Register of Selattyn*, 92.

[528] *Registers of St Mary's, Shrewsbury*, 62, 66.

[529] Moule, *Descriptive Catalogue … Weymouth and Melcombe Regis*, 71.

[530] *Early Prose and Poetical Works*, 21.

[531] W. L. Sachse, ed., *Minutes of the Norwich Court of Mayoralty 1632-1635*, NRS vol. 36 (1967), 24.

[532] Gray & Gethyn-Jones, *Registers of the Church of St Mary, Dymock*, 83.

[533] Fraser, *Durham Quarter Sessions*, 98.

[534] Fraser, *Durham Quarter Sessions*, 105.

535 Fraser, *Durham Quarter Sessions*, 112.

536 Guilding, *Reading Records*, III: 214.

537 Chakravorty, *Society and Politics*, 93.

538 Fraser, *Durham Quarter Sessions*, 140. For character and the criminal law, C. Herrup, *Common Peace*, 86-91.

539 Fraser, *Durham Quarter Sessions*, 144.

540 Fraser, *Durham Quarter Sessions*, 69.

541 Fraser, *Durham Quarter Sessions*, 88.

542 Fraser, *Durham Quarter Sessions*, 150 (1605); Axon, *Manchester Sessions*, 135.

543 Axon, *Manchester Sessions*, 33, 36, 43 (the last simply "three pence").

544 J. A. Twemlow, ed., *Liverpool Town Books*, 241.

545 Griffiths, *Household Book*, 124.

546 Headlam, *Parish Registers of St Oswald's, Durham*, 68. For this moniker, Beier, *Masterless Men*, 115-16.

547 Doree, *Parish Registers and Tithing Book*, 116.

548 J. P. Earwaker, ed., *The Court Leet of the Manor of Manchester* III (Manchester: Blacklock, 1886), 66.

549 J. Abercrombie, ed., *The Registers of Warcop*, CWPRS (1914), 58.

550 Pound, *Norwich Census of the Poor*.

551 Emmison, *Wills of the County of Essex*, II: 42 (155), 85 (316), 104 (389).

552 *Records of Maidstone*, 64 (1607); see also blind William – William Marten – buried in 1652 at Rowley Regis: P. W. L. Adams, ed., *Rowley Regis Parish Register* I, SPRS (1912) which also contains interments of John Russell called "Swash," Joan Hadley called "Jumping Jone," and William Meanely called "Clogg": pp. 89, 105, 109 (1646-53).

553 Doree, *Parish Registers and Tithing Book*, 122.

554 E. R. C. Brinkworth and R. K. Gilks, eds, *The "Bawdy Court" of Banbury. The Act Book of the Peculiar Court of Banbury, 1625-1638*, BHS vol. 26 (1997), 165, 168. The imagination might run riotously over Iddy Preston of late called Mrs Lovinge: Crawfurd, *Registers of the Parish of St Mary, Reading*, 101 (1603).

555 UN AN/PB 296/1/3.

556 UN AN/PB 296/1/3.

557 Burne, *Staffordshire Quarter Sessions Rolls* I, 234-5 (15,17).

558 Burne, *Staffordshire Quarter Sessions Rolls Volume IV 1598-1602* CHS (1936), 158.

559 Burne, *Staffordshire Quarter Sessions Rolls Volume IV*, 280.

560 Slack, *Poverty in Early-Stuart Salisbury*, 30 (1601).

561 A. J. Webb, ed., *Two Tudor Subsidy Assessments for the County of Somerset: 1558 and 1581-82*, SRS vol. 88 (2002), p. 95.

562 Guilding *Reading Records*, III: 264.

563 For insight into the social complications of the nickname, similar in context to the *alias*, Jane Morgan, Christopher O'Neill, and Rom Harré, *Nicknames: their Origins and Consequences* (London: Routledge and Kegan Paul, 1979).

Chapter 3

[564] Julian Haseldine, ed., *Friendship in Medieval Europe* (Stroud: Sutton, 1999); P. Maddern "'Best trusted friends': concepts and practices of friendship among fifteenth-century Norfolk gentry" in *England in the Fifteenth Century: Proceedings of the 1992 Harlaxton Symposium*, ed. N. Rogers, Harlaxton Medieval Studies vol. 4 (Stamford: Paul Watkins Publishing, 1994), 100-17.

[565] W. Brown, ed., *Yorkshire Star Chamber Proceedings*, YASRS vol. 41 (1909 for 1908), 148.

[566] H. Thwaite, ed., *Abstracts of Abbotside Wills 1552-1688*, YASRS vol. 130 (1968 for 1967), 33 (44).

[567] *Report on the Manuscripts of Lord Middleton* (London: Historical Manuscripts Commission, 1911), 148.

[568] Siraut and Monday, *Somerset Wills*, 129.

[569] Siraut and Monday, *Somerset Wills*, 219; Weaver, *Somerset Medieval Wills (Third Series) 1531-1558*, 92, 166, for example.

[570] J. A. Atkinson et al., eds., *Darlington Wills and Inventories 1600-1625*, SS vol. 201 (1993), 51 (1).

[571] D. O'Hara, *Courtship and Constraint. Rethinking the Making of Marriage in Tudor England* (Manchester: Manchester University Press, 2000).

[572] Sharon Farmer has ingeniously used a rather formal source – narratives in hagiographical literature – to elicit the friendships of poor women, however: S. Farmer, *Surviving Poverty in Medieval Paris. Gender, Ideology, and the Daily Lives of the Poor* (Ithaca N.Y.: Cornell University Press, 2002).

[573] For the reluctance of Henry VIII to engage personally in letters, Seth Lerer, *Courtly Letters in the Age of Henry VIII* (Cambridge: Cambridge University Press, 1997), 87-121 (chapter 3: "The King's hand: body politics in the letters of Henry VIII"), except in his correspondence with Anne Boleyn which proved a combination of intimacy and instrumentality.

[574] For a recent discussion of the advice literature, Phil Withington, *The Politics of Commonwealth. Citizens and Freemen in Early Modern England* (Cambridge: Cambridge University Press, 2005), 142-4.

[575] Nicholas Udall, *Roister Doister* (1566), Act I scene i, l. 80.

[576] Bettey, *Calendar of the Correspondence of the Smyth Family*, 15 (22) (1576).

[577] Bettey, *Calendar of the Correspondence of the Smyth Family*, 35 (68), 45 (95), 46 (96), 47 (98-9),

[578] *Report on the Manuscripts of Lord Middleton*, 158.

[579] *Report on the Manuscripts of Lord Middleton*, 126, 131, 132, 141, for example.

[580] Clark, *Boston Assembly Minutes*, 81 (716).

[581] Clark, *Boston Assembly Minutes*, 82 (717).

[582] A. E. B. Owen, ed., *The Records of the Commissioners of Sewers in the Parts of Holland 1547-1603 III*, LRS vol. 71 (1977), p. 103-4.

[583] W. P. Baildon, ed., "Some correspondence of the Maudes of Hollingwell, 1594-1599," *Miscellanea*, Thoresby Society vol. 24 (1919), 113 (5).

[584] Baildon, "Some correspondence," 120 (18) (1596).

[585] Baildon, "Some correspondence," 131 (36).

[586] Baildon, "Some correspondence," 119 (15).

[587] Philip Riden, ed., *George Sitwell's Letter Book 1662- 66*, DRS vol. 10 (1985).

[588] Sandra Bell and Simon Coleman, "The anthropology of friendship: enduring themes and further possibilities" in *The Anthropology of Friendship*, ed. Bell and Coleman (Oxford: Berg, 1999), 6-8.

[589] Bell and Coleman, "The anthropology of friendship," 1.

[590] Emmison, *Wills of the County of Essex*, I: 100.

[591] Emmison, *Wills of the County of Essex*, I: 105 (340), 114 (371), 140 (452), 190 (620); II: 39 (144).

[592] Emmison, *Wills of the County of Essex*, II: 71 (257).

[593] Emmison, *Wills of the County of Essex*, II: 168 (601).

[594] Emmison, *Wills of the County of Essex*, II: 173 (624), 193 (683).

[595] Emmison, *Wills of the County of Essex*, II: 201 (702), 205 (723), 221 (771).

[596] Evans, *Wills of the Archdeaconry of Sudbury*, 28 (67).

[597] J. D. Alsop, "Religious preambles in early modern English wills as formulae," *Journal of Ecclesiastical History* 40 (1989): 19-27; Tom Arkell, Nesta Evans and Nigel Goose, eds., *When Death us do Part. Understanding and Interpreting the Probate Records of Early Modern England* (Oxford: Leopard's Head Press, 2000).

[598] William Hunt, *The Puritan Moment: the Coming of Revolution in an English County* (Cambridge, Mass.,: Harvard University Press, 1983).

[599] Emmison, *Wills of the County of Essex*, I: 227 (733).

[600] Emmison, *Wills of the County of Essex*, I: 227 (734).

[601] Emmison, *Wills of the County of Essex*, II: 1 (1).

[602] Evans, *Wills of the Archdeaconry of Sudbury*, 39 (91).

[603] Evans, *Wills of the Archdeaconry of Sudbury*, 59 (132), 69 (155), 101 (218), 125 (264), 144 (309), 148 (318).

[604] Brinkworth and Gibson, *Banbury Wills Part 1*, 134 (32), 136 (33), 139 (36), 192 (91), 234 (142), 303 (228).

[605] S. Lang and M. McGregor, eds., *Tudor Wills Proved in Bristol 1546-1603*, BrisRS vol. 44 (1993), 14 (33), 17 (39), 58 (122), 59 (124, 126), 62 (132), 84 (170), 85 (172), 86 (174), 91 (183).

[606] Thwaite, *Abbotside Wills*, 7, 56 (10, 67).

[607] Siraut and Monday, *Somerset Wills*, 2, 5, 9, 12, 66, 73, 85, 113, 139, 191, 194, 207, 234, 238, 261.

[608] Lang and McGregor, *Tudor Wills Proved in Bristol*, 17 (39) and 29 (64).

[609] Edwards, *Derbyshire Wills Proved in the Prerogative Court of Canterbury 1575-1601*, 73 (153).

[610] Edwards, *Derbyshire Wills Proved in the Prerogative Court of Canterbury 1575-1601*, 104 (175).

[611] Edwards, *Derbyshire Wills Proved in the Prerogative Court of Canterbury 1575-1601*, 86 (165), 97 (170), 107 (177). The Latin equivalent of "welbeloved friend" was probably encapsulated by *dilectus amicus* or *dilecta amica*: E. M. Elvey, ed., *The Courts of the Archdeaconry of Buckingham 1483-1523*, BucksRS vol. 19, (1975), 157 (225), for example.

[612] G. Piccope, ed., *Lancashire and Cheshire Wills and Inventories from the Ecclesiastical Court, Chester. The Second Portion*, Chetham Society vol. 51 (Manchester, 1860), 211. For the complications of kin and friends, see below.

[613] Piccope, *Lancashire and Cheshire Wills*, 223.

[614] Emmison, *Wills of the County of Essex*, I: 244 (788).

[615] Thwaite, *Abbotside Wills* 9 (14).

[616] Thwaite, *Abbotside Wills*, 6 (9).

[617] Thwaite, *Abbotside Wills*, 15 (21).

[618] Thwaite, *Abbotside Wills*, 29 (38).

[619] Lumb, *Testamenta Leodiensia*, 45, 63, 74, 81.

[620] Lumb, *Testamenta Leodiensia*, 73.

[621] J. Clay, ed., *North Country Wills*, SS vol. 116 (1908), 203.

[622] Lumb, *Testamenta Leodiensia*, 76 (1542).

[623] R. Cook, "Wills of Leeds and district" *Miscellanea*, ThS vol. 24 (1919), 49: will of Peter Bank, esq., of Kippax: *Et volo ulterius quod expense mee funerales dicto die sepulture mee fiant per meorum executorum discrecionem ac aliorum amicorum meorum*.(1483) ("And I wish that my burial costs on that day of my burial be made by the discretion of my executors and of my other friends," where his executors were his wife and son (p. 50) suggesting that the friends were also kin.

[624] Thwaite, *Abbotside Wills*, 33 (44) (1606).

[625] G. Lumb, "Testamenta Leodiensia 1537-1559," *Miscellanea*, ThS vol. 15 (1909), 14.

[626] Piccope, *Lancashire and Cheshire Wills*, pp. 129-30.

[627] Thwaite, *Abbotside Wills*, 23 (31).

[628] Thwaite, *Abbotside Wills*, 26 (35).

[629] Piccope, *Lancashire and Cheshire Wills*, 95.

[630] Thwaite, *Abbotside Wills*, 27 (35).

[631] Thwaite, *Abbotside Wills*, 30 (41).

[632] R. Stewart-Brown, ed., *Lancashire and Cheshire Cases in the Court of Star Chamber Part I*, RSLC vol. 71 (1916), 38.

[633] Lumb, *Testamenta Leodiensia*, 27.

[634] Lumb, *Testamenta Leodiensia*, 20.

[635] Piccope, *Lancashire and Cheshire Wills*, p. 146.

[636] Clay, *North Country Wills*, 14 (xii).

[637] Clay, *North Country Wills*, 52 (xxxviii).

[638] Clay, *North Country Wills*, 95 (lxxv).

[639] Baildon, "Some correspondence," 113 (5).

[640] Baildon, "Some correspondence," 113 (6).

[641] Baildon, "Some correspondence," 115 (10); and so the same imputation at p. 114 (6-7).

[642] Evans, *Wills of the Archdeaconry of Sudbury*, 66 (147), 68 (152), 72 (163), 77 (175), 103 (223), 115 (245), 124 (262), 134 (288), 146 (315), 158 (341), 164 (356).

[643] Evans, *Wills of the Archdeaconry of Sudbury*, 74 (166), 88 (197), 90 (199), 95 (210), 113 (240), 134 (289), 140-1 (302-4), 146 (314), 148 (318), 153 (327), 157 (337-8), 163 (355), 170 (365).

[644] Evans, *Wills of the Archdeaconry of Sudbury*, 58 (129), 160 (344).

[645] Evans, *Wills of the Archdeaconry of Sudbury*, 156 (335).

[646] Evans, *Wills of the Archdeaconry of Sudbury*, 118 (251).

[647] Brinkworth and Gibson, *Banbury Wills Part 1*, 161 (58), 187 (84), 201 (106), 227 (136), 234 (142), 268 (187), 272 (193), 282 (202), 292 (213), 299 (222).

[648] Brinkworth and Gibson, *Banbury Wills Part 1*, 162 (59), 286 (206).

[649] Edwards, *Derbyshire Wills Proved in the Prerogative Court of Canterbury 1393-1574*, DRS vol. 26 (1998), 210 (112), 213 (113); Edwards, *Derbyshire Wills Proved in the Prerogative Court of Canterbury 1575-1601*, 67 (152), 74 (155), 90 (168), 92 (169).

[650] Piccope, *Lancashire and Cheshire Wills*, 42, 51, 67, 70.

[651] WRO: will of John Moore 1527. I have examined all the wills to 1534.

[652] Lang and McGregor, *Tudor Wills Proved in Bristol*, 80 (163).

[653] Lang and McGregor, *Tudor Wills Proved in Bristol*, 90 (180).

[654] C. W. Foster, ed., *Lincoln Wills* Volume II *1505-1530*, LRS vol. 10 (1918), 3-4.

[655] Edwards, *Derbyshire Wills Proved in the Prerogative Court of Canterbury 1575-1601*, 50 (145).

[656] Edwards, *Derbyshire Wills Proved in the Prerogative Court of Canterbury 1393-1574*, 216 (115).

[657] C. B. Phillips and J. H. Smith, eds., *Stockport Probate Records 1578-1619*, RSLC vol. 124 (1985), 7 (7), 14 (8), 31 (15), 36 (18), 86 (43) (1591-1607).

[658] W. H. Godfrey (and R. G. Rice), eds., *Transcripts of Sussex Wills*, 4 vols., SxRS vols. 41-43, 45 (1935-41), I: 70, 88, 92, 112, 115, 121, 133, 141, 142, 148, 165, 173, 186, 197, 202, 314, 319, 356; II: 49, 57, 70, 78, 109, 128, 133, 134, 184, 185, 193, 215, 216, 227, 228, 236, 237, 244, 255, 263, 277, 287, 288, 320, 348, 350, 351; III: 14, 35, 36, 44, 53, 58, 83, 89, 100, 110, 132, 143, 148, 160, 161, 168, 208, 222, 254, 266, 275, 281, 302, 315, 348, 349; IV: 12, 29, 53, 70, 86, 165, 166, 171, 177, 195, 198, 239, 274, 298, 312, 320, 334, 338, 356, 365, 392, 404.

[659] Many of the Sussex wills specifically included all Christian souls, a phrase probably rendered in Latin by *anima omnium fidelium defunctorum*: Elvey, *Courts of the Archdeaconry of Buckingham*, 191 (271), for example.

[660] Godfrey, *Sussex Wills*, II: 173; IV: 29, 53, 239, 404.

[661] For example only, Weaver, *Somerset Wills (1501-1530)*, 124, 128, 141, 146, 163, 172, 182, 191, 197-8, 213, 228, 326.

[662] Elvey, *Courts of the Archdeaconry of Buckingham*, 187 (266 – *omnium amicorum meorum*), 200 (282), 201 (283B), 219 (303), 231 (317), 275 (364), 277 (366), 315 (390), 316 (392), 369 (448), 397 (482 – "all my goode fryndes soules" – 1522).

[663] C W Foster, ed., *Lincoln Wills vol. III A.D. 1530 to 1532*, LRS vol. 24 (1930): good friends' souls at pp. 8, 26, 30, 35, 40, 52, 71, 72, 80; friends' souls at pp. 6, 17, 37, 38, 68, 86, 91. The year 1530 constitutes just a purposive sample.

[664] Godfrey, *Sussex Wills*, IV: 150, 419.

[665] Weaver, *Somerset Medieval Wills (Third Series) 1531-1558*, 207.

[666] B. Schofield, ed., *The Knyvett Letters 1620-1644*, NRS vol. 20 (1949), 55 (1-2), 86 (35), as examples.

[667] Schofield, *Knyvett Letters*, 55 (1-2), 57 (4), for example.

[668] Schofield, *Knyvett Letters*, 55 (1-2), 65 (13), 68 (16), 93 (32).

[669] Schofield, *Knyvett Letters*, 70 (18).

[670] Thomas Dekker, *The Shoemaker's Holiday* scene xvi ll. 56-70.

[671] William Shakespeare, *Twelfth Night*, Act II, scene 3, ll. 61-65.

[672] Gowing, *Domestic Dangers.*.

[673] Andy Wood is pursuing the language of collective rebellion; for his interim statement, *Riot, Rebellion and Popular Politics in Early Modern England* (Basingstoke: Palgrave/Macmillan, 2002), passim.

[674] Nottinghamshire Archives Office CA1/69/46

[675] Drunkenness, of course, was a male explanation for much: "that he was Dronk and in his Dronkennes he sayd that his pryvities or parts was Longer by iiij ynches then one Clerkes there." ERO D/ACA 20, fol. 29r (Henry Abbott the younger of Earls Colne) (1591).

[676] A. Bryson, *From Courtesy to Civility. Changing Codes of Conduct in Early Modern England* (Oxford: Oxford University Press, 1998), 238.

[677] Williams, *Bishop Redman's Visitation 1597*, p. 95.

[678] Angelo Raine, ed., *York Civic Records IV*, YASRS vol. 108 (1943), 70. For the imputations of *thou*, J. Hope, "The use of *thou* and *you* in early modern spoken English" in *Studies in Early Modern English*, ed. D. Kastovsky (Berlin, 1994), 142-51.

[679] Moule, ed., *Descriptive Catalogue ... Weymouth and Melcombe Regis*, 56.

[680] A. Gurr, *Playgoing in Shakespeare's London*, 3rd ed. (Cambridge: Cambridge University Press, 2004), 184-91 ("The war of railing (1599-1609)").

[681] For literary representation of gallants of this time, Ben Jonson, *Every Man in His Humour* (London, 1616) (first acted 1598).

[682] Gurr, *Playgoing in Shakespeare's London*, 191.

[683] Cited by McLuskie, *Dekker and Heywood*, 15.

[684] Thomas Middleton, *A Trick to Catch the Old One*, Act III, scene i, ll. 91-2; Act IV, scene v, ll. 75-77, 148.

[685] Williams, *Bishop Redman's Visitation*, 82.

[686] ERO D/AEA 12, fol. 184r.

[687] J. H. E. Bennett and J. C. Dewhirst, eds., *Cheshire Quarter Sessions Records 1559-1760*, RSLC vol. 94 (1940), 110.

[688] Wood-Legh, *Kentish Visitations*, 205.

[689] Wood-Legh, *Kentish Visitations*, 106. For the significance of "opprobrious," see below.

[690] M. Groombridge, ed., *Calendar of Chester City Council Minutes 1603-1642*, RSLC vol. 106 (1956), 98.

[691] Angelo Raine, ed., *York Civic Records V*, YASRS vol. 110 (1946 for 1944), 98.

[692] UN AN/PB 297/33.

[693] UNAN/PB 292/4/45.

[694] UNAN/PB 326/8/42

[695] S. Burne, ed., *The Staffordshire Quarter Sessions Rolls* volume III *1594-1597 CHS* (1933 for 1932), 130.

[696] ERO D/AEA 12, fol. 136r.

[697] B. Rosenwein, "Worrying about emotions in history," *American Historical Review* 107 (2002): 821-45; also eadem, ed., *Anger's Past. The Social Uses of an Emotion in the Middle Ages* (Ithaca, N.Y.: Cornell University Press, 1998).

[698] Atkinson, *Quarter Sessions Records*, III: 194.

[699] J. C. Atkinson, ed., *Quarter Sessions Records* vol. I, NRRS (1884), 133.

[700] Savage, *Minutes and Accounts of the Corporation of Stratford-upon-Avon I*, 51.

[701] Savage, *Minutes and Accounts of the Corporation of Stratford-upon-Avon I*, 73.

[702] E. D. Stone and B. Cozens, eds., *Norwich Consistory Court Depositions, 1499-1512 and 1518-1530*, NRS vol. 10 (1938), nos. 252, 346, 413.

[703] Bond, *Chamber Order Book of Worcester*, 152, 156.

[704] Raine, *York Civic Records IV*, 14, 42.

[705] Guilding, *Reading Records*, III: 79.

[706] Atkinson, *Quarter Sessions Records*, III: 275.

[707] B. H. Cunnington, ed., *Some Annals of the Borough of Devizes* (Devizes: Simpson and Co., 1925); for the term whore as a common insult against women, Gowing, *Domestic Dangers*, passim.

[708] Clark, *Boston Assembly Minutes*, 33 (294). He subsequently departed the borough to live in Peterborough, to the annoyance of the mayor and other aldermen.

[709] Atkinson, *Quarter Sessions Records*, II: 135.

[710] UN AN/PB 295/1/7 (1611). Churchwardens had been afforded some protection by canon 115 of the Canons of 1604: Richard H. Helmholz, *Roman Canon Law in Reformation England* (Cambridge: Cambridge University Press, 1990), 66.

[711] UN AN/PB 295/3/84 (1613).

[712] J. Wake, ed., *Quarter Sessions Records of the County of Northampton*, Northamptonshire Record Society vol. 1 (Northampton, 1922 for 1920), 42-3 (137).

[713] S. A. H. Burne, ed., *The Staffordshire Quarter Sessions Rolls Volume V 1603-1606* CHS

[714] Le Hardy, *Calendar to the Sessions Records* I: 9.

[715] William J. Connor, ed., *The Southampton Mayor's Book of 1606-8*, SoRS vol. 21 (Southampton, 1978), 77 (141).

[716] Connor, *Southampton Mayor's Book*, 93 (186).

[717] The possibility exists, however, that *Firk* was already denigrated by his own name: G. Williams, *A Glossary of Shakespeare's Sexual Language* (London: Athlone Press, 1997), 125 (beat = fuck).

[718] *Jacke Jugler*, ll. 332, 337, 340, 353, 451, 474, 498, 585, 701, 798, 810, 845, 861, 865, 867, 872, 890, 919, 923, 973, 975.

[719] It corresponds to ss. 3-4 at S. M. Kuhn and J. Reidy, eds., *Middle English Dictionary I-L* (Ann Arbor: University of Michigan, 1968), 551.

[720] F. J. Furnivall, ed., *Books of Courtesy*, EETS Extra Series vol. 8 (1869), 57.

[721] [?W. Stevenson], *Gammer Gurton's Needle* (1562x1575), Act II, scene iv, l. 541.

[722] Gowing, *Domestic Dangers*, for the frequency of whore as defamation of women and the lack of a male equivalence.

[723] [?W. Stephenson], *Gammer Gurton's Needle*, Act II, scene ii, l. 391, preceded by the contemptuous remark to Hodge: "What Devyll, be thine ars strynges brusten": Act II, scene i, l. 388.

[724] Thomas G. Barnes, ed., *Somerset Assize Orders 1629-1640*, SRS vol. 65 (1959), 49 (165)

[725] NNRO NCR Case 12a/1c, fol. 57r. It is interesting that in the deposition "you" was cancelled and "thou" interlined.

[726] Fox, *Minutes and Accounts of the Corporation of Stratford-upon-Avon V*, 86.

[727] William H. Stephenson, ed., *Records of the Borough of Nottingham* volume IV (Nottingham: Nottingham Corporation, 1889), 154.

[728] B. Howell, *Law and Disorder in Tudor Monmouthshire* (Cardiff, 1995), 48.

[729] M. Power, ed., *Liverpool Town Books 1649-1671*, RSLC vol. 136 (1999), 89.

[730] Power, *Liverpool Town Books*, 40.

[731] Power, *Liverpool Town Books*, 19.

[732] Power, *Liverpool Town Books*, 20.

[733] Power, *Liverpool Town Books*, 38.

[734] "Honour and reputation in early-modern England," *Transactions of the Royal*

Historical Society 6th ser. 6 (1996):137-248. In terms of language use, Austin and Searle predicated the impact of speech acts, which have both an illocutionary and perlocutionary force. Such utterances can thus be performative – their impact can be forceful. Austin propounded that the impact depended on the inclusion of performative verbs, but recent re-consideration has suggested that the performative verbs are not necessary to allow speech acts to have performative force. J. L. Austin, *Philosophical Papers*, 3rd ed. (Oxford: Oxford University Press, 1979), esp. chap. 10 ("Performative utterances") at pp. 233-52; J. Searle, *Mind, Language and Society. Philosophy in the Real World* (London: Basic Books, 1998), esp. chap. 6 ("How language works: speech as a human kind of action" at pp. 135-61); Thomas, *Meaning in Interaction*, 46-9.

[735] Atkinson, *Quarter Sessions Records*, III: 323.

[736] Thomas Middleton and William Rowley, *The Changeling*, Act I, scene 2, ll. 181-4.

[737] Stone and Cozens, *Norwich Consistory Court*, nos. 6, 54, 107, 333, 368. For Shakespeare's use of "whoreson," Williams, *Glossary of Shakespeare's Sexual Language*, 337. Whoreson was not confined as an insult to the priesthood or clergy, for it was liberally used by Careawaye in his dialogue with his other self: *Jacke Jugler* ll. 342, 368, 552, 612, 618.

[738] C. W. Foster, ed., *Lincoln Episcopal Records in the Time of Thomas Cooper S.T.P., Bishop of Lincoln* LRS vol. 2 (1912), 116.

[739] NNRO NCR Case 12a/1c, fol. 14r.

[740] NNRO NCR Case 12a/ld (unfoliated: 28 December 1571).

[741] NNRO NCR Case 12a/1d (unfoliated: 21 October 1567).

[742] NNRO NCR Case 12a/1d (unfoliated, n.d., but ?1567).

[743] "Star Chamber proceedings," *CHS* (1912), 67.

[744] NNRO NCR Case 12a/1a, fol. 29r.

[745] NNRO NCR Case 12a/1a, fol. 29v.

[746] Stone and Cozens, *Norwich Consistory Court*, nos. 54, 73, 144, 196, and 272.

[747] ERO D/ACA4, fol. 146r.

[748] B. H. Cunnington, ed., *Records of the County of Wiltshire* (Devizes, 1932), 27. "I had rather be a tankerd bearer in London than a maior in Wilton & more creditt to be a tankerd bearer than a maior."

[749] UN AN/PB 292/9/16.

[750] S. Burne, ed., *The Staffordshire Quarter Sessions Rolls* IV *1598-1602 CHS* (1936 for 1935), 133. For the fluency of meaning and its use for abusive purposes, Patrick Collinson, "Elizabethan and Jacobean Puritanism as forms of popular religious culture" in *The Culture of English Puritanism 1560-1700*, ed. Christopher Durston and Jacqueline Eales (Basingstoke: The Macmillan Press, 1996), 34; Chakravorty, *Society and Politics*, 10-13.

[751] Cunnington, *Records of the County of Wiltshire*, 111.

[752] For defamation of lay people: "horemaster and horemaster knave": UN AN/ LB 216/2/5/2 (Kithchinman *c.* Bardsey in defamation); AN/LB 216/2/5/1: "that he the sayd Edward Bardesey in his presence callyd the sayd William Kitchinman Whormaster and sayd that he was a Whoremaster in great malice and anger"; "that he hard the sayd Bardsey call William Kitchinman Whoremaster openly in the face of the courte" (1583). The public declamation was important for the plea

of defamation. ERO D/ACA 14, fol. 2r: "that the sayd Mr Rochester ys as Lewde a person as any within thes hundreth myles, and that yf he him selfe were a whore master the sayd Mr Rochester wolde be ready to ryde forty miles to do him a good turne...." (1585). UN AN/LB 215/1/23: "whoremaster"; AN/LB 215/2/15: "he is a whore master preist"; AN/LB 216/4/1/1: "hormayster" (1584); AN/LB 216/4/1/3 "hooremayster"; AN/LB 219/2/23/1: "whoremaster knave" (1596); AN/LB 219/2/23/2-3: "copper nosed knave and a whore maister knave" (1596); AN/LB 220/2/5/1-3: "whoremaster" (1601); AN/LB 220/6/2/3: "a whoremaster knave for hee would have ravished mee in my own hous" (1605); AN/LB 221/5/8/1: "he is a whoremaster knave and a pockie rascall" and "he is a whoremaster knave & a beggerie gentleman" (1610); and AN/LB 221/5/8/4: "an whore mayster knave & a pockie whore Maister knave" (1610).

753 UN AN/LB 216/3/2/1.

754 NNRO NCR Case 12a/1c, fol. 2r.

755 UN AN/PB 295/5/63.

756 Jennifer Coates, Women, Men and Language. A Sociolinguistic Account of Gender Differences in Language, 2d ed. (London: Longman, 1993), pp. 80-2.

757 Thomas Middleton, A Mad World, My Masters [1.1], l. 4. He later addressed them by the same epithet: [3.3], l. 14.

758 Middleton, Mad World, My Masters [2.2], ll. 138-9. Bounteous used the label habitually: [4.2] l. 16; [5.1], ll. 32, 126; [5.2], l. 128.

759 [?W. Stephenson], Gammer Gurton's Needle, Act I, scene iv, ll. 175, 178, Act I, scene v, l. 237, Act II, scene i, l. 384, Act II, scene iii, l. 490, Act III, scene ii, l. 582, Act III, scene iii, l. 643, Act V, scene ii, l. 1161 ('horsen priest').

760 "Star Chamber proceedings," CHS (1912), 13 (1518).

761 For other dramaturgical utterances of whoresons, reflecting its common usage, Udall, Roister Doister, Act I scene iv, ll. 425, 508; Act III, scene v, l. 1265.

762 Stewart-Brown, Lancashire and Cheshire Cases in the Court of Star Chamber Part I, 47.

763 On narrative strategies in courts, Gowing, Domestic Dangers, chap. 7.

764 Staffordshire Record Office D1721/1/4 (not foliated).

765 J. Lister, ed., West Riding Sessions Records Volume II Orders, 1611-1642. Indictments, 1637-1642, YASRS vol. 54 (1915), 60.

766 Fraser, Durham Quarter Sessions, 179 (6).

767 Atkinson, Quarter Sessions Records, III: 201.

768 J. C. Jeaffreson, ed., Middlesex County Records I (London, 1886), 283.

769 Connor, Southampton Mayor's Book, 57 (60).

770 Ben Jonson, The Alchemist, Act I, scene i., l. 2.

771 Ben Jonson, Bartholomew Fair, Act I, scene v, ll. 13-14.

772 J. Willis Bund, ed., Calendar of the Quarter Sessions Papers Volume I 1591-1643 WHS (1900), 317-18.

773 Jeaffreson, Middlesex County Records I, p. 283.

774 Robert Tittler, The Reformation and the Towns in England. Politics and Political Culture, c.1540-1640 (Oxford: Oxford University Press, 1998), 310.

775 Jeaffreson, Middlesex County Records I, p. 53.

776 Burne, Staffordshire Quarter Sessions Rolls, IV: 456. The allusion here must be to gonads.

[777] Jeaffreson, *Middlesex County Records*, I: 100.

[778] WSRO G23/1/3, fol. 218r. W.Van Vree, *Meetings, Manners and Civilization. The Development of Modern Meeting Behaviour* (London, 1999), proposes a higher-level development of protocols associated with state formation, closely following Norbert Elias. For an account closer to the context, Tittler, *Reformation and the Towns in England*, 306-11.

[779] Shorrocks, *Bishop Still's Visitation*, 142.

[780] Bettey, *Correspondence of the Smyth Family*, 16 (23).

[781] Burne, *Staffordshire Quarter Sessions Rolls*, IV: 354.

Chapter 4

[782] Richard Corbett, *A Proper New Ballad, Intituled the Fairies' Farewell, or God-a-Mercy Will* in *The New Oxford Book of Seventeenth-Century Verse*, ed. A. Fowler (Oxford: Oxford University Press, 1991), 177.

[783] Cited by Gowing, "Ordering the body," 59.

[784] For the relationship between spiritual kinship and naming, see now Will Coster, *Baptism and Spiritual Kinship in Early Modern England* (Aldershot: Ashgate, 2002), esp. 167-94 ("the English naming system"); also Jeremy Boulton, "The naming of children in early modern London" in *Naming, Society and Regional Identity*, ed. Dave Postles (Oxford: Leopard's Head Press, 2002), pp. 147-67.

[785] Consideration will be given below to the use of hypocorisms, perhaps as a form of self-presentation (I fight shy of repeating the New Historicist notion of self-fashioning); for a discussion of early-modern pet forms, J. Germain, "Les prénoms à Namur (Wallonie) de la fin du XVe siècle au XVIe siècle" in *Actes du XVIe Congrès International des Sciences Onomastiques 1987*, ed. J-C. Boulanger (Quebec, 1990), 279.

[786] J. Raine, ed., *Depositions and other Ecclesiastical Proceedings from the Courts of Durham*, SS vol. 21 (1845), 42.

[787] G. Weddall, *The Registers of the Parish of Howden Volume 1*, YPRS vol. 21 (1904), 69. The positive and negative aspects of informal social interaction are now considered by my colleague Barbara Misztal, *Informality*; although addressing different contexts from the above, her suggestions are powerful.

[788] Dekker, *Shoemakers' Holiday*, scene xvii, ll. 8-10.

[789] Dekker, *Shoemakers' Holiday*, scene xvii, ll. 15, 28.

[790] Dekker, *Shoemakers' Holiday*, scene x, ll. 172, 183, 191; scene xi, l. 11.

[791] Dekker, *Shoemakers' Holiday*, scene x, l. 24.

[792] Thomas Middleton, *A Chaste Maid in Cheapside* Act 1 scene i, l. 53.

[793] Middleton, *Chaste Maid in Cheapside* Act III scene iii, ll. 164-6.

[794] Bettey, *Correspondence of the Smyth Family*, 57 (116), 58 (117), 65-6 (134-5, 138), 74-6 (156-8, 160), 79 (167), 116 (255).

[795] Bettey, *Correspondence of the Smyth Family*, 124 (273), 146, 151 (327).

[796] J. Binns, ed., *The Memoirs and Memorials of Sir Hugh Cholmley of Whitby 1600-1657*, YASRS vol. 152 (2000 for 1997-8), 89, 90, 91, 92, 93, 109.

[797] Udall, *Roister Doister*.

[798] Udall, *Roister Doister*, Act I, scene i, ll. 46-7, 49, 51, 53.

[799] [?W. Stevenson], *Gammer Gurton's Nedle.*

[800] *Gammer Gurton's Nedle*, for example, Prologue, l. 10; Act I scene ii, ll. 75, 79; Act I scene iii, l. 120; Act II scene i, l. 341; Act II scene ii, l. 421; Act IV scene i, l. 712.

[801] Manley, *Literature and Culture in Early Modern London*, 343, 350.

[802] Middleton, *Chaste Maid in Cheapside* Act 1 scene i, l. 19.

[803] Chakravorty, *Society and Politics*, 86-106 (chap. 4: "Mirth and licence: Moll at the Bankside and Moll in Cheapside"); for nicknames formed by an adjective and hypocorism, see above.

[804] Middleton, *Chaste Maid in Cheapside* Act 1 scene ii, ll. 68, 76, 81.

[805] Schofield, *Knyvett Letters*, 65 (13).

[806] Schofield, *Knyvett Letters*, 72 (21), 75 (25), for example.

[807] Schofield, *Knyvett Letters*, 81 (30).

[808] Schofield, *Knyvett Letters*, 104 (48), 114 (54).

[809] Schofield, *Knyvett Letters*, 81 (29); see also p. 98 (46).

[810] Bryson, *From Courtesy to Civility*, 166, refers to hypocorisms as, in the context of gallants, "boorish one-upmanship," but the deployment of hypocorisms had, of course, a long history.

[811] Smith-Bannister cites Gouge's opinion that the "pet" form was appropriate only for servants: *Names and Naming Patterns*, 17.

[812] Headlam, *Parish Registers of St Oswald's, Durham*, 20-1, 37-41 (Barty, Bartle), 29 (Besse), 31 (Jenkin), 36 (Davy), 54 (Arche), 66 ("Isabel *alias* Eppe"): 1573-1626.

[813] Jonson, *Bartholomew Fair*, Act II, scene ii, Act II, scene iii.

[814] Fraser, *Durham Quarter Sessions*, 114 (7).

[815] Wood-Legh, *Kentish Visitations*, 75.

[816] Middleton and Rowley, *Changeling*, Act I, scene 2, ll. 99-102.

[817] Griffiths, *Household Book*, 4.

[818] Griffiths, *Household Book*, for example, 31, 33, 34, 35, 40, 43, 45, 49, 52, 55, 56, 60, 61, 62, 64, 68, 78, 79, 88, 92, 94, 95, 105, 110,, 125, 129, 143, 145, 146, 149, 161, 163, 168, 170, 175, 183, 184, 186 and passim. For the burial, p. 274.

[819] Griffiths, *Household Book*, 77, 95.

[820] Griffiths, *Household Book*, 217; also p. 227 (Henry Keble).

[821] Littlehales, *Medieval Records of a London City Church*, 128.

[822] Littlehales, *Medieval Records of a London City Church*, 126-7.

[823] Emmison, *Wills of the County of Essex*, I: 7-10 (21-2, 25, 27), 28 (82), 30 (87), 40 (121), 42 (127), 47 (143), 65 (202), 69 (214), 72 (226), 78 (248), 81 (254), 86 (276), 89 (288), 102-4 (333-4, 339), 118-19 (380, 385), 133 (430), 142 (461), 151 (482), 159 (512), 162 (523), 166 (533), 170 (551), 175 (571), 178 (579), 180 (584), 187 (609), 196 (639), 246 (792), 249 (801), 252 (817), 308 (994), 309 (999).

[824] Griffiths, *Household Book*, for example, 50, 52, 53, 54, 83, 84, 85, 86, 88, 89, 92, 99, 105, 108, 110, 112, 113, 115, 117, 121, 125, 128, 136, 141, 144, 154, 169, 235.

[825] Griffiths, *Household Book*, pp. 248, 253, 254, 271, 272, 276, 277, 284, 400, for example.

[826] "Muster roll for the Hundred of North Greenhoe (circa 1523)," NRS vol. 1 (1931 for 1930).

[827] Chibnall & Woodman, *Subsidy Roll for the County of Buckinghamshire*, 63, 64.

[828] J. Cornwall, ed., *The Lay Subsidy Rolls for the County of Sussex 1524-25*, SxRS

vol. 56 (1956), 138-65.

[829] Cornwall, *Lay Subsidy Rolls for the County of Sussex*, 155.

[830] M. M. Hulton, ed., *Coventry and its People in the 1520s*, DS vol. 38 (1999), 128-76.

[831] Hulton, *Coventry and its People*, 158.

[832] M. Faraday, ed., *Worcestershire Taxes in the 1520s*, WHS n.s. vol. 9 (2003), 11.

[833] Faraday, *Worcestershire Taxes in the 1520s*, 1-62.

[834] Faraday, *Worcestershire Taxes in the 1520s*, 33, 56.

[835] Chibnall & Woodman, *Subsidy Roll for the County of Buckinghamshire*, 2, 12, 14, 20, 42, 60,73. It's possible that Jaket Janson (p. 73) was Dutch, although this nationality is not specified.

[836] Godfrey, *Sussex Wills*, I: 314.

[837] Clark, *Boston Assembly Minutes*, 1 (2), 7 (50), 10 (77), 11 (93), 18 (152), 20 (174).

[838] Clark, *Boston Assembly Minutes*, 50 (474).

[839] Clark, *Boston Assembly Minutes*, 23 (197).

[840] Cornwall, *Lay Subsidy Rolls for the County of Sussex*, 49.

[841] Elvey, *Courts of the Archdeaconry of Buckingham*, 352 (431), and also as a witness pp. 356, 358, 402.

[842] UN AN/PB 292/9/44.

[843] Emmison, *Wills of the County of Essex*, I: 149 (477)

[844] Maslen, *Woodstock Chamberlains' Accounts*, 89.

[845] Maslen, *Woodstock Chamberlains' Accounts*, 110, 119, 125, 130.

[846] Maslen, *Woodstock Chamberlains' Accounts*, 147.

[847] Maslen, *Woodstock Chamberlains' Accounts*, 117.

[848] Maslen, *Woodstock Chamberlains' Accounts*, 118, 122, 125, 131.

[849] Littlehales, *Medieval Records of a London City Church*, 172, 184.

[850] Littlehales, *Medieval Records of a London City Church*, 359.

[851] P. M. Briers, ed., *Henley Borough Records*, (ORS vol. 41 (1960), 223.

[852] Cornwall, *Lay Subsidy Rolls of the County of Sussex*, 95, 113, 115. Other random hypocorisms were associated with the lower end of taxation: Nele Raynold, Huch Tayler, Huch Moresbe, and Simkyn Thetcher; all on £1: pp. 81, 100-2.

[853] Emmison, *Wills of the County of Essex*, II: 96 (358).

[854] Griffiths, *Household Book*, 131.

[855] Chibnall and Woodman, *Subsidy Roll for the County of Buckinghamshire*, 82, 86, 88.

[856] Chibnall & Woodman, *Subsidy Roll for the County of Buckinghamshire*, 1, 19, 20, 23, 27, 28, 30 (*bis*), 64, .

[857] Emmison, *Wills of the County of Essex*, I: 43 (131), 58 (176), 133 (430); II, p. 102 (379).

[858] Webb, *Two Tudor Subsidy Assessments for the County of Somerset*, 105, 108-10.

[859] Griffiths, *Household Book*, 36 (John); 8, 10, for example.

[860] Griffiths, *Household Book*, 3, 116, 119, 120, 144, 159, for example.

[861] Griffiths, *Household Book*, compare 250 and 258.

[862] Thwaite, *Abbotside Wills*, 20-1 (27, 30).

[863] *Early Prose and Poetical Works*, 185.

[864] *Early Prose and Poetical Works*, 32.

[865] Emmison, *Wills of the County of Essex*, I: 21 (62).

[866] Emmison, *Wills of the County of Essex*, I: 112 (363).

[867] Emmison, *Wills of the County of Essex*, I: 162 (565).

[868] Emmison, *Wills of the County of Essex*, I: 178 (581).

[869] Emmison, *Wills of the County of Essex*, I: 187 (609).

[870] Emmison, *Wills of the County of Essex*, I: 183 (595).

[871] Brinkworth and Gibson, *Banbury Wills Part 1*, p. 196 (98).

[872] Brinkworth and Gibson, *Banbury Wills Part I*, p. 133 (31).

[873] Lang and McGregor, *Tudor Wills Proved in Bristol*, 52 (107) (1599).

[874] Griffiths, *Household Book*, 112 (Elizabeth); 3, 5, for example.

[875] Griffiths, *Household Book*, 131. He also mentioned Besse Staveley: p. 168.

[876] Emmison, *Wills of the County of Essex*, II: 85.

[877] Record Office for Leicestershire, Leicester and Rutland 1D41/13/24 (not foliated; 1600).

[878] Atkinson, *Quarter Sessions Records*, I: 170 (1609).

[879] Griffiths, *Household Book*, 394.

[880] Maslen, *Woodstock Chamberlains' Accounts*, 85.

[881] Emmison, *Wills of the County of Essex*, III: 346 (814).

[882] Atkinson, *Quarter Sessions Records*, II: 21.

[883] Udall, *Roister Doister*, Act IV scene iii, ll. 1477, 1505; scene vii, l. 1649.

[884] Emmison, *Wills of the County of Essex*, I: 116 (375), 128 (416), 143 (462).

[885] Emmison, *Wills of the County of Essex*, I: 251 (813), 269 (870); Emmison, *Wills of the County of* Essex, II: 41 (150), 98 (365), 205 (720), 220 (765).

[886] For legacies to other Parnels, Emmison, *Wills of the County of Essex*, III: 64-5 (159), 77 (200), 88 (228), 92 (237), 96 (247), 124 (310), 236 (549), 400 (934). Petronilla is invisible.

[887] Maslen, *Woodstock Chamberlains' Accounts*, 80, 89.

[888] Marshall, *Registers of Worksop*, 4, 14 (1570, 1586).

[889] Emmison, *Wills of the County of Essex*, I: 278 (898).

[890] Emmison, *Wills of the County of Essex*, II: 22 (77).

[891] Emmison, *Wills of the County of Essex*, II: 139 (502), 140 (505), 145 (522); III, pp. 129 (321-22), 238 (557), 454 (1040). Benedict is not discernible.

[892] Chibnall & Woodman, *Subsidy Roll for the County of Buckinghamshire*, 48, 94.

[893] Maslen, *Woodstock Chamberlains' Accounts*, 181-3, 188, 191, 204.

[894] "Three letters of Thomas Draxe concerning the recusants at Colwich," *CHS* (1933 for 1931), 268.

[895] NNRO NCR Case 12a/1c, fols. 25r, 34r.

[896] Brinkworth and Gilks, eds, *"Bawdy Court" of Banbury*, 129.

[897] David Cressy, *Birth, Marriage, and Death. Ritual, Religion, and the Life-cycle in Tudor and Stuart England* (Oxford: Oxford University Press, 1997), 162-3, has some interesting comments; the material below is different from, but complements, his assertions.

[898] The term "hortatory" is borrowed from David H. Fischer, *Albion's Seed. Four British Folkways in America* (New York: Oxford University Press, 1989), 97; at pp. 93-7, Fischer describes the importation of forenames into New England. The exaggeration of the significance of "Puritan" forenames is addressed by Smith-Bannister, *Names and Naming Patterns*, 181-2. Still the most effective discussion of these "grace" names is Nicholas Tyacke, "Popular Puritan mentality in late Elizabethan

England" in *The English Commonwealth, 1547-1640. Essays in Politics and Society Presented to Joel Hurstfield*, ed. P. Clark, G. T. Smith and Tyacke (Leicester: Leicester University Press, 1979), 77-92.

[899] Webb, *Two Tudor Subsidy Assessments for the County of Somerset*, 189.

[900] See also, Coster, *Baptism and Spiritual Kinship*, 182-5 ("the role of religion," including saints' days and injunctions of the clergy).

[901] For Puritan gentry, J. T. Cliffe, *The Puritan Gentry: the Great Puritan Families of Early Stuart England* (London, 1984).

[902] J. Gibson, ed., *Oxfordshire and North Berkshire Protestation Returns and Tax Assessments 1641-1642*, ORS vol. 59 (1994), 38-9; such names recurred in nearby Cropredy: pp. 43-4. For Banbury, we should take into account nine additional men described only by the title master and their surname.

[903] Smith-Bannister, *Names and Naming Patterns*, 155-61, considers the contribution of Biblical names in the early-modern naming process.

[904] N. Fillmore and J. S. W. Gibson, eds., *Baptism & Burial Register of Banbury, Oxfordshire* I, BHS vol. 7 (1966).

[905] Fillmore and Gibson, *Baptism & Burial Register of Banbury*. Needless to recount, the labeling of a child Temperance did not always socialize the child sufficiently: Temperance Strickland was presented as a scold in 1620 and ducked: Moule, *Descriptive Catalogue … Weymouth and Melcombe Regis*, 63.

[906] J. B. Blackenfield, "Puritans in the Provinces: Banbury, Oxon., 1554-1660" (Ph. D. diss., Yale University,1985).

[907] A. T. Michell, ed., *The Parish Registers of Marsham* (Norwich, 1889), 1-11.

[908] Mitchell, *Parish Registers of Marsham*, 12, 15-16, 18, 20, 29, 38, 54, 56, 65, 71-3, 78, 84, 86.

[909] "The Staffordshire Quarter Sessions rolls II 1590-93," *CHS* (1932 for 1930), 14.

[910] "Elizabethan Chancery proceedings, Series II, 1558-1579," *CHS* (1933 for 1931), 228.

[911] W. Stavert, ed., *The Registers of the Parish Church of Bingley*, YPRS vol. 60 (1901), pp. 33, 36, 38, 41, 45, 49, 54, 141, 268. One wonders whether the potential contrast of Mary (contemplative) and Martha (active) was realized.

[912] Braddick, *State Formation in Early Modern England*.

[913] Smith and Baker, *Papers of Nathaniel Bacon III*, 146 (1591).

[914] Smith and Baker, *Papers of Nathaniel Bacon III*, 147 (1591).

[915] Christopher Haigh, *Reformation and Resistance in Tudor Lancashire* (Cambridge: Cambridge University Press, 1975).

[916] NRO X614/27, fols. 92v and 98r (visitation and correction book, 1595).

[917] Smith-Bannister, *Names and Naming Patterns*, 3-6

[918] Tyacke, "Popular Puritan mentality in late Elizabethan England" for the most extensive investigation.

[919] Smith-Bannister, *Names and Naming Patterns*, 5.

[920] Atkinson, *Quarter Sessions Records*, II: 58-81; Fraser, *Durham Quarter Sessions*, 330-6. Nor is there anything distinctive about the forenames of recusants listed at the Staffordshire Quarter Sessions in the mid 1580s, although these adherents to Catholicism might have received their names in more fluid times: S. A. H. Burne, ed., *The Staffordshire Quarter Sessions Rolls Volume 1 1581-1589 CHS* (1931 for 1929), 134-41.

[921] Dom H. Bowler, *Recusant Roll No. 2 (1593-1594)* Catholic Record Society vol. 57 (1965), passim and 127, 149.

[922] C. Clark, "Onomastics" in *The Cambridge History of the English Language, 2: 1066-1476*, ed. N. Blake (Cambridge: Cambridge University Press, 1992), 542-606, for the comparison by gender for the middle ages.

[923] For these last two names, M. C. S. Cruwys, ed., *The Register ... of St Andrew's, Plymouth*, Devon and Cornwall Record Society vol. 24 (Exeter, 1954), 502, 544, 546, 549.

[924] That regional dimension was exhibited also in the male name Digory: Cruwys, *Plymouth*, 38, 61, 70, 125, 150, 165 for example.

[925] NNRO microfiche: Norwich St Giles fiche 1.

[926] K. E. Cubbs, ed., *The Parish Registers of Aldenham, Hertfordshire, 1559-1659* (St Albans, 1902), 8, 18.

[927] Cubbs, *Parish Registers of Aldenham*, 22, 31, 32, 33, 42, 44, 45, 48, 55.

[928] Lang and McGregor, *Tudor Wills Proved in Bristol*, 36 (78).

[929] Propositions by, amongst others, cognitive psychologists that the phonemic ordering of some names implied female status have been dispelled by Carole Hough, "Towards an explanation of phonetic differentiation in masculine and feminine personal names," *Journal of Linguistics* 36 (2000): 1-11.

[930] R. Hovenden, ed., *The Parish Register of Chislet, Kent* (London, 1887), 23, 25-7, 29, 31, 33, 35, 36.

[931] Hovenden, *Parish Register of Chislet*, 35.

[932] Hovenden, *Parish Register of Chislet*, 24. One possibility, of course, is that it is a variant of Godlif.

[933] Hovenden, *Parish Register of Chislet*, 24-7, 31.

[934] Walton and Riden, *Chesterfield Parish Register 1558-1600*; Nolan, Watkinson and Riden, *Chesterfield Parish Register 1601-35*.

[935] Edwards, *Derbyshire Wills Proved in the Prerogative Court of Canterbury 1575-1601*, 90 (168), 92 (169).

[936] Edwards, *Derbyshire Wills Proved in the Prerogative Court of Canterbury 1575-1601*, 86 (165).

[937] J. Parker, *The Parish Register of Thirsk*, YPRS vol. 42 (1911), 134.

[938] T. B. Willis, ed., *The Parish Register of Pontefract 1585-1641*, YPRS vol. 122 (1958), 15, 25, 31, 75, 77, 98.

[939] Stavert, *Registers of the Parish Church of Bingley*, 12, 21, 27, 40, 60, 67.

[940] Stavert, *Registers of the Parish Church of Bingley*, 35 (first instance).

[941] Stavert, *Registers of the Parish Church of Bingley*, 10.

[942] Stavert, *Registers of the Parish Church of Bingley*, 53.

[943] For other exceptions, Perpetua at Childwall in 1593: R. Dickinson, ed., *The Registers of the Parish of Childwall Part 1*, LPRS vol. 106 (1967), 45; Peregrina and Florence in Gisburne: Simpson and Charlesworth, *Parish Register of Gisburne Part 1*, 13, 45.

[944] Siraut and Monday, *Somerset Wills*, 9.

[945] J. Freeman, ed., *The Parish Register of Arksey I*, YPRS vol. 166 (2001), 41, 45, 49.

[946] Stavert, *Registers of the Parish Church of Bingley*, 25.

[947] Smith-Bannister, *Names and Naming Patterns*, 8, is dismissive of this connection because of the diminutive numbers involved.

[948] Hovenden, *Parish Register of Chislet*, 21.

[949] Weddall, *Registers of the Parish of Howden Part 1*, 143.

[950] Hovenden, *Parish Register of Chislet*, 39, 40.

[951] P. W. L. Adams, ed., *Gnosall Parish Register*, SPRS (1922), 58.

[952] Wake, *Quarter Sessions Records of the County of Northampton*, 55 (166).

[953] Miss Edleston, ed., *The Registers of Coniscliffe*, DNPRS vol. 18 (1908), 3-4.

[954] Stavert, *Registers of the Parish Church of Bingley*, 49.

[955] J. Arrowsmith, ed., *The Registers of the Parish Church of Ormskirk*, LPRS vol. 13 (1902), 101.

[956] Arrowsmith, *Registers of the Parish Church of Ormskirk*, 74, 85, 95, 99-101, 104, 111, 123..

[957] Weddall, *Registers of the Parish of Howden Part 1*, 129.

[958] Parker, *Parish Register of Thirsk*, 17, 120.

[959] For the attribution of social stigma, but also how its effects can be subverted, Goffman, *Stigma*.

[960] *Tamworth Parish Register Part 1*, SPRS (1917), 196. This unfortunate female trespasser died in the same year.

[961] *Tamworth Parish Register Part I*, 206.

[962] *Tamworth Parish Register Part I*, 174.

[963] Nolan, Watkinson and Riden, *Chesterfield Parish Register*, 213.

[964] Weddall, *Registers of the Parish of Howden Part 1*, 226, 228.

[965] Weddall, *Registers of the Parish of Howden Part 1*, 262.

[966] C. E. Whiting, ed., *The Parish Register of Cantley*, YPRS vol. 112 (1941), 64.

[967] A. Sabin, ed., *The Registers of the Church of St Augustine the Less, Bristol*, Bristol and Gloucestershire Archaeological Society Records Section vol. 3 (Gloucester, 1956), 61.

[968] E. Dodds, ed., *The Registers of Berwick-upon-Tweed Part 1*, DNPRS vol. 11 (1905), 105.

[969] T. B. Willis, ed., *The Parish Register of Pontefract 1585-1641*, YPRS vol. 122 (1958), 119, 124.

[970] Access to names thus confirms the recent emphasis on the complexities of any relationship between or separation into elite and popular culture(s): Tim Harris, "Problematicising popular culture" in *Popular Culture in England, c. 1500-1850* ed. idem (Basingstoke: The Macmillan Press, 1995), 1-27, 216-22.

Conclusion

[971] Steve Hindle, *The State and Social Change in Early Modern England c.1550-1640* ((Basingstoke: The Macmillan Press, 2000); Braddick, *State Formation in Early Modern England c.1550-1700*; Bryson., *From Courtesy to Civility*.

[972] For a critical résumé of these aspects of Elias's sociology of the past, John Fletcher, *Violence and Civilization. An Introduction to the Work of Norbert Elias* (Cambridge: Polity 1997), esp. 89-93.

[973] Here, I extend Michel de Certeau's spatial considerations: de Certeau, *The Practice of Everyday Life*, 96-7.

[974] Gowing, *Domestic Dangers*; Jane Kamensky, *Governing the Tongue. The Politics*

of Speech in Early New England (Oxford: Oxford University Press, 1997).

Appendix

[975] Richard H. Helmholz, *Roman Canon Law in Reformation England* (Cambridge: Cambridge University Press, 1990), 66-9. I am extremely grateful to him for his expert advice about this material by e-mail. What I hope to do here is to provide some illustrations of his interpretation of what was happening. His point is an important one in fully understanding the proceedings on defamation in ecclesiastical courts.

[976] UN AN/LB 215/1/32

[977] UN AN/LB 215/3/1/8

[978] UN AN/LB 220/2/5/1-2

[979] UN AN/LB 220/2/5/1/3

[980] UN AN/LB 220/4/17/2

[981] UN AN/LB 220/5/5/1

[982] UN AN/LB 220/6/1/1/2

[983] UN AN/LB 220/6/1/2

[984] UN AN/LB 220/6/4/5

[985] UN AN/LB 220/6/4/5-6

[986] UN AN/LB 221/1/24

[987] UN AN/LB 221/34

Bibliography

Manuscript sources

Cambridge University Library
    EDR D2 Diocese of Ely: office act books
Essex Record Office
    D/AEA Archdeaconry of Essex: office act books
    D/ACA Archdeaconry of Colchester: office act books
Norfolk and Norwich Record Office
    NCR case 16 shelf c no. 5 city of Norwich: assembly minute books.
    NCR Case 12a city of Norwich: assembly minute books
    Microfiche of parish registers in the searchroom
Northamptonshire Record Office
    NBR 3/1 Northampton borough: assembly minutes
    X614 Diocese of Peterborough: visitation books and correction act books
    Marriage registers P (xerox copies in the search room – e.g. 50P/1, 46P-204)
Nottinghamshire Archives Office
    CA1 Nottingham borough records: constables' presentments
Record Office for Leicestershire, Leicester and Rutland
    1D41/1 Archdeaconry of Leicester: office act books
Staffordshire Record Office
    D1721/1/4 borough of Stafford: memoranda book
University of Nottingham Department of Manuscripts and Special Collections
    AN/PB Archdeaconry of Nottingham: churchwardens' presentments
    AN/LB Archdeaconry of Nottingham: libels, depositions and other cause papers
Wiltshire and Swindon Record Office
    G23/1/3 Salisbury borough records: assembly minutes
Worcestershire Record Office wills
    Microfilms of wills (deposited in the University of Leicester Library)

Secondary works

Adair, Richard, Courtship, Illegitimacy and Marriage in Early Modern England. Manchester: Manchester University Press, 1996.

Alsop, J. D., "Religious Preambles in Early Modern English Wills as Formulae." Journal of Ecclesiastical History 40 (1989): 19-27

Arkell, Thomas, N. Evans and N. Goose, eds., When Death us do Part. Understanding and Interpreting the Probate Records of Early Modern England. Oxford: Leopard's Head Press, 2000.

Austin, John L., Philosophical Papers, 3rd ed. Oxford: Oxford University Press, 1979.

Beattie, John, Crime and the Courts in England, 1660-1800. Oxford: Oxford University Press, 1986.

Beattie, John, Policing and Punishment in London, 1660-1750: Urban Crime and the Limits of Terror. Oxford: Oxford University Press, 2001.

Becker, Howard, Outsiders. Studies in Sociology of Deviance. Rev. ed. London: Simon and Schuster, 1963.

Beier, A. L. (Lee), Masterless Men. The Vagrancy Problem in England, 1560-1640. London: Methuen, 1985.

Beier, A. L. (Lee), "Anti-language or Jargon? Canting in the English Underworld in the Sixteenth and Seventeenth centuries." In Languages and Jargons. Contributions to a Social History of Language, edited by. Peter Burke and Roy Porter. Cambridge: Polity, 1995.

Bell, S., and S. Coleman, eds., The Anthropology of Friendship. Oxford: Berg, 1999.

Blackenfield, J. B., "Puritans in the Provinces: Banbury, Oxon., 1554-1660." Ph.D. diss., Yale University, 1985.

Botelho, Lynn, and Pat Thane, eds., Women and Ageing in British Society since 1500. Harlow: Longman, 2001.

Boulton, Jeremy, 'The Naming of Children in Early Modern London.' In Naming, Society and Regional Identity, edited by Dave Postles, 147-67. Oxford: Leopard's Head Press, 2002.

Braddick, Michael, State Formation in Early Modern England c.1550-1700. Cambridge: Cambridge University Press, 2000.

Bryson, Anna, From Courtesy to Civility. Changing Codes of Conduct in Early Modern England. Oxford: Oxford University Press, 1998.

Butler, Judith, Gender Trouble. Feminism and the Subversion of Identity. London: Routledge, 1990.

Chakravorty, S., Society and Politics in the Plays of Thomas Middleton. Oxford: Oxford University Press, 1996.

Charlesworth, Simon J., A Phenomenology of Working Class Experience. Cambridge: Cambridge University Press, 2000.

Clark, Cecily, "Onomastics." In The Cambridge History of the English Language, 2: 1066-1476, edited by Norman Blake, 542-606. Cambridge: Cambridge University Press, 1992.

Cliffe, J. T., The Puritan Gentry: the Great Puritan Families of Early Stuart England. London, 1984.

194   Bibliography

Coates, Jennifer, Women, Men and Language. A Sociolinguistic Account of Gender Differences in Language. 2d ed. London, 1993.
Cohen, Anthony, Self Consciousness. An Alternative Anthropology of Identity. London: Routledge, 1994.
Collinson, Patrick, "Elizabethan and Jacobean Puritanism as Forms of Popular Religious Culture." In The Culture of English Puritanism 1560-1700, edited by Christopher Durston and Jacqueline Eales. Basingstoke: The Macmillan Press, 1996.
Coster, Will, Baptism and Spiritual Kinship in Early Modern England. Aldershot: Ashgate, 2002.
Cressy, David, Birth, Marriage, and Death. Ritual, Religion, and the Life-cycle in Tudor and Stuart England. Oxford: Oxford University Press, 1997.
de Certeau, Michel, The Practice of Everyday Life. Trans. Steven Rendall. London: University of California Press, 1988.
de Certeau, Michel, The Writing of History. Trans. Tom Conley. New York: Columbia University Press, 1988.
Dutton, R., A. Findlay, and R. Wilson, eds., Region, Religion and Patronage. Lancastrian Shakespeare. Manchester: Manchester University Press, 2003.
Elliott, Anthony, Concepts of the Self. Cambridge: Polity, 2001.
Fairclough, N., Language and Power, 2d ed. Harlow: Longman, 2001.
Farmer, Sharon, Surviving Poverty in Medieval Paris. Gender, Ideology, and the Daily Lives of the Poor. Ithaca, N.Y.: Cornell University Press, 2002.
Fischer, David H., Albion's Seed. Four British Folkways in America. New York: Oxford University Press, 1989.
Fletcher, John, Violence and Civilization. An Introduction to the Work of Norbert Elias. Cambridge: Polity, 1997.
French, Henry, "Social Status, Localism and the Middling Sort of People in England, 1620-1750." Past and Present 166 (2000): 66-99.
Germain, J., "Les prénoms à Namur (Wallonie) de la fin du XVe siècle au XVIe siècle." In Actes du XVIe Congrès International des Sciences Onomastiques 1987, edited by J-C. Boulanger (Quebec, 1990),
Giddens, Anthony, "Erving Goffman as a systemic social theorist." In idem, Social Theory and Modern Sociology. Stanford, Calif.: Stanford University Press, 1987.
Goffman, Erving, Behaviour in Public Places. Notes on the Social Organization of Gatherings. New York: Basic Books, 1963.
Goffman, Erving, Stigma. Notes on the Management of Spoiled Identity. New Jersey, Prentice-Hall Inc., 1968.
Goffman, Erving, The Presentation of Self in Everyday Life. New York: Anchor Books, 1959.
Gowing, Laura, Common Bodies. Women, Touch and Power in Seventeenth-century England. New Haven, Conn.: Yale University Press, 2003.
Gowing, Laura, Domestic Dangers. Women, Words, and Sex in Early Modern London. Oxford: Oxford University Press, 1996.
Gowing, Laura, "Ordering the Body: Illegitimacy and Female Authority in Seventeenth-century England." In Negotiating Power in Early Modern Society. Order, Hierarchy and Subordination in Britain and Ireland, edited by Michael

Braddick and John Walter. Cambridge: Cambridge University Press, 2001.

Greenblatt, Stephen, Renaissance Self-fashioning: from More to Shakespeare. Chicago: University of Chicago Press, 1980.

Griffiths, Paul, "Overlapping Circles: Imagining Criminal Communities in London, 1545-1645." In Communities in Early Modern England, edited by Alexandra Shepard and Phil Withington, 115-33. Manchester: Manchester University Press, 2000.

Gurr, A., Playgoing in Shakespeare's London. 3d ed. Cambridge: Cambridge University Press, 2004.

Hage, Per, and Frank Harary, Structural Models in Anthropology. Cambridge: Cambridge University Press, 1983.

Haigh, Christopher, Reformation and Resistance in Tudor Lancashire. Cambridge: Cambridge University Press, 1975.

Hall, Stuart, & Tony Jefferson, eds., Resistance through Rituals. Youth Subcultures in Post-War Britain. London, Hutchinson, 1975.

Harris, Tim, "Problematicising Popular Culture." In Popular Culture in England, c. 1500-1850 edited by idem,1-27, 216-22. Basingstoke: The Macmillan Press, 1995.

Hartman, A. A., "Criminal Aliases: a Psychological Study." Journal of Psychology 32 (1951): 49-56

Haseldine, Julian, ed., Friendship in Medieval Europe. Stroud: Sutton, 1999.

Helmholz, Richard H., Roman Canon Law in Reformation England. Cambridge: Cambridge University Press, 1990.

Herrup, Cynthia, The Common Peace. Participation and the Criminal Law in Seventeenth-century England. Cambridge: Cambridge University Press, 1987.

Hey, David, Family Names and Family History. London: Hambledon, 2000.

Hindle, Steve, The State and Social Change in Early Modern England c.1550-1640. Basingstoke: The Macmillan Press, 2000.

Hindle, Steve, On the Parish? The Micro-politics of Poor Relief in Rural England c.1550-1750. Oxford: Oxford University Press, 2004.

Hindle, Steve, "The Political Culture of the Middling Sort in English Rural Communities." In Politics of the Excluded, edited by Harris, 125-52.

Hope, J., "The Use of thou and you in Early Modern Spoken English." In Studies in Early Modern English, edited by D. Kastovsky, 142-51. Berlin, 1994.

Hough, Carole, "Towards an Explanation of Phonetic Differentiation in Masculine and Feminine Personal Names." Journal of Linguistics 36 (2000): 1-11.

Howell, B., Law and Disorder in Tudor Monmouthshire. Cardiff, 1995.

Hunt, William, The Puritan Moment: the Coming of Revolution in an English County. Cambridge, Mass.: Harvard University Press, 1983.

Jütte, R., Poverty and Deviance in Early Modern Europe. Cambridge: Cambridge University Press, 1994.

Kamensky, Jane, Governing the Tongue. The Politics of Speech in Early New England. New York and Oxford: Oxford University Press, 1997.

Keenan, Siobhan, Travelling Players in Shakespeare's England. Basingstoke: The Macmillan Press, 2002.

Kinney, Arthur F., ed., A Companion to Renaissance Drama. Oxford: Blackwell, 2002.

Kuhn, S. M., and J. Reidy, eds., Middle English Dictionary I-L. Ann Arbor: University of Michigan, 1968.

Lakoff, George, & Mark Johnson, Metaphors We Live By. Chicago: University of Chicago Press, 1980.

Laslett, Peter, Karla Oosterveen and Richard M. Smith, eds., Bastardy and its Comparative History. Studies in the History of Illegitimacy and Marital Nonconformism in Britain, France, Germany, Sweden, North America, Jamaica and Japan. London: Edward Arnold, 1980.

Lerer, Seth, Courtly Letters in the Age of Henry VIII. Cambridge: Cambridge University Press, 1997.

Loyal, Steven, and Simon Quilley, eds, The Sociology of Norbert Elias. Cambridge: Cambridge University Press, 2004.

Maddern, Philippa, "'Best trusted friends': Concepts and Practices of Friendship among Fifteenth-century Norfolk Gentry." In England in the Fifteenth Century: Proceedings of the 1992 Harlaxton Symposium, edited by Nicholas Rogers, 100-17. Harlaxton Medieval Studies 4, Stamford: Paul Watkins Publishing, 1994).

Manley, Lawrence, Literature and Culture in Early Modern London, Cambridge: Cambridge University Press, 1995.

McLuskie, Kathleen E., Dekker and Heywood. Basingstoke: The Macmillan Press, 1994.

Misztal, Barbara, Informality. Social Theory and Contemporary Practice. London: Routledge, 2000.

Mitchell, W. J. T., ed., On Narrative. Chicago: University of Chicago Press, 1981.

Morgan, Jane, Christopher O'Neill, and Rom Harré, Nicknames: their Origins and Consequences. London: Routledge, 1979.

Mukherji, Subha, "Women, Law and Dramatic Realism in Early Modern England." English Literary Renaissance 35 (2005): 248-72.

Norbrook, David, Poetry and Politics in the English Renaissance. Rev. ed. Oxford: Oxford University Press, 2002.

O'Hara, Diana, Courtship and Constraint. Rethinking the Making of Marriage in Tudor England. Manchester: Manchester University Press, 2000.

Ottaway, Susannah, The Decline of Life. Old Age in Eighteenth-century England. Cambridge: Cambridge University Press, 2004.

Pelling, Margaret, "Old Age, Poverty, and Disability in Early Modern Norwich: Work, Remarriage, and Other Expedients." In Life, Death and the Elderly. Historical Perspectives, edited by eadem and Richard M. Smith, 74-101. London: Routledge, 1991.

Redmonds, George, Surnames and Genealogy. A New Approach. (Boston, Mass.: New England Historical Genealogical Society, 1997).

Riggs, David, Ben Jonson. A Life. Cambridge, Mass.: Harvard University Press, 1989.

Rosenwein, Barbara, ed., Anger's Past. The Social Uses of an Emotion in the Middle Ages. Ithaca, N.Y.: Cornell University Press, 1998.

Rosenwein, Barbara, "Worrying about Emotions in History." American Historical Review 107 (2002): 821-45

Scott, John, Social Network Analysis. A Handbook. London: Sage, 1991.

Searle, John, Mind, Languages and Society. Philosophy in the Real World. London, 1999.

Shepard, Alexandra, The Meanings of Manhood in Early Modern England. Oxford: Oxford University Press, 2003.

Smith-Bannister, Scott, Names and Naming Patterns in England 1538-1700. Oxford: Oxford University Press, 1997.

Smith, D., R. Strier and Bevington, The Theatrical City. Theatre and Politics in London, 1576-1649. Cambridge: Cambridge University Press, 1995.

Smith, Richard M., "Marriage Processes in the English Past: Some Continuities." In The World We Have Gained, edited by Lloyd Bonfield, Richard M. Smith and Keith Wrightson. Oxford: Blackwell, 1986.

Stryker, S., Symbolic Interactionism. A Social Structural Version. Menlo Park, Calif.: Benjamin/Cummings, 1980.

Taylor, Charles, Sources of the Self. The Making of Modern Identity. Cambridge: Cambridge University Press, 1989.

Thomas, I., Meaning in Interaction. An Introduction to Pragmatics. Harlow: Longman, 1995.

Tittler, Robert, The Reformation and the Towns in England. Politics and Political Culture, c.1540-1640. Oxford: Oxford University Press, 1998.

Tyacke, Nicholas, "Popular Puritan Mentality in Late Elizabethan England." In The English Commonwealth, 1547-1640. Essays in Politics and Society Presented to Joel Hurstfield, edited by Peter Clark, G. T. Smith and Tyacke, 77-92. Leicester: Leicester University Press, 1979.

Underdown, David, Fire from Heaven. Life in an English Town in the Seventeenth Century. 1992. Reprint. London: Pimlico, 2003.

Van Vree, W., Meetings, Manners and Civilization. The Development of Modern Meeting Behaviour. London, 1999.

Williams, G., A Glossary of Shakespeare's Sexual Language. London: Athlone, 1997.

Wilson, Stephen, The Means of Naming. A Social and Cultural History of Personal Naming in the West. London: UCL Press, 1998.

Withington, Phil, The Politics of Commonwealth. Citizens and Freemen in Early Modern England. Cambridge: Cambridge University Press, 2005.

Wood, Andy, "'Poore men woll speke one daye': Plebeian Languages of Deference and Defiance in England c.1520-1640." In The Politics of the Excluded, c.1500-1850, edited by Tim Harris, 67-98. Basingstoke: Palgrave/Macmillan, 2001.

Worden, Blair, "Ben Jonson Among the Historians." In Culture and Politics in Early Stuart England, edited by Kevin Sharpe and Peter Lake, 67-89. Basingstoke: The Macmillan Press, 1994.

Wrightson, Keith, English Society 1580-1680. Rev. ed. London: Routledge, 2003.

Wrightson, Keith, "'Sorts of people' in Tudor and Stuart England." In The Middling Sort of People. Culture, Society and Politics in England, 1550-1800, edited by Jonathan Barry and Christopher Brooks, 28-51. Basingstoke: The Macmillan Press, 1994.

Wrightson, Keith, "The Politics of the Parish in Early Modern England." In The Experience of Authority in Early Modern England, edited by Paul Griffiths, Adam Fox and Steve Hindle, 10-46. Basingstoke: The Macmillan Press, 1996.

"Honour and Reputation in Early-modern England," Transactions of the Royal Historical Society 6th ser. 6 (1996): 137-248

Index

Printed in the United Kingdom
by Lightning Source UK Ltd.
108711UKS00002B/188